"Let's be honest: we all have questions about life, God, and the Scriptures. If you're looking for a book that provides answers in a perfectly packaged and simplistic manner, it's probably best that you pass on this book. But if you're looking for a resource that gives permission, space, and grace to engage many of those deeper questions, this book is truly a gift. Krish Kandiah's *Paradoxology* is honest, sincere, theologically robust, and biblically engaging. A Christian spirituality that leaves no room for doubts, questions, and messiness will inevitably lead to challenging consequences. A false illusion of faith and discipleship sets people up for epic failures, bouts with disillusionment, and, at times, a slow but sinking spiral into cynicism. Read this book. Engage your questions. Grow in your faith."

Eugene Cho, pastor and humanitarian, author of *Overrated*

"Read this book, and you'll be concerned and comforted. You'll question and doubt—and believe more deeply than ever. You'll despair at times . . . and hope like never before. In short, you'll be doing the best Christian theology, which takes you to places dark and mysterious and to vistas bursting with light and beauty, often both at the same time. That's what it means to live by paradox, where the deepest truths lie."

Mark Galli, editor, *Christianity Today*

"Apologetics in a postmodern world is looking less for historical proof, scientific demonstration, and systematic omniscience. Rather, it is looking for honest, open, and genuine probings that have less certitude while holding firm to belief in a good God who loves us but who has not created a world where everything ends up with happy emojis. Krish Kandiah explores here the genuine paradoxes of the Bible in an open and honest manner. *Paradoxology* will bless a new generation with a new kind of apologetics."

Scot McKnight, Julius R. Mantey Professor of New Testament, Northern Seminary

"Being able to live within the tensions created by paradox is one of the most essential capacities for true spiritual deepening and growth. So to have an entire book devoted to reflecting on the reality that the life of faith is full of paradox, to acknowledge some of the most confounding ones, and then learn how to be with God in the midst of them—wow! What a gift! I am most grateful for this offering that clearly emerges from Krish Kandiah's honest wrestling with the great paradoxes of life."

Ruth Haley Barton, founder and CEO, Transforming Center, author of *Life Together in Christ*

"As I read this book I thought, *I wish I had this book when I was in college*—when I was studying theology and wrestling with life's challenges. As I continued to read I realized that a book like this is always timely because the more difficult biblical narratives are still there, and our life and faith will always present us with challenges. Krish Kandiah has given us a valuable treasure in his new book. Rich in theology, warmth, and honesty, *Paradoxology* offers a safe place to explore and engage tough questions."

Jo Saxton, chair of the board, 3D Movements

"Following Jesus is a paradox: Christianity asks its followers to place their total faith in a 'personal friend and savior' who is likely to be quite 'silent' for most of that follower's remaining time on earth. Any normal person, Christian or not, would wonder how to keep these kinds of tensions in balance. *Paradoxology* shows that these tensions—even apparent contradictions—actually provide texture and truth to Christianity. After reading *Paradoxology* you may think that some of the doubts and contradictions you were so certain disproved Christianity were a result of seeing the world in two dimensions, rather than the robust 3D nature of the gospel."

David Kinnaman, president of Barna Group, author of *unChristian* and *You Lost Me*

"In a complex, unpredictable world, we yearn for simplicity and easy answers. Christianity can become a safe haven for many who just want to pull their boat into a port and enjoy life. In *Paradoxology*, Krish Kandiah dispels that myth with biblical clarity. God is God, and we are invited into a journey with Christ, out in the wild deep where the Spirit is moving across the waters. This book is for pastors and spiritual leaders, Christ-followers and seekers who truly wonder about the character of God and the nature of faith. Kandiah proposes a biblical way to construct a sturdier boat and a truer spiritual journey."

MaryKate Morse, author of *A Guidebook to Prayer* and *Making Room for Leadership*

"In *Paradoxology*, Krish Kandiah explores some of the most fascinating characters in the Scriptures, specifically highlighting some of the paradoxes in their lives. He treats difficult issues with grace and humility, handling the texts well and explaining theological truths clearly."

Ed Stetzer, Billy Graham Distinguished Chair, Wheaton College

"With theological wisdom, a storyteller's craft, and, most importantly, a pastoral hand, Krish Kandiah shows the reader that Christianity's paradoxes do not refute faith. Rather, when cherished and contemplated, they lead us into the ever-deepening mystery of God's love."

Mark Sayers, senior pastor, Red Church, Melbourne, Australia, author of *Disappearing Church*

"This is a book that dares to ask the questions we seldom voice, even to ourselves. We believe in a loving God yet see suffering on a global scale. We believe in a powerful God yet see unfettered injustice everywhere. Krish dares to bring all we see and all we believe together. It's a powerful work of unshakable faith."

Sheila Walsh, author, cohost of LIFE Today

"We have always believed that all our greatest truths (the Trinity, the Incarnation, predestination and free will, good and evil) are in the end paradoxical and invite us into mystery and propel us to worship. Here is highly readable book from a very credible voice in British Christianity about engaging paradox. What's not to like?"

Alan Hirsch, author, founder of Forge Mission Training Network

"Jesus didn't write books about theology or church doctrine; he spent his life telling stories. Why? Because stories are the most powerful way to share a message that triggers questions, starts conversations, and changes lives. That's why Krish Kandiah's book *Paradoxology* is so powerful and timely. If we could recapture this incredible idea, it would transform the way we connect with and engage today's culture."

Phil Cooke, filmmaker, media consultant, author of *Unique*

"*Paradoxology* is one of the most straightforward and honest books I have read on the inherent tension of faith. Krish's seminal work leads us deeper into faith not by erasing doubt or the awkwardness of trust, but by moving us through it—as was the experience of the prophets of old, and as is the witness of Scripture. *Paradoxology* has a clean structure that should make it easily accessible for churches, small groups, and book clubs, which is good, because this book deserves a wide reading."

Ken Wytsma, president of Kilns College, author of *Pursuing Justice* and *Create vs. Copy*

PARADOXOLOGY

WHY CHRISTIANITY
WAS NEVER MEANT
TO BE SIMPLE

KRISH KANDIAH

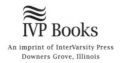
IVP Books

An imprint of InterVarsity Press
Downers Grove, Illinois

InterVarsity Press
P.O. Box 1400, Downers Grove, IL 60515-1426
ivpress.com
email@ivpress.com

US Edition ©2017 by Krish Kandiah
UK Edition © 2014 by Krish Kandiah

Published in the United States of America by InterVarsity Press, Downers Grove, Illinois. Originally published by Hodder & Stoughton as Paradoxology *by Krish Kandiah. ©2014 by Krish Kandiah. All rights reserved. Published by permission of Hodder & Stoughton.*

InterVarsity Press® is the book-publishing division of InterVarsity Christian Fellowship/USA®, a movement of students and faculty active on campus at hundreds of universities, colleges, and schools of nursing in the United States of America, and a member movement of the International Fellowship of Evangelical Students. For information about local and regional activities, visit intervarsity.org.

While any stories in this book are true, some names and identifying information may have been changed to protect the privacy of individuals.

Cover design: David Fassett
Images: © Paul Taylor/Getty Images

ISBN 978-0-8308-4504-0 (print)
ISBN 978-0-8308-9772-8 (digital)

Printed in the United States of America ∞

 As a member of the Green Press Initiative, InterVarsity Press is committed to protecting the environment and to the responsible use of natural resources. To learn more, visit greenpressinitiative.org.

Library of Congress Cataloging-in-Publication Data
Names: Kandiah, Krish, author.
Title: Paradoxology : why Christianity was never meant to be simple / Krish Kandiah.
Description: Downers Grove : InterVarsity Press, 2017.
Identifiers: LCCN 2016046183 (print) | LCCN 2016046928 (ebook) | ISBN 9780830845040 (pbk. : alk. paper) | ISBN 9780830897728 (eBook)
Subjects: LCSH: Bible—Theology. | Paradox—Religious aspects—Christianity.
Classification: LCC BS543 .K36 2017 (print) | LCC BS543 (ebook) | DDC 230/.041—dc23
LC record available at https://lccn.loc.gov/2016046183

P	22	21	20	19	18	17	16	15	14	13	12	11	10	9	8	7	6	5	4	3	2	1
Y	35	34	33	32	31	30	29	28	27	26	25	24	23	22	21	20	19	18	17			

Contents

The Preface (paradox)

There is a famous philosophical paradox derived from the custom for an author to acknowledge substantial help in the preparation of a book, and also to accept full responsibility for any mistakes. In other words I believe there are no errors in this book, thanks to my incredible team of experts acknowledged below. I also admit my (and their) fallibility, and therefore I simultaneously believe there are errors in this book. Although this statement itself may be one of the erroneous ones.

If you can pardon the paradox both that I believe there are, and there are not errors in this book, there is some hope as you tackle the rest of the book.

As you ponder this paradox, let me say my heartfelt thanks to Ian Metcalfe, a publisher with a passion and a good friend who has helpfully stretched me as an author. Also to my mother June who, as you will read, taught me to pray and trust from the beginning of my life to the end of hers. Also to Olive Baxter, a patient and godly Sunday School teacher whose lessons she taught me when I was seven years old are still being learned today. To Bruce Milne, author of *Know the Truth*, a book foundational to my adult faith, who has been gracious enough to read mine. To Pete Greig, Mark Galli, Malcolm Duncan, Andy Croft, Adrian Reynolds, Michael

Jensen, Ann Holt, David Kinnaman, Alan Hirsch and Lucy Peppiatt, who have given me considerable encouragement (not to mention generous endorsements). To Ruth Roff and Kate Craigie, editors extraordinaire. To my wife Miriam who has cajoled me and crafted the manuscript from conception to completion. To my children, Joel, Luke, Anna, and Elly who I hope will one day read and be encouraged by this book, just as I have learned many of its lessons from them.

And, yes, notwithstanding these fine contributors, any errors found herein are mine alone.

Introduction

It was much easier to keep my eyes on the floor than to meet the mother's gaze as she knelt by the bedside, with thick black lines of makeup smearing down her face. The boy's father glared accusingly at me as though I was implicated in the tragedy that God had brought to his family. The one-year-old in the hospital bed had been babbling and bubbly just a few days earlier – gorgeously boyish. Now he was blind, crying incessantly, his body rigid. It was supposed to be a routine operation; now his screams expressed how we were all feeling – his piercing cries made audible the pain of the tragedy, the panic for the future, and the ever-present question, 'Why?'

Why does God allow such meaningless suffering?

And what sort of God do we worship, anyway?

I have always struggled to understand God. As a child, I remember sitting on a shrunken brown wooden chair with my hand in the air and my toes just about reaching the polished parquet floor. My young, smiling Sunday School teacher never let on that she was fed up of my regular interruptions to her well-intentioned story-telling. 'Who made God, miss? Is God bigger than the universe, miss? Why does God tell Abraham to kill his son? Will he tell me to hit my sister? If I do hit my sister, then isn't God responsible, because he is in charge of the universe? If I'm only

half-sorry for hitting her, will I only get halfway to heaven, miss?'
My Sunday School teacher always had an answer. One of the
following usually seemed to be enough to shut me up, if only until
the following Sunday morning:

'If we could understand God, then we would be God.'
'God works in mysterious ways.'
'Don't be awkward – get on with your colouring.'

As I sat in that hospital, with tragedy all around, I knew I could
not pass on her advice. I needed more than a pat answer, a slick
one-liner or a handy proof-text. I sat in silent prayer, asking God
for wisdom, grace and hope. It was in that moment that I began a
journey that would lead me to discover that it is often in the mysteries
of life that we learn most about the mysteries of God. It is the very
paradoxes of Scripture that help us to come to God most effectively
when life itself is a paradox.

A paradox, just to be clear, consists of true statements that lead
to an apparent or real contradiction in logic or intuition. The
birthday paradox is a classic example. How can you reconcile these
two statements?

The boy has had three birthdays.
The boy is thirteen years old.

They appear to contradict logic and intuition. But once we discover
that the boy's birthday is 29 February, the contradiction disappears.
Easy.

However, the paradoxes that come to light when we try to think
about God deeply are nowhere near as easy to resolve. How can

2

God both be always with us, and yet so often seem alarmingly distant? How can Jesus' death bring us life? How can a God who tells us to love our enemies ordain the wiping out of a whole generation, or command genocide? Why do we bring our prayers for healing to a God who, we are forced to recognize from experience, often doesn't oblige?

Facing up to hard questions about God can be disconcerting. Believers may feel we are letting the side down if we dare to admit we still have questions. Perhaps we fear that in admitting to unresolved questions in our faith, we might lead other people into doubt and destabilize, or even destroy, their faith. Often we are taught – or at least we pick up by osmosis – that Christian maturity means giving confident, slick answers without a hint of uncertainty. But this is simply wrong. False assurance is no assurance at all, and taking time to tackle the difficult passages of the Bible head on may in fact be exactly what we need to help strengthen and life-proof our faith. If what we believe is true, it will stand up to questioning.

One of the paradoxes of faith is that years of living the Christian life and studying the Bible do not give us immunity from the troubling questions of faith. In fact, sometimes the longer we have been Christians, the more questions, doubts and struggles we have. Just like in any other field of study, the more you know, the more you know you don't know. As we will see during the course of this book, the Bible itself gives us many examples of our heroes in the faith who dare to direct their questions straight at God himself. Knowing that it is OK to raise and struggle with the mysteries about God can be extremely liberating. Far from challenging our faith, it can be exactly what our faith needs. If our faith is true – the truth – then our God must be big enough to face our questions. They don't need to be a dirty secret.

Most of the time, what we hear about in church and what we might study in our own personal reading of the Bible focuses on the same safe Bible passages, with the same comforting texts, even recycling the same anecdotes. We become expert not in wrestling with the big questions of faith, but in filing them away. We put them into a mental folder marked 'unanswered'.

And then, one day, we find ourselves sitting in an intensive-care unit somewhere, wondering whether we know God at all. Suddenly we realize that those questions weren't actually safely filed away; instead, the files are overflowing, mounting up and ready to spill over the floor, or like an over-crowded email inbox just waiting to crash the whole system.

Paradoxology was going to be a book of troubling questions that everyone asks. But instead it is a book of troubling questions that many people never ask, because we have become convinced that it is unhealthy to discuss them. We worry that, exposed to the light, our faith will fade away; tested on difficult ground, it may shatter. But if our faith is that fragile, it was never true; if our God is that easily defeated, he is not the true God. Whether we have built castles of doctrine on what prove to be flimsy foundations, or we have metaphorically curled ourselves up in a ball around the fundamentals of the gospel, avoiding good questions is not going to lead to any kind of answers.

What I want to ask is, what if we've been going about this all wrong?

What if the tension between apparently opposing doctrines is exactly where faith comes alive?

What if this ancient faith we call Christianity has survived so long not in spite of but precisely because of its apparent contradictions?

What if we have settled for neatly packaged, simplistic answers, instead of seeking out the deep and rich realities of our faith?

What if it is in the difficult parts of the Bible that God is most clearly revealed?

What if it is in and through our doubts that we learn the meaning of true relationship with the God who created us – of true worship?

What if Christianity was never meant to be simple?

Paradoxology makes a bold claim: that the paradoxes that seem to undermine belief are actually the heart of our vibrant faith, and that it is only by continually wrestling with them – rather than trying to pin them down or push them away – that we can really worship God, individually and together. As we search the Scriptures we find that even the most heroic figures, the models of courageous faith in the Bible, those to whom we habitually look for strength, struggled with the conundrums of God's character. Their struggles illuminate and validate our struggles, and their faith and worship in the midst of despair can help us in our faith and worship too.

Whether you are exploring the Christian faith for the first time, or have been leading a church for years, the premise of this book is based on the liberating fact that the Bible has more room for doubt, uncertainty and struggle than we have ever allowed ourselves to believe. God is fully able to handle our inquiries and our inconsistencies. We don't need to protect God or the faith he has given us from our difficult questions.

We can bring our questions into the open with confidence, and with humility we can listen to what God says, following clues the Bible gives us, and our faith will grow, not founder.

It is my desire that this book, argumentative and opinionated as it is, should be a form of doxology – that is to say, an expression of praise to God. Expressing problems and praise together is not a contradiction, as we will discover. In fact, worry and worship, doubt and devotion frequently go hand in hand in Scripture. As we tackle head on these tough questions about a God who allows suffering, instigates genocide, demands the impossible, promises to speak yet remains deafeningly silent, we will discover that, paradoxically, it is in the parts of the Bible we find most difficult that we find the most treasured and valuable truths about God. When God seems most difficult to understand, it is then that we can see him most clearly and love him most dearly.

My hope is that *Paradoxology* will help our faith to grow stronger by daring to flag up some of the paradoxes about God that challenge us, rather than covering them up. My belief and my prayer is that together we can lift our eyes off the hospital floor and up to God who can help us as we face the joys, tragedies and mysteries of life.

Chapter 1

The Abraham Paradox
The God who needs nothing but asks for everything

The teenager stood trembling on the stage, wearing her smart black school uniform, dwarfed by the huge platform and a very tall lectern. Four thousand pairs of eyes were trained on her. Gyeoung[1] was born in Pyeong Yang, the capital of North Korea. Her father had the lofty position of being an assistant to President Kim Jong Il himself. But then one day, out of the blue, the president's attitude towards her father changed – they became undesirables and were immediately subjected to political persecution. Aged six, she and her parents fled as refugees to China. There her parents became Christians. What a good news story – exiled by a dictator from North Korea, only to be converted in communist China – just the kind of poetic justice I like. It proves not only that God is in control of the universe but also that he has a sense of humour.

Unfortunately, the story didn't end there. Her hands still shaking, the girl carried on reading. After only a few short months, Gyeoung's mother, pregnant with her second child, contracted leukaemia and died. Not long after that, her father was arrested by the Chinese

---

1 You can read more of Gyeoung Son's story in Cameron, J. E. M. (ed.) (2013), *Christ Our Reconciler: The Third Lausanne Congress on World Evangelization*, IVP, pp. 17ff.

7

authorities and sent back to North Korea. He spent three years in prison, tirelessly sharing his faith, before finally being released and allowed to leave the country. Again, I was ready to cheer; maybe not quite so loudly this time, but God still wins, turning the tragedy of widowerhood and imprisonment into opportunities for others to hear the good news of the gospel. Grief wouldn't mute this minister of the gospel, prison bars couldn't contain him.

But the story was still not finished. Shortly after being reunited with his daughter, Gyeoung's father felt called by God to return to North Korea to help others come to know Jesus. He was discovered by the authorities in 2006, and he disappeared. In her soft voice, Gyeoung explained: 'I have heard no word from my father nor about him ever since. In all probability, he has been shot dead on charges of treason and espionage, as is so often the case for persecuted Christians in North Korea.'[2] A hush fell over the room as this petite teenager paused to glimpse up from the script she was holding. Now I didn't feel like cheering. I wanted someone to go and embrace this young girl and let her know that she was not alone in the world after all. Silence descended on the auditorium.

Questions were crowding into my head faster than I could acknowledge or record them. How far should believers be willing to go to serve God? What price should we put on the cost of discipleship? What would it take to put this situation right? These were closely followed by deeper, darker questions. A big part of why Gyeoung's story so disturbed me is because as a father and foster carer, I have seen the damage done to children when they are left without parents. I have seen children emotionally crippled and unable to form attachments with others because they felt so abandoned by their parents.

2 Ibid., p. 18.

Should a father be willing to sacrifice his daughter's well-being for God? Would God really ask a father to do that? How could this girl stand up there as a follower of a God who would ask that of her, that she give up her own father?

As a young Christian, hearing stories like this would have inspired me – I could afford to be a lot more reckless then about my personal safety. But now, as a husband and father I feel the responsibility of providing and caring for those who depend on me. I find it nerve-wracking enough to cross the road and invite my neighbours to church – I have grave doubts that my courage would stand up to the life-and-death decisions that my brothers and sisters in the persecuted church face every day. On my best days, I'd like to think that with great help from God I might have enough courage to choose to be faithful to Christ even in the face of death. But deliberately taking risks that might orphan my own children seems a wholly different question.

Gyeoung's story struck a chord at the Lausanne conference, a global gathering of Christian leaders;[3] her story has inspired thousands around the world. So why am I left more perplexed than encouraged? How, after losing his home, his unborn child and his wife and after surviving three years in a North Korean prison, could a father abandon his one and only daughter, whom he loved? Why would one teenage girl have to pay such a high price for her father to follow God?

Why would God demand such an outrageous, impossible thing? What kind of God could possibly need his followers to make these kinds of sacrifices?

Why does worshipping God cost so much to those who love him, and those whom he supposedly loves? The more we reflect on the

---

3 You can watch her story here: http://www.krishk.com/2013/11/northkorea/

nature of God, the less these kinds of sacrifices make sense, as God is supposed to be all powerful and all sufficient.

This is not an isolated problem. Every day Christians face, not the life of peace and contentment we might hope for, but impossible situations – situations in which God seems to want them to take the hardest path. Not just those who are facing persecution in places like North Korea, Pakistan or Sudan. Recently I met a young woman who had been abused by her foster parents while she was a child in their care, and yet she told me she had felt called by God to phone them and forgive them. How could God ask her to do that? But he did, and she did, and she is now training as a social worker so as to devote her life to helping children in care. I have met countless Christians who have heard God's call to move into difficult neighbourhoods. I have met single women who have felt God lead them to leave jobs they love and friends they care for to nurse elderly parents. I have met Christians who are trying to break long-term addictions out of honour for God. I have met converts who have been rejected and disinherited by their family because of their new-found love for Jesus. I have met parents who have received physical abuse from adopted children whom they felt led to welcome into their homes.

To be perfectly honest, when I hear these stories I sometimes wonder if God is insecure, cruel or greedy.

First, sometimes God seems to behave like a jealous or hopeless lover who demands huge sacrifices and outrageous demonstrations of devotion because he needs reassurance that he is still loved. Perhaps when God asks the impossible of us, he is not actually testing our ability to survive, but testing our affections? Is he just insecure? When we look at the Job Paradox, this possibility will come up again.

Second, God can appear to be behaving like a nasty child slowly pulling the wings off a butterfly, simply to watch how it struggles, to see how much pain it can endure before it dies. As God asks people to make sacrifices for him, gradually stripping away so much of what they hold dear, it may feel as though he is just testing their resolve, seeing how much loss can be coped with – and all just for the fun of it. There are moments when we experience the terrible cost of worshipping God, or watch while others have to face these impossible decisions, and the idea of a cruel God seems like it might fit the reality better than a loving one.

Third, and perhaps most complex of all to try and work through, when God asks the impossible, it makes him look greedy. With all the riches at his disposal, why would he ask for more? I would feel a lot happier sacrificing my coat to a homeless person shivering in the tube station, than offering it to a fellow commuter huddled over his laptop because he left his designer jacket in the office. When a poor person asks you to give them something, you may not feel comfortable about it but you can see the point; the request has greater plausibility than when a wealthy person asks.

The Bible makes it very clear that God needs nothing from us:

> I have no need of a bull from your stall
> or of goats from your pens,
> for every animal of the forest is mine,
> and the cattle on a thousand hills.
> I know every bird in the mountains,
> and the insects in the fields are mine.
> If I were hungry I would not tell you,
> for the world is mine, and all that is in it.[4]

---

4 Psalm 50:9–11.

In the New Testament Paul explains that God 'is not served by human hands, as if he needed anything. Rather, he himself gives everyone life and breath and everything else.'[5] The term that captures this idea is 'aseity' which, according to theologian J. I. Packer, means that God 'has life in himself and draws his unending energy from himself' (*a se* in Latin means 'from himself').[6] God needs nothing – yet he demands everything.

Here lies the heart of the paradox: an all-powerful, self-sufficient God who asks for costly worship. This paradox challenges us not just at an intellectual level, but at an emotional one. It strikes at the core of our faith, because it is about the very character of God. Is God loving, kind and compassionate? Or is he cruel, insecure and greedy? If we don't resolve this issue we will either become miserly towards God – refusing to give him what he demands – or miserable with God – resenting giving him what he deserves.

The Bible, however, acknowledges and indeed encourages us to explore this paradox of a God who asks the impossible. In fact, it is highlighted early on in Scripture when we are given a heart-rending account of a dark episode in biblical history – when a father is asked to participate in child-sacrifice in the name of devotion to God.

Abraham is a key figure in the Old Testament. His story is the first in-depth biography we come to in the Bible, and is thus significant as the bridge point between the primeval story of creation and the history of the patriarchs of the Jewish and Christian faith. Abraham's story is the link between cosmology and genealogy.[7] We

---

6 Packer, J. I. (1993), *Concise Theology: A Guide to Historic Christian Beliefs*, Wheaton, IL: Tyndale House, p. 26.

7 Wenham, G. J. (1998), *Vol. 1: Genesis 1–15*, Word Biblical Commentary, Dallas: Word, Inc.

are given a long and detailed account of Abraham's family tree. It gets more space than was given to describe the creation from nothing of billions of constellations and galaxies.[8] But then, after we have heard over and over about who 'begat' whom and went on to 'beget' someone else, there is an abrupt stop. This family line will not continue, because Sarai, Abraham's wife, 'was childless because she was not able to conceive'.[9]

In an ancient culture where your identity was defined by your ancestors and your future would be defined by your descendants, being childless was a particularly heavy burden to carry.[10] In today's culture, of course, some make a conscious decision to live a childless life. But sadly, there are many other families who do want children and live with the continual pain of childlessness. Our televisions, social networks, supermarkets and workplace policies constantly take for granted the expectation that we will get married, have babies, raise a family, have children to make small talk about. It is an unspoken heartache, because the corollary of the Me Culture is that you can't talk about things that haven't worked out. Too many people silently identify with the prayer of Rachel, wife of the patriarch Jacob: 'Give me children, or death.'[11] The sense of shame and public exposure as one who cannot have children was then, and still is now, unbearable for the many women who suffer it.

For Sarai and Abram, without children there was quite literally

---

8 Genesis 10:10–26.

9 Genesis 11:30.

10 'In the ancient Near East, children were needed to care for aging parents, attend to the family's work and inherit the family name and estate.' Magnusson, K.T. (2000), 'Childlessness' in Alexander, T. Desmond & Rosner, Brian S. (eds.) (2000), *New Dictionary of Biblical Theology, Digital Edition,* IVP.

11 Genesis 30:1.

no future – they had no one to pass on their inheritance to, no one to care for them in old age.[12] They would become a genealogical dead end. Despite being materially wealthy, they carried a huge burden of shame. They may well have felt their lives had been worthless – we are told Abram's body was 'as good as dead',[13] and Sarai's womb 'was also dead'. Into this story of an elderly couple entering their twilight years and about to fade into the night of genealogical obscurity, God steps in.

The God who created the stars in Genesis chapter 1 asks Abraham to count the stars in Genesis chapter 15. The Creator's promise to this humble and ageing creature is that his offspring – none of which are yet born – will one day outnumber the stars. The cosmic, universe-creating God becomes intimately involved in the life of an elderly couple living in an out-of-the-way corner of a major landmass in the northern hemisphere of the third rock from a pretty ordinary star in a forgotten backwater of one of the spiral arms of the Milky Way. Abraham's story links the big story of the creation of the universe and the one-on-one story of God's involvement in the creation of a new family.

The God who spoke the stars into being gives Abraham a new name, a new vocation and a new location. The God of creation becomes the God of the covenant, establishing relationship with one man from amongst the wealth of his creation.

The LORD had said to Abram, 'Go from your country, your people and your father's household to the land I will show

---

12 See note on Genesis 11:30 in Matthews, V. H., Chavalas, M. W. & Walton, J. H. (2000), *The IVP Bible Background Commentary: Old Testament* (electronic edn.).

13 Hebrews 11:12.

you. I will make you into a great nation, and I will bless you; I will make your name great, and you will be a blessing. I will bless those who bless you, and whoever curses you I will curse; and all peoples on earth will be blessed through you.'[14]

Our nightmare story begins like the ultimate fairy tale. An elderly couple are plucked from obscurity and told their dreams are coming true: they will be given significance, inheritance and innumerable descendants in God's plans for the world. This feel-good plotline could be the story of Cinderella, or *Pretty Woman*, or Harry Potter. A nobody will become a somebody. When we are first introduced to Abraham, the details are sparse. Even his name is shorter than it becomes later: at the moment, he is just plain Abram.

As God's plans come to pass, Abram and Sarai become the poster couple for the transforming power of God.

God is revealed as the Lord of the second chance, no matter what stage of life we are at. God turns mourning into dancing, obscurity into fame, shame into glory, tragedy into triumph and barrenness into a family that he promises will expand to stellar proportions. God is the one who invented the rags-to-riches plotline. God is the one who gives the impossible.

At the end of their lives, this living-dead couple are offered a new start, and after several scrapes – a sexual liaison with a servant girl, a surrogate child, Abram pretending his wife is really only his sister, not forgetting a rebrand to the new names 'Abraham' and 'Sarah' – the couple are finally en route to the Promised Land with their new-born son, their miracle baby, Isaac.

When you think about it, it seems like a picture-perfect patriarch

---

14 Genesis 12:1–2.

origin story. There can be no doubt that the nation of Israel owes its existence not to human endeavour or wisdom, but to the direct intervention of God. The God who speaks the universe into being from nothing, creates his nation from scratch too. God has stepped in to rescue Abraham from obscurity, anonymity and genetic redundancy. Here is hope for the living dead.

I have heard preachers use this passage to promise everything from fame to fertility, from recognition to riches. This part of the story, they argue, reveals God as the deity who knows our dreams and longings and wants to meet them. This is the kind of God we like the sound of. It's the American dream,[15] if you like, embodied in a personal transformation – one family given the ultimate opportunity to achieve 'life, liberty and the pursuit of happiness'.[16] This is the kind of faith that makes total sense – trusting a God who will fulfil our dreams.

This is the kind of God we can love without question – a God who enables the ugly duckling to become a beautiful swan, the prostitute to marry the millionaire, the washed-up boxer to become the world heavyweight champion, the busker to become a multi-platinum-selling recording artist. Our culture loves these stories of people achieving the impossible; they fill our cinemas, our television screens and our imaginations.

This way of thinking starts young: a recent survey found that 'the top three career aspirations for five- to eleven-year-olds in

---

15 Missiologist Andrew Walls describes the cultural captivity of the gospel message in Walls, A. F. (1996a), 'The Gospel as Prisoner and Liberator of Culture', in Walls, A. F. (1996), *The Missionary Movement in Christian History: Studies in the Transmission of Faith*, Edinburgh: T&T Clark, pp. 3–15. (First published in 1982, *Faith and Thought* 108 (1&2), pp. 39–52.)
16 United States Declaration of Independence.

Britain were sports star, pop star and actor, compared with teacher, banker and doctor 25 years ago'.[17] Thanks to TV talent shows, these zero-to-hero stories form part of the narrative that shapes us as citizens of the twenty-first century. From a young age children are offered the hope that they too can be plucked from obscurity and become household names, and see their disappointments turn to dreams.

End the story here and we can cheer for a God who fits our expectations neatly.

But God is not just a chaplain to our consumerism, or a catalyst for our consumption.[18] We are only part-way through this story. God gives the impossible – and he also demands the impossible. We need the painful paradox of the story, the challenge of what is yet to unfold, in order to see God most clearly. While God is busily fulfilling our dreams, it is easy to trust him. When his actions fit with our aspirations and conform to the flow of our culture, it is easy to ask people to follow him. The danger is that rather than worshipping the true and living God who created us, we have simply created our own designer god, a god who meets our specifications and measures up to our expectations.

This is why paradoxes are so critical for us. When things are going smoothly we can assume we have a good relationship with God – but we may just be worshipping a projection. Sociologists like Émile Durkheim have long challenged believers, claiming they construct gods that suit their needs; psychologists such as Freud have accused Christians of worshipping their own desires. So when

---

17 http://www.guardian.co.uk/lifeandstyle/2010/apr/17/i-want-to-be-famous
18 For more on this idea see Bartholomew, C. & Moritz., T. (eds.) (2000), *Christ and Consumerism: Critical Reflections on the Spirit of our Age*, Paternoster.

God surprises us – when God demands of us what we would never expect – this is a good sign that we are connecting with the real God. When God acts as an iconoclast – smashing our self-constructed idols – we know we are really in a relationship with the true and living God.

We are about to see that the God of Abraham is a dream-shattering God. This part of the story makes for uncomfortable reading; God does not always give fame or fortune or fertility, as many of us know from bitter experience. He is the God who both gives the impossible and asks the impossible.

All seems to be going so well for Abraham; then, out of the blue, God makes an apparently ridiculous demand. This story, too, is well known and yet at its heart it is way off-beam – a paradox that is hidden in plain sight. It's a Sunday School story staple and a foundational story for Judaism, Islam and of course Christianity, yet it illustrates a conflict of values that draws us right into the most important and fundamental questions of life – what is God really like, and what does having faith in him mean practically? Here we come face to face with the God who needs nothing, yet asks the impossible. Having given so much to Abraham, God demands it back, smashing that image of God as a supernatural sugar daddy.[19]

Take your son, your only son, whom you love – Isaac – and go to the region of Moriah. Sacrifice him there as a burnt offering on a mountain I will show you.[20]

---

19 Bosch, D. (1980), *Witness to the World*, John Knox, p. 202 describes an emaciated gospel that focuses solely on personal fulfilment and 'eternal healing' and not on the transformation of the universe.
20 Genesis 22:2.

This command effectively conveys three death sentences. Innocent Isaac will be killed. So will Abraham's aspirations, and Sarah's maternal pride and joy. In a few words from this God they'd been learning to trust, all joy, hope and life were being snatched away from this tiny family.

God knows exactly what he is asking Abraham. Three times he specifies just who he's talking about in his demand: God asks not just for a son, but for Abraham's 'only son', not just his only son but the son 'whom you love'. It's easy to see where the charge of divine cruelty comes from. God has given a precious gift to an elderly couple and now he is going to snatch it back. It seems petty and unexpected, like a jealous child demanding back a gift at the end of a friend's birthday party.

When God asked Abraham to leave his country and go to a new place, Abraham didn't really have much to lose. In the stories the ugly duckling, the washed-up boxer and the busker are always willing to take a risk – they have hit rock bottom. But in Abraham's story, it is only after the happy ending has arrived that the story really hots up, and when God asks for a child-sacrifice, Abraham has everything to lose. His reputation would no longer be as the founder of a great nation, but as a fool, even a murderer, who killed his only child when he knew he was too old to have another. Abraham would no longer be known as blessed by God, but instead as someone cursed by God. Instead of seeing his family line multiply, it would be cruelly cut short. Abraham may have given up his past without qualms, but when he was asked to raise the knife to Isaac, 'he was asked to surrender his future as well'.[21]

---

21 Lane, W. L. (1991), *Hebrews 9–13*, Word Biblical Commentary, Dallas: Word, Inc., p. 360.

Had the God that Abraham knew and trusted turned into a monster? Atheist Christopher Hitchens uses this story as ammunition to argue his case that *God is not Great*.[22] He is appalled by the fact that 'All three monotheisms . . . praise Abraham for being willing to hear voices and then to take his son Isaac for a long and gloomy walk. And then the caprice by which his murderous hand is finally stayed is written down as divine mercy.'[23]

If Abraham did as God asked, he had everything to lose – including his faith. What sort of God is it that asks a father to kill his young son? Who would want to follow a monster like this? Now the contradictions come thick and fast. Is the God that forbids murder[24] telling Abraham to kill his son? Is the God that expressly forbids child-sacrifice[25] demanding the blood of an innocent boy? Are all the promises that God made to Abraham now to be revoked? When God asks the impossible, what are the faithful to do? Do we just close our eyes and hope for the best? Is faith in God ultimately irrational?

The nature of Abraham's faith is pivotal as we consider these paradoxes. Abraham is given the nickname 'father of faith' in the New Testament[26] – he is held in high esteem as an archetype or 'worked example' of faith in the Old Testament. We are told: 'Abraham believed God and it was credited to him as righteousness.'[27] It was because of Abraham's faith that he was promised a son, and

---

22 Hitchens, C. (2007), *God is not Great: The Case against Religion*, Atlantic Books.

23 Ibid., p. 53.

24 Genesis 9:5–6.

25 Deuteronomy 12:31; 18:9–12.

26 Romans 4:11.

27 Genesis 15:6; Romans 4:3.

it was also because of his faith that he was prepared to go through with God's incongruous and apparently irrational demand that he execute that son. So what kind of faith is he the father of? A blind, unquestioning faith? Or what? We are told that Abraham sets out 'early the next morning'[28] for Mount Moriah to do the terrible deed. The terse story-telling does not enlighten us as to how Abraham agonized over the issue. We can only imagine his internal turmoil. Did he unquestioningly take a blind leap of faith?[29] Does Abraham's example of belief demonstrate that pursuing faith is intellectual suicide?[30] Can the 'life of faith' be reduced to the simple maxim, 'When God says jump, I jump' – no questions, no hesitations?

The belief that faith is by definition a blind leap into the unknown is so prevalent that often unbelieving friends will say things to me like, 'I wish I could believe like you do, but I think too much.' This might sound like a gracious compliment but it is actually an insult – perhaps unwitting – and might be better phrased: 'I respect your faith, but I'm just not as gullible as you.' They may as well have said: 'I used to believe in the tooth fairy too.'

Many people have described faith as believing what you know isn't true. Richard Dawkins, the vocal atheist and zoology professor, dismisses it as 'the process of non-thinking called faith'.[31] But the Bible refutes this.

---

28 Genesis 22:3.

29 Kierkegaard.

30 Some argue that this is what Kierkegaard is saying about Abraham's leap of faith in his complex reflection on the relationship between ethics and faith exhibited in Abraham's dilemma. Kierkegaard, S. (1986), *Fear and Trembling*, Penguin Classics.

31 *Root of All Evil*, Part 1: 'The God Delusion', Channel 4.

Looking more closely at Abraham's story, there are three things that we can establish about the nature of true faith.

First, faith is not a leap in the dark. The Bible's stories, including this episode in Abraham's life, are all intended to refute this mis-definition of faith. The Bible is full of testimonials that present reasons for trusting in God. Jesus himself described his words and his miracles as 'evidence' for belief.[32] The step of faith is an informed decision. This may sound like a paradox, but it is one we live with every day. Take, for example, the mundane but potentially life-changing decision to cross a road.

We cross the road every day without even thinking about it, but in a philosophical sense we cannot be certain that we are going to make it to the other side. There are all sorts of factors that might prevent a successful crossing. A reversal of gravity that sends you flying up off the surface. Some super-powerful glue on the road that you get stuck in and, wouldn't you know it, a steamroller inching its way towards you. A falling meteor fragment that blows a crater in the road right in front of you. Or something more commonplace, like a pothole in the road in which you catch your foot and sprain your ankle, or a speeding car careering round a blind corner. We can never be 100 per cent certain – but this lack of absolute certainty doesn't mean that the only option is to just leg it without looking, sticking your fingers in your ears, closing your eyes and screaming at the top of your voice.

When it comes to crossing a road, we gather evidence with our eyes and ears, and when we are reasonably confident that it is safe, we step out in faith and aim for the other side of the road. Similarly, when as Christians we take a step of faith, we use judgement based

---

32 John 14:6.

on gathered evidence and previous experience, and, trusting in our convictions, we move forward. Abraham had his eyes wide open when he decided to lead his son to Mount Moriah and offer him as a sacrifice. He had evidence that God would fulfil his promises. He had already experienced the miracle of God's provision of Isaac. He had seen that God could bring dead things to life. He knew that his future was safest in God's hands. So it was an immensely challenging, but not an intrinsically irrational, step to keep trusting God.

Second, Abraham's faith was not only based on evidence that he had seen, it was also set within the context of a relationship. One of my earliest memories is of being taken to a musty room with an odd smell. My mother was present, and two strangers. There was some brief discussion, which I did not understand, and as my mother looked on, one of the strangers proceeded to stab me, causing intense pain. My eyes welled up with tears, and my mother took me home. At the time I could not understand why my mother had allowed this to happen, yet I don't remember feeling angry with her. Despite understanding that she had knowingly and willingly allowed something painful to happen to me, I did not assume she had evil intent – I trusted her. I had only experienced good things from my mother up until that point, and our home was a happy one. In the years to come I would meet the same stranger again and have other vaccinations that protected me from all manner of unpleasant diseases. The wider relational context helps me to understand the strange episode stored up in my memory. All events take place within a bigger story, and it is impossible to understand the snapshot without knowing the bigger story within which it is set.

When God asks Abraham to do the impossible, there is a narrative and a relational context. Abraham had heard many times from

God. He knew first-hand of God's power, of God's ability to intervene, of God's kindness, of God's patience, and, too, of God's unusual ways of working. More than that, he had developed over time a trust-based relationship with God, which meant that even when God seemed to act out of character, Abraham had enough experience to continue to trust. Perhaps in this light it is easier to understand why Abraham was willing to go to such great lengths to follow God's call on his life.

Third, what we see in Abraham's obedient actions may in fact be not a bypass of but an engagement of his critical faculties. The New Testament letter to the Hebrews describes a 'hall of fame' of men and women who were distinguished for their faith in God. Abraham, constantly held up in the Bible as the model of faith, takes up the lion's share of the wall space in this virtual room. In Hebrews we are given insight into the inner working of Abraham's mind and heart as he approached his test of faith.[33] First, Isaac is referred to specifically as the starting point for a nation of descendants – Abraham knew that Isaac was essential to the fulfilment of God's promise.[34] Second, Abraham is referred to both here and in Romans as 'as good as dead'.[35,36] In Isaac's very existence, Abraham had already experienced the power of God overcoming the power of death. The writer to the Hebrews says: 'Abraham reasoned'.[37] There was no disengaging of his brain here. The three-day journey to the top of Mount Moriah gave him plenty of time to think this through. His conclusion was that he knew that God had the authority

---

33 Genesis 22:1.
34 Genesis 21:12.
35 Hebrews 11:12.
36 Romans 4.
37 Hebrews 11:9.

to demand the impossible; he knew that God had the power to perform the impossible; and he knew that God had been unchanging in his love and faithfulness in the past. So even though he couldn't understand the reason why, he still needed to trust God's promises and lift the knife to kill his son.

Faith in God is not unreasonable – it is based on evidence, on the character of God, and on our experience of him in our lives; it is seeing the bigger picture and knowing that God is bigger than any earthly outcome. God can give us the impossible, and God can demand the impossible, and based on all that we know about God, we can make a considered judgement that either way, he is to be trusted.

However, that still leaves us with the question of why God demands so much of us in the first place. When Abraham has climbed the mountain and built the altar and laid out Isaac as a sacrifice and raised the knife, God intervenes and tells him to stop and use a ram instead. What was the point? Why submit Abraham to all that emotional torment, only to let him off right at the end? What did God achieve by putting Abraham through this ordeal?

C. S. Lewis wrote:

We are half-hearted creatures, fooling about with drink and sex and ambition when infinite joy is offered us, like an ignorant child who wants to go on making mud pies in a slum because he cannot imagine what is meant by the offer of a holiday at the sea. We are far too easily pleased.[38]

These words are taken from Lewis' celebrated essay 'The Weight

---

38 Lewis, C. S. (1949), *Transposition and Other Addresses*, Geoffrey Bles.

of His Glory'. Lewis concludes that the problem with humanity is not that we desire great things, but that we settle for mediocrity. Our desires should lead us to God, but instead we take as the objects of our affections the gifts that God offers us, rather than God himself. We allow this to happen, not because our desires are too strong but because they are too weak. If we discerned the true trajectory of our desires we would see that only God himself could satisfy them. Sometimes God asks us to give up what seems impossible for us to give up, only so that we can appreciate all that he has for us. The appetites mentioned by Lewis – sex, drink and ambition – are not bad in themselves, they are good gifts from God to be enjoyed and celebrated. But these good gifts of God can be misused, and when they prevent us from relating with God himself, then they cease to be good for us. Lewis reminds us that our worship is to be directed at the God who gives the gifts, not the gifts themselves. Abraham's choice between God and Isaac forces him to recognize that the Giver is always more important than the gift.

In his dealings with us, God pursues our affections through both his provision and his withholding of that provision. Every good thing that we experience in life is a gift from God. Life, breath, even the fact that the sun's rays warm our planet sufficiently to sustain life at all – all this is a gift that God offers humanity.[39] God provides for us through nature so that our hearts will be filled with joy, and he provides for us through the circumstances of our life so that we might seek him and find that his love and compassion are not far from us.[40] A genuine gift is not given because it is deserved

---

39 'God sends the sun to shine on the righteous and the wicked' (Matthew 5:45).

40 See Acts 14:8–20 and Acts 17:16–32.

or merited, and so God's gifts are given freely. But God's gifts are given to help us experience his loving kindness.

Sometimes, though, it is not abundance that helps to deepen a relationship most effectively, but absence. As the old proverb puts it, 'absence makes the heart grow fonder'. Sometimes we really don't appreciate what we have until it is gone. This principle is at play in the spiritual discipline of fasting and the idea of the Sabbath, where God asks believers to forgo the undeniable goods of food and work in order to deepen our relationship with himself, turning or expressing our hunger for food or for satisfaction or for identity into a hunger for God. When God asks Abraham to sacrifice Isaac, the same principle is at work – God knows that in being prepared to forgo something good and valuable, Abraham will discover a greater intimacy with God, a greater appreciation of both the Giver and the gift.

Whether we experience the pleasure of God's abundant gifts, or the pain of their absence, we have an opportunity to encounter God in more profound ways. We can learn to direct our affections to him, and know his affection for us. But why is this affection so important that it is worth losing so much? Why does God so desperately want us to know him – even calling us to make seemingly impossible sacrifices for him? Is God insecure, egotistical or both?

As foster carers,[41] Miriam and I welcome children into our home who are in most cases very needy. We can give them balanced and tasty meals, clothes that fit and that they enjoy wearing, pocket money and advice on how to spend it, playmates, help with homework, a place to store their precious things and a room of their

---

41 For more on the opportunity of deeper intimacy with God through caring for vulnerable children, see Kandiah, K. & Kandiah, M. (2013), *Home for Good*, Hodder.

own, but all this doesn't even begin to meet their real needs. What those children crave is a parent-figure who will love them and pour themselves into their lives.[42]

It seems counter-intuitive, but it is plain truth that *I* am the best thing that I can give a child – my attention, my commitment, my time, my discipline, my love. Of course, no analogy is perfect, but in a much more profound way God too sees our lives and our needs and knows, as our Creator, that he himself is the best thing that he can give us.[43] Gifts, talents, relationships and property are all secondary to the love he can invest in us. We have often seen that fostered children find it difficult to trust us and accept the love and affection that we want to invest in their lives. When God adopts us into his family, he knows that we are broken and needy and he wants to help us learn to trust him and accept his affection and love. This is not out of some petty insecurity or narcissist preoccupation but because that is the best thing for us. This bond of trust and love and affection and commitment is the heart of true worship – worship that both we and God can enjoy together.

Sometimes it is hard to give God our affections, because they are already reserved for other things or other people. It is possible God may need to help us reorient those affections – he may need to loosen our grip on the things we cling to instead of him. As we shall see when we explore the Job Paradox, it is simplistic, not to mention judgemental and arrogant, to assume that all suffering and difficulties can be explained by God's discipline or punishment in

---

42 For a psychotherapist's take on this, see Gerhardt, S. (2004), *Why Love Matters*, Routledge. For a Christian child psychologist's perspective, see Purvis, K. (2007), *The Connected Child*, McGraw-Hill.

43 The logic of this position is further expressed by Piper, J. (1989), *Desiring God*, IVP.

a person's life. For example, we cannot simply argue that Gyeoung's father was idolizing his wife and daughter to such an extent that God forced him to sacrifice them and punished him by sending him as a missionary to North Korea. As we shall see, God has harsh words for those who dare to assume they know his mind and assert that suffering is a cause of discipline. If we believe God is acting out of cruelty, greed or insecurity, then we will react with fear and suspicion. But if we believe he is acting out of our best interests, out of perfect love and compassion, perhaps even the most painful of God's demands can become more bearable.

Psychopaths and surgeons have something in common – both can inflict considerable pain with a knife, both can cause scarring, loss of limbs and terrible disfigurement. But whereas we would fight off an attack by the psychopath, we would willingly put ourselves under the surgeon's knife because we trust their expertise and their motives. We recognize that in order to save a life, sometimes pain and loss have to be endured.

As the father of faith lifts his knife to kill the son of the promise on the Mount of Moriah, Abraham trusts that his God is more like the surgeon than the psychopath. But at the last moment, the angel of the Lord calls out to Abraham to stop the killing. In place of his one and only son, God tells Abraham to sacrifice a ram caught in a nearby thorn bush. En route to the mountain-top, the inquisitive Isaac had asked where the sacrificial lamb would come from. Abraham had replied to the young boy with the words, 'God himself will provide.'[44] In this terse dialogue these words are pregnant with meaning. God had provided Isaac, without a shadow of doubt. Now God seemed to be asking for Isaac back, but Abraham knew that

---

44 Genesis 22:9.

God had promised to provide him offspring through whom all the nations would be blessed, and he knew him to be a God who kept his promises. So Abraham both knew and foresaw God's provision. The letter to the Hebrews argues: 'Abraham reasoned that God could even raise the dead.'[45] Because of his unrelenting trust in God, Abraham believed God would return Isaac to him. He led his beloved son up the mountain and raised the knife because he had unshakable confidence in God's character, and a vision for the future.

It was a future he could only have begun to imagine. Hundreds of generations of descendants later, and thousands of years later, a city was built in that wilderness: Jerusalem was built on that same hill, and close to the spot where Isaac was prepared as a sacrifice, King Solomon built God's temple.[46] That temple was the place where God's people would be able to confess their sins and sacrifice animals to be killed in their place.

Hundreds of years later John, reflecting on another sacrifice, would write:

For God so loved the world that he gave his one and only Son, that whoever believes in him shall not perish but have eternal life.[47]

In the most famous verse in the Bible, there's an echo of the Abraham story. It is no accident that the Bible records that God gave 'his one and only Son', reprising God's command to Abraham. It is no accident that the only other time in the Bible that we are told about

---

45 Hebrews 11:19.

46 2 Chronicles 3:1.

47 John 3:14–17.

Mount Moriah is in 2 Chronicles 3:1, where it is identified as the place where God halted the plague of Jerusalem and where Solomon built the temple. In New Testament terms, this is the vicinity of Calvary.[48] This is the place where Jesus died. And on that occasion the innocent Son was fully aware of the plan, and knew there would be no last-minute reprieve. He himself was the Lamb of God, pierced with branches from a thorn bush, dying an agonizing death on a cross for the sins of the world, sacrificing even his own life for us.

When God asks us to sacrifice much for him, we are reminded that he sacrificed everything for us. He was the Father who watched his Son climb up the lonely hill, knowing he would be the sacrifice for the world. When Abraham is asked to do what God, not he, will later bring to fulfilment, he is being brought into God's inner circle. This shared experience helps Abraham to understand God to a much greater degree. The apostle Paul speaks of the same experience when he says he knows Christ through his suffering.[49] The suffering that both Paul and Abraham experienced connected them relationally to God at a different level than would have been possible simply through knowledge of the Bible, or the experience of blessing from God. Somehow it is in this co-suffering with God that we know God more deeply.

We read in the book of Romans, in the context of a church population facing suffering, that:

---

48 Kidner, D. (1967), *Vol. 1: Genesis: An Introduction and Commentary*, Tyndale Old Testament Commentaries, IVP, p. 154.

49 Paul writes: 'I want to know Christ – yes, to know the power of his resurrection and participation in his sufferings, becoming like him in his death, and so, somehow, attaining to the resurrection from the dead' (Philippians 3:10–11).

If God is for us, who can be against us? He who did not spare his own Son, but gave him up for us all – how will he not also, along with him, graciously give us all things?[50]

If God did not withhold even the life of his own Son from us, there can be no doubting the generosity or benevolence of God. The cross of Christ is the place where God dealt with our sin and gave himself up for us. If God loves us this much, we know that anything he does to us or asks us to do for him is not to be taken in isolation, but understood in the context of love. It is through the times of loss and trauma and sacrifice that we can learn most about trust and faith, God's heartbeat and God's resurrection power.

God continues to make difficult demands of his followers. Jesus used a huge range of images to make sure his followers didn't miss the normal mode of discipleship. The Christian life involves daily sacrifice – taking up our cross.[51] His followers were to be 'light in the darkness'.[52] He said they were being sent out as 'lambs amongst wolves',[53] and challenged them to 'resist the devil',[54] loving one another as God had loved them, learning to trust him in the face of tragedy. If the God we believe in never asks the impossible of us, it is possible that we are not worshipping the true God at all, but a substitute, imitation, knock-off, lower-case god. In today's culture of instant gratification, it is little wonder that our Christianity

---

50 Romans 8:31–32.
51 Luke 9:23.
52 Matthew 5:14.
53 Luke 10:3.
54 James 4:7.

can seem to tally exactly with this kind of deity.[55] As Renee Padilla, a Latin American theologian, put it, this 'is a gospel that the "free consumers" of religion will want to receive because it is cheap and demands nothing of them'.[56]

Dietrich Bonhoeffer, a German Christian leader who was executed by the Nazis, called this soft substitute for Christianity 'cheap grace':

Cheap grace is the grace we bestow on ourselves. Cheap grace is the preaching of forgiveness without requiring repentance, baptism without church discipline, Communion without confession . . . Cheap grace is grace without discipleship, grace without the cross, grace without Jesus Christ, living and incarnate.[57]

The God of the Bible, the God of Abraham, is a God who can be trusted because of the weight of evidence and the consistency of his character. He is a God who gives the impossible, and sometimes asks the impossible. To come close to this God we need to know what it is to enjoy relationship with him, to sacrifice like he sacrificed, to love even when it hurts, and to experience resurrection. Just as he did with Abraham, God wants to involve us in his great story of creation and rescue and redemption.

I left the global leaders' gathering in Cape Town with Gyeoung's story rattling around my mind. She, like her father, had lost much, but the story she shared was having an impact all around the world.

---

55 Latin American theologian Renee Padilla calls this 'culture christianity'. Padilla, R. (1975), 'Evangelism and the World', in Stott, J. (ed.) (1975), *Let the Earth Hear His Voice*, World Wide Publications, p. 137.

56 Ibid., p. 138.

57 Dietrich Bonhoeffer's life and writings have long challenged believers to beware of cheap grace. See especially Bonhoeffer, D. (1996), *The Cost of Discipleship*, SCM, p. 36.

What was I willing to sacrifice? How would God use me in his bigger picture? Could I show the same unflinching trust in God? Her story, that of Abraham, and the stories of millions of others who have trusted God through difficult times of sacrifice could lead me to reject a God who seems irrational. Or, like Gyeoung herself, these stories could lead me to worship a God who knows the bigger picture and painstakingly involves us in it. We may not understand, but we can see enough to know we need to follow.

Chapter 2

The Moses Paradox
The God who is far away, so close

It's the question the children nag us with at bedtime. It's the question that echoes through literature, art and science. It's the question that a young Russian was supposed to have answered definitively on 12 April 1961 when he became the first human in space: *Where is God?* If nobody can answer the question 'Where is God?' it is easy to see why some people would decide that the answer is that God is nowhere. Even if Yuri Gagarin did utter those infamous (but contested) words, 'I do not see God', as he peered out of the tiny window of his Soyuz capsule, his search can hardly be described as exhaustive. The young cosmonaut had only ventured a few hundred miles from earth. Though that was more than any before him had achieved, it is a giant leap of faith to extrapolate from this that God does not exist anywhere in the vast unexplored universe. To have been logically consistent, Gagarin should really have concluded that he was agnostic about the subject of God, because he had only searched a miniscule fraction of space.

Yet for many people around the world, the inability to see or locate God is taken as grounds enough to deny his existence altogether.

The need to reconcile the fact that a supposedly omnipresent God feels impossibly distant from us is a paradox believers have wrestled with throughout history. It has led to architects through the centuries designing ever-larger churches and cathedrals, to try and find a way of mediating the presence of God through majestic buildings. It has led millions to set off on pilgrimage to try and find God either on the journey or at the destination – a holy place or sacred space. Musicians, artists, sculptors, preachers, technical wizards all continue to pursue the 'holy grail' of making God's presence felt. Christians worldwide talk about and seek out sacred spaces, 'mountaintop experiences' and hallowed ground to worship God.

Without a clear grasp of the location of God we could easily end up compartmentalizing our lives, assuming he is distant from us when we are not in our church buildings. We could think God is not available to us any more when the 'mountain-top' worship experiences have been left behind and we are in the valley of the mundane, stuck in the drudgery of the domestic. We could accuse God of not caring when we don't feel him by our side in times of crisis. If we don't wrestle with this paradox, we run the risk of not knowing how to find God in the loneliness of leadership, the sting of suffering or the darkness of doubt. The paradox of the whereabouts of God needs to be addressed, both to commend the faith to those who don't believe and to strengthen the faith of those who do.

If God is as the Bible describes him, then he surely shouldn't be hard to find. The Bible teaches that God is present everywhere:[1] if we were to go up to the heavens or to the depths of the oceans, God is there. God is the one in whom all of creation holds together, we are told,[2] and he is described as being not far from us.[3] The heroes of the Old Testament certainly seem to physically see and

---

1 For example: Psalm 139:7–10; Jeremiah 23:23–24.
2 Colossians 1:14–18.
3 Acts 17:27–28.

hear God, walk with him and talk to him. In the New Testament Paul reminds us that 'in him we live and move and have our being'.[4] Scripture declares that God is unmissable in his universe,[5] and involved in the intricacies of our personal lives. He promises his presence with us wherever we go.[6] In fact he promises all believers that he will never leave us or forsake us.[7]

However, the Bible also teaches that God is elusive and distant. His ways 'are above our ways'.[8] He is the 'Lord of Heaven and earth and does not live in temples built by human hands'.[9] The Psalmists call on a God who seems to have hidden himself[10] and abandoned his people;[11] time after time they talk about seeking God, thirsting for God, longing for God, or remembering God – all suggesting he is currently unavailable.[12] Even in the New Testament we are reminded that 'no one has ever seen God',[13] at least not in his glory.

Paradoxically, even God himself experienced the absence of God – Jesus, the Son of God himself, cried in despair from the cross: 'My God, My God, why have you abandoned me?'[14]

---

4 God is an ever-present help, and in him we 'live and move and have our being', as the Greek philosopher Epimenides wrote in his poem *Cretica* in the sixth century BC. He is approvingly quoted by the apostle Paul in Acts 17:28.

5 Romans 1:18–20.

6 Matthew 28:20.

7 Hebrews 13:5; Joshua 1:5.

8 Isaiah 55:8–9.

9 Acts 17:24.

10 Psalm 10.

11 Psalm 22.

12 Psalm 63, for example.

13 John 1:18. See also Exodus 33:20: 'But,' he said, 'you cannot see my face, for no one may see me and live.'

14 Psalm 22. Matt 27:46.

And so the Bible itself is caught up in this problem. How can God be both everywhere present, promising he will be with us at all times, and yet also so intangible that for much of our lives we don't see, hear or feel him at all? How can we worship a God who says he is here with us, when so often it feels like he is nowhere to be found?

We call this the Moses Paradox, because although Moses himself regularly had unique encounters with God's presence, he also stands alone in his understanding of the limitations of access to God. Moses is the only person who is described as seeing God face to face,[15] but he is also the one who has to protect and prevent others from seeing him; he builds the Tabernacle to house the presence of God, and is given the laws to restrict who had access to it. Moses knew the presence of God – he also knew the distance of God. How did Moses reconcile this tension in himself, and what can we learn from this for our own lives?

Moses' life began in tension – the country was in the middle of a crisis. God's promise to Abraham, that he would be the father of a great nation, had begun to be fulfilled, but his descendants, the Israelites, had been forced to move from the Promised Land to Egypt to escape a famine. There was then such rapid demographic growth that the Egyptian authorities got nervous and, in an attempt to control the population, they enslaved the Israelites and culled a whole generation of baby boys. The Jews' experience in Egypt was not dissimilar to what their descendants would go through in the Nazi concentration camps. In both situations the Jews slaved under increasingly harsh working conditions. The motto over the entrance to Auschwitz read '*Arbeit macht frei*'

---

15 Deuteronomy 34:10.

– 'work makes us free'. It was true neither in Egypt nor in the Nazi concentration camps, however. In the middle of both of these tragedies the Jews cried out to God. In the Exodus story, we are given a God's-eye perspective of the situation: 'God heard their groaning'. God 'remembered his covenant with Abraham' – he 'looked on the Israelites and was concerned about them'.[16] God is not far from his people physically or emotionally, even though they may not feel his presence.

Through the providence of God, a pair of courageous midwives, and some quick thinking by his mother and sister, the baby Moses escaped the slaughter and was raised by an Egyptian princess inside the Pharaoh's palace. Moses grew up living in the tension of two identities – his Hebrew heritage, and his status as a royal Egyptian. After killing an abusive slave-driver, he fled to the countryside of Midian where he started a new life as husband, father and shepherd; that is, until God called him to start a new life as a freedom-fighter.

As Moses was at work one ordinary day, he noticed an extraordinary bush fire.[17] As the fire burned, the bush strangely remained intact, and then a voice from the bush called Moses' name. Now that God had attracted his attention, and drawn him towards the bush, he warned Moses to stand back:

> 'Do not come any closer,' God said. 'Take off your sandals, for the place where you are standing is holy ground.' Then he

---

16 Exodus 2:24–25.

17 'The initial encounter between God and Moses reflects a remarkable mixture of ordinary elements of human experience with the extraordinary.' Childs, B. (1974), *The Book of Exodus: A Critical, Theological Commentary*, Westminster, p. 72.

said, 'I am the God of your father, the God of Abraham, the God of Isaac and the God of Jacob.' At this, Moses hid his face, because he was afraid to look at God.[18]

In Moses' very first direct encounter with God we face the paradox of the simultaneous presence and distance of God. Why does God first call Moses to approach him and then tell him to stay where he is? Why does God tell Moses to take his shoes off as he declares a remote corner of Midian wasteland to be 'holy ground'? This tension between the closeness and distance of God will recur throughout Moses' life.

God then introduces himself to Moses with the name 'I AM', affirming that his presence is real, his character is unchanging and his power is almighty.

But we are left with a mystery. If God is everywhere, why would he appear in a bush? Should we draw close, or must we stand back? If we now understand God to be everywhere all the time, should we walk around barefoot all the time?

In this first direct encounter with God, Moses receives a commission: he is to liberate God's people from Egyptian tyranny. God has heard the cry of his people, and Moses is going to be (part of) the answer to their prayers. God promises Moses that his mission will be successful, indeed that the people of God will come and worship on this very mountain where God has manifested himself through the burning bush.[19]

These questions of how we should understand God's whereabouts,

18 Exodus 3:5–6.
19 Exodus 3:1–12. It seems that Mount Horeb and Mount Sinai are the same place. See Cole, A. (1973), *Exodus*, Tyndale Old Testament Commentary, IVP, p. 70.

and how we should worship him aright, appear again later in the Moses story. After God had completed his mission of transforming Moses from a shepherd of sheep to the shepherd of his people, from a frightened criminal fleeing arrest to a courageous leader, and after all the action sequences of the book of Exodus, where the Egyptian superpower's military force is obliterated and God's people are liberated, just as God promised, Moses leads the Israelites back to Mount Sinai, the place of the burning bush. Moses is called up the mountain to meet God, but the rest of God's people are warned not to approach.[20] God commands Moses to 'Put limits for the people around the mountain and tell them, "Be careful that you do not approach the mountain or touch the foot of it."' It's another spatial paradox. God goes to all the effort of liberating his people from Egyptian captivity, calls them to worship him in the desert – but then he refuses to allow them into his presence. Moses alone receives the laws to pass on, laws that were to enable the Israelites to show their allegiance to the God who had rescued them. The bulk of these laws relate to how God's people will experience his presence and worship him appropriately.

God wants his people to build him a Tabernacle, a special tent where God's presence will manifest itself. The relation, in minute detail, of how this special tent was to be built sadly means that for many well-intentioned readers who set out to read the Bible from cover to cover, their journey ends in this part of Exodus! But understanding the big picture, knowing why these details matter, can help you get through this section without missing its significance.

The very precise instructions given about the size, shape and

---

20 Exodus 19.

furnishings of the Tabernacle are laced with meaning, and indeed illustrate the paradox under consideration. For example, the tent was erected 'outside of the camp' of the travelling Israelites.[21] But the whole point of the Tabernacle was that God had promised that he would 'dwell among his people'.[22] God is not a three-day walk away – but he is not within the camp either. He is distinct but not distant. He is, to quote a U2 song: far away, so close.[23]

Within the Tabernacle there were different zones, and specific locations for each of the furnishings. At the heart of the Tabernacle was the Most Holy Place – sometimes called the Holy of Holies. This was where the Ark of the Covenant was kept – that is, the gold-plated box made of acacia wood containing the two stone tablets with the Ten Commandments on them. No one had access to the Ark, or even into the Holy of Holies except once a year when, on the Day of Atonement, the chief priest would go and offer a sacrifice for all the sins of the people of Israel. The paradox of the presence and distance of God is clearly demonstrated here: setting up a tent of meeting as a year-round visible reminder of God's presence among them, yet restricting access to the actual 'presence of God' to just one man once a year.[24]

This brings us back to our original question. Where is God, exactly? Why does the God of the universe, the ruler of creation, need a Tabernacle tent, if he is everywhere? When God is in the Tabernacle, does he cease to be present elsewhere at that moment?

---

21 Exodus 33:7–11: 'Now Moses used to take a tent and pitch it outside the camp some distance away, calling it the "tent of meeting". Anyone inquiring of the LORD would go to the tent of meeting outside the camp.'

22 Exodus 25:8–9.

23 *Stay (Faraway, So Close)* U2 (1993)

24 Hebrews 9:6–8.

From the time of Moses to today, believers have wrestled with the paradox represented by the Bible's teachings about the presence and the distance of God. There are two nineteenth-century terms[25] that will help us with this paradox of the whereabouts of God: first, 'transcendence' and second, 'immanence'.

We have seen that the Bible teaches that God is present everywhere. As the Psalmist so eloquently puts it:

> Where can I go from your Spirit?
> Where can I flee from your presence?
> If I go up to the heavens, you are there;
> if I make my bed in the depths, you are there.
> If I rise on the wings of the dawn,
> if I settle on the far side of the sea,
> even there your hand will guide me,
> your right hand will hold me fast.
> If I say, 'Surely the darkness will hide me
> and the light become night around me,'
> even the darkness will not be dark to you;
> the night will shine like the day,
> for darkness is as light to you.[26]

This psalm is comforting. Even if we are taking our lives in our hands going paragliding or deep-sea diving, we are equally in God's care, we have his attention and protection. There is no place where God is out of reach, and no time when God is off duty. This is

---

25 Packer, J. I., 'God', in Ferguson, S. B. & Packer, J. I. (eds.) (2000), *New Dictionary of Theology*, IVP, p. 277.
26 Psalm 139:7–12.

what we mean by the 'immanence' of God: he is close by and available to each of us, as he is equally present in time and space, permeating the whole of creation.

But at the same time, God is not to be confused with his creation – he may permeate everything, but God is not the same as 'everything'. God is distinct, other, separate, holy or, to put it technically, 'transcendent'. Solomon knew this. He turned the blueprint of the mobile Tabernacle that Moses built into the solid structure of the temple on Mount Moriah. The temple was complete with its own Holy of Holies, and a giant curtain separated it off from the rest of the sanctuary. In the middle of his prayer of dedication of the temple, Solomon asks:

> But will God really dwell on earth? The heavens, even the highest heaven, cannot contain you. How much less this temple I have built![27]

Solomon recognized that God could not be contained or restricted or locked in a building or put in a box. Yet in building the temple he acknowledged the paradox of God's location – he is both present with and yet distinct from his creation. He is both transcendent and immanent.[28]

Often in our churches, as we gather for worship, we emphasize one aspect of this paradox to the detriment of the other. If we focus on the immanence of God, we can lose sight of his transcendence.

---

27 1 Kings 8:27.

28 Stanley Grenz and Roger Olson have argued that the tension between transcendence and immanence has been a central concern of theology in the twentieth century. See Grenz, S. & Olson, R. E. (1992), *20th Century Theology: God and the World in a Transitional Age*, IVP.

There are at least three different problems this could lead to: mistaking the creation for the Creator, over-sentimentalizing God, or misunderstanding the will of God.

Many of us have experienced the wonder of nature and felt a renewed connection to God through it. We have felt jaw-dropping awe when we are looking down from the top of a mountain, or a sense of wonder when surfing a powerful wave, or even been stuck for words watching a nature documentary. This sense of resonance comes because we have a common ancestry and vocation with the natural world; we and it were both created by God and for God; so it is no surprise that we are deeply connected. The beauty and majesty of nature is supposed to give us a spiritual experience – not so that we should worship nature, but instead so that we worship alongside nature. If we over-emphasize the immanence of God, though, we can confuse the creation with the Creator, and begin to look for God in nature. This is called pantheism and can be found in the New Age movement and some spiritualities associated with environmentalism.[29] There are strong similarities to the way that many religions such as Buddhism and Hinduism conceptualize God.

In reaction against the fear of worshipping the creation instead of its Creator, some Christians have disengaged from our responsibility to care for the environment. But this is to pass up both a responsibility and an opportunity. Creation care is part of the original vocation of humanity:[30]

God blessed them and said to them, 'Be fruitful and increase

---

29 For a brief introduction to pantheism, look at Sire, J. (2009), *The Universe Next Door*, IVP, pp. 144–65.

30 Bookless, D. (2008), *Planetwise: Dare to Care for God's World*, IVP.

in number; fill the earth and subdue it. Rule over the fish in the sea and the birds in the sky and over every living creature that moves on the ground.'[31]

We were called to make something of the world that God has given us responsibility for. We are to rule over it, but not by raping and pillaging its resources; rather, our rule ought to be modelled on God's compassionate care for his creation. This initial charge is nowhere rescinded in Scripture.

Many activists of other faiths engage in care for God's creation. Are they not responding to the fingerprints of God in the beauty of creation and the latent memory of humanity's God-given responsibility to care for it? If Christians retreat from this vocation we pass up opportunities to work alongside others and help them to discover the Creator rather than just enjoying his creation. As we live with the paradox of a transcendent yet omnipresent God, we are called to worship by caring for nature and by joining in the praise as 'the heavens declare the glory of God'.[32]

Let me tell you a story about a little boy who had no fear of walking into the Oval Office in the White House, the centre of the US government. No matter what meetings were going on, whichever global dignitaries were present, no matter what the topic of conversation, this little boy would march in and no one stopped him. For the rest of the world the man who sat behind the oak desk was known as President J. F. Kennedy. But for little John-John, that man was known as 'Daddy'.[33]

---

31 Genesis 1:28.

32 Psalm 19.

33 Stanley Tretick took some wonderful candid photographs in 1963 of John Jr. hiding under the president's wooden desk while his father engages in important diplomatic business.

Similarly, throughout the Bible we are encouraged to foster a familiar intimacy and access to our all-powerful God. Through word pictures God is described to us as a loving father, a caring mother,[34] a faithful friend,[35] a genuine helper.[36] The Scriptures are full of personal and affectionate language for God, and to neglect them is to resist God's desire for genuine intimacy with us. But if these are the only words we hear associated with God, they can lead us to over-familiarity and the second danger, of focusing exclusively on the immanence of God. One theological student coined the phrase 'Jesus is my girlfriend'[37] to describe the over-sentimentalized approach taken in some contemporary worship music. On the one hand, we risk hyping up the emotional side of our relationship with God; on the other, we are guilty of bringing God down to our level. Once we romanticize[38] our relationship with God, it will not be long before we start expecting God to deliver what we demand. In a world where we are increasingly encouraged to think that everything revolves around us, the seeming lack of immediate compliance to our material and emotional requests can leave us feeling shocked or outraged.

Writing at the end of the twentieth century, theologian David Wells lamented:

---

34 'Can a woman forget her nursing child / And have no compassion on the son of her womb? / Even these may forget, but I will not forget you' (Isaiah 49:15–16).

35 John 15:15; James 2:23.

36 Psalm 46:1–4.

37 See Hargreaves, S., '"Jesus is my girlfriend"? A critique of romantic imagery in youth orientated worship songs, and a doctrinal framework for intimacy in worship', unpublished dissertation at London School of Theology.

38 To be fair, there has been a mystic tradition which has emphasized this perspective too. For example, Catherine of Siena in the fourteenth century wrote about Christ as the 'sweet bridegroom of my soul'.

Much of what should be understood as transcendent is either disappearing or is now relocated to what is immanent . . . A God with whom we are on such easy terms and whose reality is little different from our own – a God who is merely there to satisfy our needs – has no authority to compel and will soon begin to bore us.[39]

Neglecting the transcendence of God, we will end up suffering from boredom with God. If we become over-familiar with (our idea of) God, it is likely that familiarity will breed contempt. If our view of God is biased towards the immanent, when we face trouble, our question, 'Where is God?' betrays not so much a true interest in where God is to be found, but rather our self-interest. What we are really asking is, 'Where is the God that I ordered?' Neglecting the transcendence of God, it becomes easy for us to diminish God, both at a personal level and a national one. At a personal level God can become simply a mascot or a supplier. He exists to reconstruct our self-esteem, to meet our 'felt needs', to deliver our dreams and aspirations. He exists to make my life easier, to make me richer, to help me feel more secure and at ease. Our prayer lives end up revolving around asking for success in business, for a parking space or for a boost of confidence before a blind date. At a national level, we expect God to fight on our side when we are at war, protect our soldiers, rubberstamp our tactics and ensure the economic prosperity and military might of our country.[40]

But God is bigger than our nation, and bigger than our dreams

---

39 Wells, D. (1994), *God in the Wasteland: The Reality of Truth in a World of Fading Dreams*, IVP, p. 93.

40 See, for example, Grudem, W. (2010), *God's Politics*, Zondervan. Grudem includes a section where he argues that waterboarding is justified and that only capitalism is biblically justifiable.

or ambitions. He is not partisan, but the judge of all the earth. He loves the whole world. He is the holy and transcendent one who cannot be boxed in or cut down to size. When he doesn't comply with our demands, we can be sure that he has good reason.

A further danger of focusing exclusively on the immanence of God comes when we wrestle with how to relate what happens in our world to God's will. Steve Jobs, the inspirational CEO of Apple computers, made the following connection, as recorded by his biographer Walter Isaacson:[41]

Even though they were not fervent about their faith, Jobs's parents wanted him to have a religious upbringing, so they took him to the Lutheran church most Sundays. That came to an end when he was thirteen. In July 1968 *Life* magazine published a shocking cover showing a pair of starving children in Biafra. Jobs took it to Sunday school and confronted the church's pastor.

'If I raise my finger, will God know which one I'm going to raise even before I do it?'

The pastor answered, 'Yes, God knows everything.'

Jobs then pulled out the *Life* cover and asked, 'Well, does God know about this and what's going to happen to those children?'

'Steve, I know you don't understand, but yes, God knows about that.'

Jobs announced that he didn't want to have anything to do with worshipping such a God, and he never went back to church.[42]

---

41 Isaacson, W. (2011), *Steve Jobs: The Exclusive Biography*, Little, Brown.
42 Ibid., pp. 14–15.

Like many of us, Jobs struggled with the idea that God could see and know the details of the injustice in the world and do nothing to prevent it. This is something that is fundamental to the Job Paradox. When we consider that God not only knows about the suffering but is actually present where it occurs, it is no wonder this can be a major stumbling block to faith. For some the omnipresence of God and the omniscience of God must add up to God having responsibility for everything that takes place. In other words, if God is present everywhere and knows what is going on there, then everything that happens must effectively be God's will, and every bad thing that happens must be God's fault. We end up with a kind of fatalism that attributes to God evil motives, evil actions and evil outcomes. This is more like the impersonal 'Force' of the *Star Wars* universe, which implies no distinction between what takes place in the physical world and what God 'wants'.

But there is a distinction between God the Creator and his creation, between his perfect presence and his giving permission to allow things to happen. This distinction is vitally connected with the balance between God's immanence and his transcendence. He is omnipresent, even in the midst of the suffering; we know from the Bible that he both sees and cares, but that does not imply malicious intent when he allows bad things to happen or when the Almighty chooses not to intervene.

In order to resolve some of the challenges posed by exclusive attention to the immanence of God, many have overcompensated and overemphasized the transcendence of God. The dangers here include thinking that God is both physically and emotionally distant, believing he is unable to intervene, or that he is unwilling to do so.

Traditionally, many in this camp have ended up describing God as a watchmaker who constructed the intricate mechanism of our world, wound it up and then let it play out its existence. This way of thinking was popularized in the eighteenth and nineteenth centuries under the name of Deism.[43] The watchmaker theory appeared to give God an excuse for non-involvement in human tragedy. The argument states that the brokenness in the world is not God's fault, as he set up the world correctly, and any flaws are our responsibility for misuse of what was a good creation. We still hear echoes of this view when people talk about places as being 'God-forsaken' or in some apologists' arguments around suffering, where God is portrayed as being deliberately distant and taking a non-interventionist stance to our problems, simply watching our tiny planet from afar.

In a well-known sociological study a woman was asked: 'Do you believe in a God who can change the course of events on earth?'

'No, just the ordinary one.'[44]

The God that many people assume exists is one that can't actually effect change in our world. He is portrayed as an impotent deity who listens to our prayers but can't actually act on them. Prayer becomes less about God changing situations and just about God changing the person praying. In a landmark study in the United States, exploring the beliefs of thousands of twenty-first-century teenagers,[45] it was found that in the churches of America the beliefs of young people were 'almost Christian' – their thinking differed

---

43 Brown, C. (1990), *Christianity and Western Thought: From the Ancient World to the Age of Enlightenment*, IVP, p. 214.

44 Abercrombie et al. (1970), p. 160, cited in Grace Davie, 'An Ordinary God: The Paradox of Religion in Contemporary Britain', *The British Journal of Sociology*, Vol. 41, No. 3, Special Issue: *Britain as a European Society?* (Sept. 1990), p. 395.

45 Creasey-Dean, K. (2010), *Almost Christian: What the Faith of Our Teenagers is Telling the American Church*, Oxford University Press.

from orthodox Christianity in three key ways that the report summarized as 'Moralistic Therapeutic Deism'. The word 'moralistic' is used because acceptance by God is based on doing good things to earn merit with God. The 'therapeutic' element is because the chief point of human life is our personal satisfaction. It is 'Deist' because God does 'not need to be particularly involved in one's life except when he is needed to resolve a problem'.[46] This view might be expected among young people outside of the church, holding on to some vestige of belief; but it has become the norm within churches too. The study argues that the main reason young people believe these things about God is because of what they see and hear in their parents' generation. For many Christians God has very little to do with daily life: when we go to work, play sports, watch television, travel, vote or shop, God's presence and purposes are hardly on our radar.

Some writers have described this as the sacred–secular divide. If we focus exclusively on the transcendence of God, first, we do not expect to engage with God in the mundane aspects of life. God is reserved for 'special occasions', good and bad: Sundays, church holidays – and crises. God is assumed to be a distant higher power, too far away to be interested in our work, the way we do business, or our public life in general. Separating out the transcendence of God from his immanence echoes similar separations that have been taking place in our culture. Sociologists such as John Murray Cuddihy have observed that modern culture sunders things that had once been held to be united: 'home from work, fact from value, individuals from community, religion from politics, nuclear from

---

46 Smith, C. (2010), '"Moralistic Therapeutic Deism" as U.S. Teenagers' Actual, Tacit, De Facto Religious Faith', in Collins-Mayo, S. & Dandelion, P. (eds.) (2010), *Religion and Youth*, Ashgate, p. 1.

extended families, medium from message, form from content, art from belief, economy from ethics, the present from the past, time from eternity'.[47] What God has joined none of us should put asunder. In our understanding and practice we must lash together the immanence and transcendence of God: the truth is not one or the other, but both.

Second, when we focus on the transcendence of God, we can end up picturing him a bit like a time traveller from a science-fiction movie who has been warned not to touch anything when he goes back to the past, for fear of the repercussions. This can lead to some fascinating conundrums in approaching prayer. If we were to pray for sunshine on our daughter's wedding day, are we depriving someone else on the planet from receiving enough rain to nourish their crops? If God intervened to delay a train on our behalf, would that prevent somebody else from meeting their future wife and their child becoming the next Prime Minister of Kenya?[48] We may acknowledge God is close enough to intervene, but sometimes we act as though he were prevented from doing so by the laws of physics. This will lead to our prayer life stagnating and we will miss out on opportunities to worship him as we see him in action in our lives.

Third, even if we reject the idea of a wholly transcendent God, it is easy to jump to the conclusion that even if God were able to intervene, he doesn't want to. We may imagine him being emotionally distant, or worse, like an uncaring parent neglecting his children and refusing to help. Focusing on the otherness of God can lead to

---

47 Adapted from Ken Myers reflecting on John Murray Cuddihy's work in *Mars Hill Audio Journal*, Vol. 118.

48 For a mind-bending exploration of this kind of theme with a romantic twist, you might enjoy Peter Howitt's 1998 film *Sliding Doors*.

a lack of intimacy. The polar opposite of the 'Jesus is my girlfriend' romanticism is the cold formalism of an overly distant relationship with God, of which the most extreme version has been dubbed 'worm theology' by its critics. Mark Galli, editor of the market-leading US magazine *Christianity Today*, describes it succinctly: 'God's holiness is set against our sinfulness to such a degree that the only appropriate response seems to be self-loathing.'[49] This kind of outlook on life earned the Puritans the (mostly unfair) definition assigned to them by H. L. Mencken: 'Puritanism: The haunting fear that someone, somewhere, may be happy.' The dour formalism and joyless judgementalism that this stereotype engenders is, sadly, well known to many people around the world. It finds frequent expression in literature and films, from the corruption of Warden Norton in *The Shawshank Redemption* to the judgemental and moralizing leaders in Nathaniel Hawthorne's *The Scarlet Letter*.

The name 'worm theology' may in fact come from a line in a hymn by Isaac Watts:

> Alas, and did my Saviour bleed
> And did my Sovereign die?
> Would He devote that sacred head
> For such a worm as I?[50]

It is actually a fair question, and Watts raises a critical point here. When we do get a glimpse of the transcendent majesty of God, it is hard not to reflect on our humble status in comparison to him.

---

49 http://www.christianitytoday.com/ct/2010/aprilweb-only/23-51.0.html?
paging=off
50 Watts, I. (1707), 'Alas! and Did My Saviour Bleed' in Watts, I.

In front of an eternal God, our transience is inescapable; alongside a holy God our sinfulness becomes clear; next to an omnipotent God our insignificance is obvious. But right humility in front of God's awe-inspiring magnitude and guilt-inspiring holiness needs to be held in check against the gracious acceptance of a Father who wants to embrace lost and broken people. Jesus subverted the idea of a distant and dour God, by bringing joy and celebration as he lived, then bleeding and dying to bridge the gap between us and the Father.

What we want and need – and what God offers – is neither cold formalism nor romantic sentimentality. The twentieth-century writer and speaker A. W. Tozer strikes a helpful balance when he writes:

When we come into this sweet relationship, we are beginning to learn astonished reverence, breathless adoration, awesome fascination, lofty admiration of the attributes of God and something of the breathless silence we know when God is near.[51]

By taking the time to explore the dangers of paying inadequate attention to either the transcendence or the immanence of God, we can see the importance of this paradox. The truth will be found by holding in tension our understanding of the God who is with us and present everywhere in his universe, against our knowledge that he remains distinct from what he has made. Unless we face up to this struggle to reconcile the paradox of the closeness and the distance of God, we are in danger of leaving out a vital aspect of

---

51 Tozer, A. W. (1986), *Whatever Happened to Worship?*, OM Publishing, p. 27.

God's nature. If we don't wrestle with this tension we deprive ourselves of knowing God in his fullness and will be settling for a mediocre picture of God.

So how do we understand where God is in relation to his universe? Just as software is present in every computer but is distinct from the hardware, just as your mind is more than the chemical reactions of your brain, so God is more than his universe. God is both physically present and morally distinct from the world. He comes to draw alongside us, wanting to live with and among his people. But God also has to tell us to stand back from his perfect glory – because it would destroy us. He has to let us know that though earthly, time-bound points in space may form a focus for his approaches to us at a particular moment, he is far more than just a burning bush or a cloud in a tent. We have to understand that he is not a mascot, ready to cheerlead for us, at our beck and call. He is the Lord of all creation and he deserves to be feared, honoured and worshipped, intimately and reverently. God invites us into his presence but for our own protection he warns us to keep our distance. The Exodus story is full of examples of this particular paradox. The God who rescues his people from slavery is deemed inadequate by those he rescued. The food he provides is complained about, and instead, Israel's selective memory allows them to recall only the good bits about their time in Egypt: they ignore the forced labour and the killing of their children, but optimistically remember 'pots of meat' and eating 'all the food they wanted'.[52] Similarly, when Moses is up the mountain receiving the law from God, it seems the Israelites do not have any patience for a God they cannot touch and see right in front of them. So they

---

52 Exodus 16:3.

swap a transcendent, mighty God for an immanent, cast-from-gold calf.

After this depressing experience, Moses asks to see the glory of God, so that he might know that God is truly with him. He craves the presence of God, and to encourage his servant, God gives him unique access to himself.[53] But even Moses still needs to shield himself in a cleft of the rock – God forbids him from seeing his face.

God is transcendent, but he is also involved; he is neither distant nor disinterested nor distracted. But the question remains: why is it that, if he is not far from us, we still so often fail to feel God's presence? Why does God deprive us of experiential access to himself? Why are we left longing to know where God is, where to find him, how to see him?

My collar was a bit tight and the dinner jacket, which I had borrowed from a teenager in our church, was a bit too long in the sleeve. But I was there, at London's Leicester Square, on the red carpet and with paparazzi all around. I was loitering with intent: this was no ordinary movie premiere, this was a royal premiere with the Queen herself due to join us in the auditorium. The red carpet was disappearing fast under a layer of real snow (topped up by some fake) as I mingled with the stars. I had spotted former Wimbledon tennis champion Boris Becker, various C-list celebrities from a reality TV talent contest and Qui-Gon Jinn (or, as non-members of the *Star Wars* fan club call him, Liam Neeson). I was poised, ready with my camera to snatch an exclusive of Her Majesty, when suddenly two huge men with sunglasses appeared. I was about to ask them why they were wearing sunglasses in winter at night-time,

---

53 Deuteronomy 34:10.

but before I could say anything, they ushered me and my camera into the empty cinema while all the important people carried on their loitering outside of the cinema. Apparently riff-raff weren't allowed to be on the red carpet at the same time as the elites. I never did snatch a picture of the Queen wearing her first ever pair of 3D glasses, and Qui-Gon didn't have time to sign my *Star Wars* calendar. As I sat there, far away from the stars I had come to see, I reflected on my own experience of God. Normally I don't think about my proximity to the Queen of England, but just when I was actually the closest to her, I felt the furthest away.

There have been times when I have felt very close to God, but there have also been many times when I have sensed a distance from him; in retrospect, perhaps the occasions overlapped. But when I experienced distance from God, I did not feel like I was being ushered away from a celebrity who had no time for little, insignificant people. Quite the opposite: when I felt distant from God, I knew that the desire to draw close to him came from God himself.

Sometimes I know that my feeling of distance from God is not just due to God's transcendence, but due to my own stupidity, sin or selfishness. It is not always he who is distant; often it's me. He calls me closer, but I feel ashamed or fearful or inadequate. It is no accident that the first time the question 'Where are you?' appears in the Bible, it was not from people looking for God, but from God, looking for his people.[54] Adam and Eve's sin and shame had caused them to try to hide from God, and millions have followed in their footsteps. Similarly, it was not Moses looking for God in the desert – he too was trying to hide from the consequences of his sinful

---

54 Genesis 3:9.

actions – but God seeking out Moses as he called to him from the burning bush.

It was no accident, either, that God appeared to Moses as a flame. The movement of a flame and its bright colours attract us, and yet the heat of the flame pushes us away. This is the 'fearful and fascinating Mystery' of God that the German theologian Rudolf Otto celebrated.[55] The burning bush drew Moses' attention and yet he was told not to come too close because of the dangerous holiness of God: this encounter gives us a visual aid of our presence–distance paradox. Fire is a symbol of purity.[56] The moral purity of a perfect God draws us to him, but his holiness and our sinfulness separate us. God has to bar us from his presence in order to protect us – we would survive in the white-hot radiance of God's moral perfection no longer than an ice cube on the surface of the sun. It is for our protection that God keeps his distance, but it is for our salvation that God comes close.

The moment this was most perfectly symbolized was when the sky turned black and the Son of God, feeling the pain of the unique occasion of separation from his Father, cried out, 'My God, My God, why have you forsaken me?' Then, the huge curtain in the temple was torn in two from the top to the bottom, allowing anybody and everybody access to the most restricted part, called the Holy of Holies. This was the moment when God invited us – all of us

---

55 The German theologian Rudolf Otto attempted to engage a predominantly liberal theological context with a greater sense of mystery and humility. In his most famous work (Otto, R. (1923), *The Idea of the Holy*, translated by John W. Harvey, Oxford University Press) he writes about *mysterium tremendum et fascinans*, 'the fearful and fascinating mystery'.

56 'Fire seems to speak of God's holiness and, in particular, his anger in relation to sin.' Cole, R. A. (1973), *Exodus: An Introduction and Commentary*, Tyndale Old Testament Commentaries, IVP, p. 71.

– to get close and personal with the King of Heaven. It ushered in a new era when God could be accessed not only at the physical temple, but through Jesus, by the Holy Spirit.[57]

Jesus' death seemed like the end for this so-called prophet and 'King of the Jews'. But instead it was a final blow to the problem that separated us from God's presence. Now, when we search for God, we can find him, as millions around the world can testify. And one day we will be with him and see him face to face. One day the dwelling of God will truly be with his people.

In the meantime, because of the nature of the character of God, there is no escaping the apparent absence of the everywhere-present God. We are required to wrestle with it in our public life and in our private life, in our personal life and our corporate life, in our worship in the world, and in the church. The tension between these elements, though, is exactly what will help us cross the secular–sacred divide, pray well and relate well to God. We have not resolved all of the questions this issue raises, and more clarity will come as we explore the paradoxes surrounding Job and Judas, but the Moses Paradox helps us to understand – and accept – that we simply must live in, rather than trying to avoid, the tension between the distant but ever-present God. Sometimes we will feel God especially close, and sometimes we will wish he felt closer. Both states of being are essential to our spiritual health.

---

57 Ephesians 2:18.

Chapter 3

The Joshua Paradox
The God who is terribly compassionate

We weren't sure what to believe. We saw jets flying in formation, heading north. Stories were circulating of families being rounded up in the middle of the night and locked in cafés which were then set alight. Reports were spreading of pregnant women cut open to settle bets on the gender of babies that would now never be born. Our student friends had been called home to help with the visitors that had arrived from across the border. Then the BBC reported that the NATO bombardment had begun.

My wife and I were living in neighbouring Albania during the Kosovo crisis, and we heard first-hand the horrific stories of how Serbia was trying to rid itself of all the ethnic Albanians within Kosovo (which was a region of Serbia). It started with the banning of the language, and eventually led to full-scale 'ethnic cleansing'. It was inexcusably evil, yet this atrocity was taking place in the name of Jesus. The Kosovars were ethnically Albanian and culturally Muslim, and the Serbs were culturally Christian, so this was pitched as a religious battle – one group systematically exterminating another. It is, sadly, not an isolated case in history. From the bloody massacres of the Crusades, through the mass killings of Mayans by the Spanish Conquistadors, to Afrikaaner oppressing black South Africans, or sectarian violence in Northern Ireland between Catholics and Protestants, so-called Christians have justified all sorts of atrocities, taking inspiration from the apparent ethnic cleansing God commanded in the Old Testament. When I read these portions of our history, or meet somebody who has suffered at the hands of religious persecution in the name of Jesus, I am frankly ashamed to call myself a Christian.

This kind of sectarian warfare seems to be exactly what we find in the Bible. Jews encouraged to kill Canaanites. The Israelite army commanded to raze cities to the ground and execute everyone inside. They are specifically commanded not to show mercy.[1] One incident may help to illustrate where inspiration for these killings might come from.

When the people of God arrive in the Promised Land, having been liberated from Egyptian slavery, they come to the city of Ai and are told to completely destroy it. This involves some subterfuge. The Israelite army is divided into two – a small force comes up against the city and then flees, baiting the soldiers to follow them. Meanwhile the primary force is in hiding, and when the soldiers pursue the fleeing Israelites, the rest of them swoop in, capture the city, set it ablaze and then head out of the city, where they outflank the force pursuing their compatriots. The tactics pay off: it is recorded that 'Twelve thousand men and women fell that day – all the people of Ai';[2] the only recorded survivor is the king, who is taken to Joshua, then impaled on a pole and left on public display.

How do we reconcile the paradox of a God who has compassion on the Jewish nation through all their failures, but then commands them to show no compassion towards other nations? How can a God

---

1 Deuteronomy 7:10.
2 Joshua 8:25.

of love order the annihilation of a whole people-group, the mass slaughter of men and women, old and young, and even animals too? How can we take seriously the command of God to love our enemies, when he appears to ignore those injunctions himself? How can we trust a God who looks so partisan, who gives his own people the ultimate weapon of mass destruction; namely, his own presence and power? How can we praise a God who seems to leave the poor pagan nations of the Old Testament without a fighting chance? Equally, why would he defend and protect the Jews of Bible times, yet then keep himself completely aloof during the extermination of 16 million Jews in Europe during the lifetime of our own grandparents?

Let me be honest. I feel embarrassed about my faith when these questions crop up. And I am not alone. Many of us would rather edit such violent episodes out of the Scriptures. We try and forget about them when praying or praising God. We skim over the bits of the Bible we don't like, latching on to uplifting phrases instead – underlining them in our Bibles, copying them out and attaching them on to the doors of our kitchen appliances, using them to help us through the day and support our hopes, dreams and desires. The awkward bits that seem blatantly evil or that we don't have the moral, spiritual or emotional capacity to deal with, we quietly ignore, leaving whole swathes of the Bible unread. Lots of us effectively edit our Bibles to avoid those difficult passages where God appears more terrible than compassionate.

This is not a new problem, the consequence only of highly developed twenty-first-century moral consciences. Marcion of Sinope[3] (lived AD 80–160) believed that there were in effect two

---

3 Marcion was excommunicated for this view in AD 144. McGrath, A. (1997), *Christian Theology*, 2nd edn., Blackwell, p. 197.

Gods. The Creator God of the Old Testament was obsessed with the law and was mostly angry and judgemental. Then there is a second God, the good and gracious Father of Jesus, unknown to us before the New Testament. Marcion was denounced as a heretic for views that were way outside the scope of what the church was teaching. But many Christians live as if Marcion was actually right – we are practising Marcionites without knowing it. Maybe we don't actually believe in two separate Gods, but with the scant attention we give the Old Testament, we might as well.

We don't articulate any of this, of course – it's just that since we like and feel we can connect with the stories of the patriarchs, the prophets' predictions about Jesus and the comfort of the Psalms, that's what we spend our time reading and studying. But in doing so we effectively deem the rest of the Old Testament redundant.

Ironically, we are happy to allow children access to the full horrors of the Old Testament – even at bedtime. We tell the story of Noah, and how his whole generation was wiped out by a massive flood. We love the story of Joseph, which itself doesn't really dwell on the fact that the nations around Egypt were slowly starving to death in a famine. We tell the story of Moses and the crossing of the Red Sea, while the Egyptian soldiers (who have already, with the rest of the nation, had to face boils, plagues of locusts, and the divine execution of their eldest sons) get drowned in the waves.

Children do love the stories of the Old Testament (though that doesn't stop them asking some challenging questions of their own!). And Jesus loved the Old Testament too – he quotes it at key moments in his life, he uses its thought forms and imagery in the majority of his teaching,[4] he explains his mission as fulfilling the Old Testament, not (as some may have been claiming) abolishing it.[5] If we want to know God and follow Jesus, then it is not OK just to love some parts of the Old Testament – we need to learn to love it all. If we want a genuine relationship with our God and Saviour, we cannot edit his written word.

So, we avoid the genocide stories in the Bible because we find them difficult to cope with ourselves. In addition, we may avoid them because they do not fit our agenda. We want to preach a God of love, of peace and of forgiveness, and to see those values spread. Surely that is a good thing?

Ironically, though, if we manipulate God's word to ignore the difficult passages for our purposes, we become tragically like those who manipulate God's word in the other direction and use these same passages to justify violence[6] against other people-groups. It is always a tragedy for God's word to be twisted in order to support things that God expressly forbids.

But another and probably the biggest reason why we avoid reading and thinking about much of the Old Testament is because we are

---

4 Jesus cites Deuteronomy when facing temptation; Isaiah 6:9–10 on why he spoke in parables; Psalms 35:19; 69:4 on his rejection and persecution; Psalm 22 on his death.

5 'Do not think that I have come to abolish the Law or the Prophets; I have not come to abolish them but to fulfil them' (Matthew 5:17).

6 'We are particularly disturbed by the violence of the Old Testament when we contemplate the way in which it has been used to justify violence down through the ages . . . crusades against Muslims, genocide of North American Indians or aboriginal Australians, apartheid against black South Africans, discrimination and violence against African Americans, expropriation of land from Palestine – even attitudes towards Roman Catholics in Northern Ireland.' Wright, C. (2008), *The God I Don't Understand: Reflections on Tough Questions of Faith*, Zondervan, p. 74.

afraid. After all, if we don't like what we see when we've given these things just a cursory look, looking closer might make the problem even worse. We fear it might even lead us to losing our faith, or at least our confidence to share that faith. The new atheists, of course, have played on that fear as they have lambasted the God of the Old Testament. Militant atheists such as Richard Dawkins have caused the confidence of many Christians to wobble over this issue, of whether the Bible can be taken seriously. Here's a single sentence from *The God Delusion* which encapsulates these allegations:

> The God of the Old Testament is arguably the most unpleasant character in all fiction: jealous and proud of it; a petty, unjust, unforgiving control-freak; a vindictive, bloodthirsty ethnic cleanser; a misogynistic, homophobic, racist, infanticidal, geno-cidal, filicidal, pestilential, megalomaniacal, sadomasochistic, capriciously malevolent bully.[7]

This statement hits us hard, because we can see exactly where Dawkins gets his ammunition from. In the Exodus story God sends the angel of death to Egypt to kill off the firstborn sons of all those who had not painted the blood of a lamb over their door posts. The Old Testament law that Moses receives from God on Mount Sinai did make it legal for an unruly child to be stoned to death.[8] God does command Joshua to rid the land of the Canaanites.

Dawkins is not a lone voice of critique: he is joined by such luminaries as Daniel Dennett, Christopher Hitchens, Philip Pullman, David Attenborough, Sam Harris and a host of others. They bandy

---

7 Dawkins, R. (2008), *The God Delusion*, Black Swan Books, p. 51.
8 Deuteronomy 21:18–21.

around what seem like pretty convincing arguments that the Bible message is horrific, unbecoming and irrelevant (not to mention untrue). But in fact it is only by looking squarely at these difficult parts of the Bible that our faith can grow. When we come across difficult questions, we should learn that ignoring them does not build faith. We must be brave enough to face our challengers head on: then, perhaps, our faith will become stronger, not weaker.

Preachers often avoid such passages, or skate over the implications when they do teach on them, and we are fearful of asking the awkward questions, so we become vulnerable to the poison in Dawkins' vociferous litany of difficult-to-swallow Old Testament sound-bites.

The best place to explore the paradox of God's conflicting cruelty and compassion is in the difficult yet celebrated story of Joshua, the very man whose exploits have already highlighted the problem for us. The undisputed hero of faith in his generation, Joshua was one of twelve spies sent out by Moses on a reconnaissance trip into the land of Canaan.[9] After a forty-day mission, they came back to base camp. Everyone was agreed that this place was all that God had promised, 'a land flowing with milk and honey'.[10] But ten of the spies reported that the people in the land were so big, they looked like they were descended from an ancient tribe of warrior giants. Joshua and another spy, Caleb, saw things very differently. Nonetheless, on hearing this report, fear spread like wildfire through the camp, and the people of Israel turned back from the border and were cursed by God to wander in the desert for another forty years.[11] That day Joshua was hand-picked to succeed Moses as leader of God's people,

---

9 Numbers 13.

10 Exodus 33:3.

11 Numbers 34:32–35.

because of his faith and his vision. He was willing to trust in God's power and provision despite the challenges ahead. While the other ten spies, along with that whole generation of Israelites, were destined to die in the desert, Joshua and Caleb were shown mercy.

Joshua knew the compassion of the God who spared his life, but he also knew the terrifying anger of a God who sentenced a generation to die in the desert. Forty years later, he had presumably had a lot of time to think this over. He and Caleb had outlived Moses and the whole of the cursed generation. Returning to the border of Canaan, they were faced once more with the challenge of taking possession of a land that was already inhabited. And Joshua was faced again by a God who was both terrible and compassionate.

God had made clear in the book of Deuteronomy what he expected his people to do when they got to the Promised Land:

> However, in the cities of the nations the LORD your God is giving you as an inheritance, do not leave alive anything that breathes. Completely destroy them – the Hittites, Amorites, Canaanites, Perizzites, Hivites and Jebusites – as the LORD your God has commanded you. Otherwise, they will teach you to follow all the detestable things they do in worshipping their gods, and you will sin against the LORD your God.[12]

So Joshua's task as they crossed into the Promised Land was to undertake a shock-and-awe exercise which looks like nothing short of genocide. The land was to experience ethnic cleansing, ordained by God. So that was precisely what Joshua did. We have already looked at the taking of the city of Ai, but it is in the well-known account of

---

12 Deuteronomy 20:16–20.

the fall of Jericho that we see most clearly God's relationship with this violence.

The story is taught and even acted out by children in Sunday Schools across the world. The people of Israel marched around the city walls once a day for six straight days. But on the seventh day they marched round seven times, and then there was a long blast from the trumpets and a great shout from the army, 'and the walls came tumbling down'.[13] I remember getting very dizzy in my Sunday School re-enactments of this event, and we would all fall down just like those walls. But we didn't reconstruct what happened after the walls fell:

> When the trumpets sounded, the army shouted, and at the sound of the trumpet, when the men gave a loud shout, the wall collapsed; so everyone charged straight in, and they took the city. They devoted the city to the LORD and destroyed with the sword every living thing in it – men and women, young and old, cattle, sheep and donkeys.[14]

It's right there in black and white: 'destroyed with the sword every living thing in it'. This is the Joshua Paradox. This is not, after all, a nice child-friendly story. Yes, God is the saviour who helps his weak people because he loves them; he even saves Rahab, the prostitute who had helped the spies on their reconnaissance mission – but what about everyone else in Jericho? This is the story of a God-ordained, systematic extermination of an entire city. Whatever happened to the promise to Abraham that through his offspring God would bless the nations? In Jericho and Ai the Israelites razed

---

13 Joshua 6:4–5.
14 Joshua 6:20–21.

the cities to the ground, and all the inhabitants were killed. The words used are uncompromising: 'not sparing anyone that breathed'. What kind of blessing is that?

How can we reconcile this action with the God who is so compassionate to an elderly childless couple, or to a murderer on the run, a God who acts to save individuals, let alone whole nations? When God hears the cry of his enslaved people in Egypt, he comes to rescue them through Moses. The Egyptians suffer only until they let God's people go. But when it comes to the inhabitants of the region of Canaan, whose land he has chosen to give to his people, he shows no mercy and orders their slaughter. Is God racist? Is God schizophrenic? Is God cruel? What's going on?

This paradox has plagued my mind ever since I was a brand-new Christian trying to work my way through reading the Old Testament. How can we believe in, let alone worship, such a 'vindictive, bloody ethnic cleanser', to use Dawkins' phrase?[15]

I have never heard a sermon on this subject. It doesn't come up in Bible reading notes. Many preachers and teachers I have talked to evade these questions. Academics all come to very different conclusions.

Unfortunately, there are indeed no quick-fix answers to be found. However, there are clues that will help us as we seek to navigate the Joshua Paradox. And navigate it we must, if we seek a strong faith rather than merely a superficial one.

Firstly, there is a 'prequel', if you like. There is history, not just between God and Israel but also with the people living in the Promised Land. God did not lose his temper with the Canaanites suddenly and on a whim because he needed somewhere to give to

---

15 See Dawkins, R. (2008), *The God Delusion*, Black Swan Books, p. 51.

his people. Nor was it a divinely mandated smash-and-(land)-grab mission for Israel. Centuries before, God had asked Abraham to leave his home in Ur and go to a country that God would show him. That country was the land of Canaan. Abraham did spend time in the Promised Land, but God did not allow him to settle there. Instead he gave him a glimpse of the future:

> He also said to him, 'I am the LORD, who brought you out of Ur of the Chaldeans to give you this land to take possession of it.' . . .
>
> 'Know for certain that for four hundred years your descendants will be strangers in a country not their own and that they will be enslaved and ill-treated there. But I will punish the nation they serve as slaves, and afterwards they will come out with great possessions. You, however, will go to your ancestors in peace and be buried at a good old age. In the fourth generation your descendants will come back here, for the sin of the Amorites has not yet reached its full measure.'[16]

Abraham and his descendants would be homeless nomads for four centuries. Abraham was not given a reason for the hardships his descendants would face – although, ironically, it was during this time in captivity that one might argue they found their identity as a nation – but it appears that God was giving the indigenous inhabitants[17]

---

16 Genesis 15:7, 13–16.

17 It can be quite confusing that the inhabitants of the Promised Land are variously called 'Amorites' and 'Canaanites'. The more common term is 'Canaanites', but even then there can be confusion, as sometimes 'Canaanites' refers to an individual tribe/nation and other times 'Canaanites' is used as a collective term for the surrounding peoples which include the Hittites, Jebusites, Amorites, Hivites and Girgashites.

time: time to show their true character; either to get worse, or to change their sinful practices. If God was being merciful to the Canaanites, he did so at the great expense of his chosen people, letting them be slaves and strangers in the land of Egypt, then bringing them out only for them to become starving wilderness campers.

God's patience in giving the Canaanites extra time stands in stark contrast to the first impression we get, if we just jump in at Joshua, of God randomly wiping out the Canaanites on a whim. God is not a bad-tempered bully who annihilates nations without cause. He is more like a compassionate gardener, who wants to see good come, but will take action eventually if it doesn't. Jesus himself illustrates this in the parable of the fig tree.[18] The owner wants it destroyed, as it has not produced any fruit, but the gardener negotiates extra time, during which he will care for and fertilize it. The parable finishes with the gardener saying: 'If it bears fruit next year, fine! If not, then cut it down.' God's patience is very long, but in the end he has to act. This is a consistent message in the Bible. God is patient in the extreme, continuing his faithfulness to us despite our unfaithfulness to him, sacrificing what is precious to him for the sake of whoever may turn to him. But eventually the time will come when he must take action. From the length of time he is prepared to wait, it seems like he relishes that task little more than we relish reading about it.

This is the first clue that there is more going on behind the scenes than meets the eye – perhaps God's extremes of patience are more the point than the extreme judgement that is so much more noticeable on our initial reading.

---

18 Luke 13.

The second clue has to do with the place of judgement within any moral framework.

When we hear about harsh judgements far away or long ago, we wonder if we have heard the whole story, fear that the punishment has been too harsh, and perhaps want to side with the 'underdog'; but this is a natural consequence of our modern sensibilities, the desire to question everything. We need to consider this issue from the other side.

If we actually stop and think about our reaction when we hear stories of injustice where nothing seems to have been done, it is very hard for us not to feel disgust and anger against the perpetrators. Whether it is a local troublemaker smashing shop windows, or a gunman halfway round the world firing indiscriminately into a class-room of children, there is something within all of us that cries out for justice. We want the perpetrators to be held to account and punishment to be meted out. Without judgement and accountability for how individuals or nations act, then, there is no moral framework – the universe would be in anarchy. Or we could put it the other way around, as Dostoyevsky's character Ivan Karamazov states: 'Without God and without a future life? Why in that case, everything is allowed.'[19]

Our sense of outrage and desire for justice go hand in hand with our expectation of a God who should hold the world to account. We expect the wicked to be punished, and we do not want to let them get away with careless and callous behaviour. If there is a God, then, we do want him to be the righteous judge. Sometimes when we read the account of the genocide stories in the Old Testament, we see God as the perpetrator, the people-group as the

---

19 Dostoyevsky, F. (1983), *The Brothers Karamazov*, translated by David Magarshack, Penguin, p. 691.

victims, and we set ourselves up as the judge. If we recalibrate our minds to see God as the judge, and the people-group being wiped out as the perpetrators of crimes against victims unknown to us, we may react very differently.

So what was it that the Canaanites could possibly have done so very wrong over such a long period? What crime had they, including their children, committed? We are given some insight in these verses in the book of Deuteronomy:

> The LORD your God will cut off before you the nations you are about to invade and dispossess. But when you have driven them out and settled in their land, and after they have been destroyed before you, be careful not to be ensnared by enquiring about their gods, saying, 'How do these nations serve their gods? We will do the same.' You must not worship the LORD your God in their way, because in worshipping their gods, they do all kinds of detestable things the LORD hates. They even burn their sons and daughters in the fire as sacrifices to their gods.[20]

God is not just clearing the land for his people; he is holding the Canaanites accountable for atrocities committed. It is hard to imagine anything worse than the slaughter of children – the taking of innocent lives. They have sunk as low as it is possible to go. We should be relieved that people will not get away with murder – God will hold the world to account. Far from indicating the lack of a moral framework for us to count on, these passages show clearly that there is just such a framework, and God is in charge.

It's a start. But even so, it appears that God is being hypocritical.

20 Deuteronomy 12:29–31.

God brings judgement against the Canaanites for killing children – but then commands the Israelites to conduct a total extermination of all life. To kill children as a punishment because children were being killed does not seem just or fair. The concept of God punishing wickedness may be comprehensible to us, even welcomed, but the idea of God commanding his people to slaughter innocents is not so easy to swallow. We will need to take account of this issue, too.

A third clue, then, brings us on to look more closely at the uniqueness of the accounts themselves. God did not send the Israelites out on a campaign of global domination, with a *carte blanche* mandate to wipe out all the nations or to obliterate every city on earth. In Deuteronomy God makes a specific distinction between how to treat hostile peoples outside the Promised Land as against how to treat those inside in situations of war:

> When you march up to attack a city, make its people an offer of peace. If they accept and open their gates, all the people in it shall be subject to forced labour and shall work for you. If they refuse to make peace and they engage you in battle, lay siege to that city. When the LORD your God delivers it into your hand, put to the sword all the men in it. As for the women, the children, the livestock and everything else in the city, you may take these as plunder for yourselves. And you may use the plunder the LORD your God gives you from your enemies. This is how you are to treat all the cities that are at a distance from you and do not belong to the nations nearby. However, in the cities of the nations the LORD your God is giving you as an inheritance, do not leave alive anything that breathes.[21]

---

21 Deuteronomy 20:10–16.

The command to kill all the inhabitants of a city is limited to the Canaanite invasion. In other warfare contexts 'terms of peace' are always to be offered. The 'total destruction' clause is reserved specifically to the judgement on the Canaanites, and God specifically tells the Israelites not to use the Canaanite conquest as a model for how they should relate to other nations. And later, when Israel as a nation reflects back on receiving the Promised Land, they show they have understood the special nature of the circumstances: they do not celebrate their great military prowess or tactical superiority, but rather attribute their victory to God.[22] The Canaanite conquest was uniquely God's judgement on Canaan and God's gift to Israel of a homeland. It is not appropriate for any nation to take these texts and use them as a model or a mandate for military conquest, and when these events have been used this way to justify war, it is an abuse of Scripture.

For our fourth clue, we need to perhaps understand more of the cultural context of these passages. These are bronze-age peoples. Chris Wright argues that the annihilation of cities and their inhabitants was far from unique to Israel[23] – it was standard practice in the warfare of the day. In fact, God's institution of the rule that conquered nations outside Canaan must be offered 'terms of peace' was quite revolutionary. God continually argues with Israel that they must not become like the nations that surround them, but must show themselves as his unique people – a holy, just and compassionate people.

Nonetheless, it could still be argued that God should not be

---

22 See Wright, C. (2008), *The God I Don't Understand: Reflections on Tough Questions of Faith*, Zondervan, p. 91.

23 Ibid., p. 88.

accommodating the methods of war of the surrounding nations in the way the Canaanites are dealt with. Is he just racist against the Canaanite peoples? The following passage suggests otherwise:

> Do not defile yourselves in any of these ways, because this is how the nations that I am going to drive out before you became defiled. Even the land was defiled; so I punished it for its sin, and the land vomited out its inhabitants . . . And if you defile the land, it will vomit you out as it vomited out the nations that were before you.[24]

God warns the Israelites that the land itself was defiled by sin – this accentuates the need for judgement, and indeed this passage says that the land itself rose up against its inhabitants. The same fate will await the Israelites if they commit the same sins as the Canaanites. Just because God uses Israel as an instrument of his judgement does not give them immunity from facing the judgement of God themselves. Indeed, sadly, little by little the Israelites do become immoral and ignore God, and are captured and taken off into exile in Babylon and Assyria. God stands against wickedness and has to punish it wherever he finds it.

Wright goes on to argue, 'in a fallen world where struggle for land involves war, and if the only kind of war at the time was the kind described in the Old Testament texts, this was the way it had to be'.[25] He makes a connection between war and issues such as divorce and slavery in the Old Testament. God is clear that he hates

---

24 Leviticus 18:24–25, 27.

25 Wright, C. (2008), *The God I Don't Understand: Reflections on Tough Questions of Faith*, Zondervan, p. 89.

divorce[26] and that all human life is equally valuable,[27] but he allows both divorce and slavery to be practised among his people, as a concession to the reality of the broken and unjust world of the time. In the same way, the annihilation of whole towns was a given, considering the way warfare was conducted in that time. It could also be argued that God was taking the drastic action of wiping out a people who practised child-sacrifice from the Promised Land in order to prevent Israel being corrupted. A bit like a surgeon, forced to take the drastic action of amputating a patient's limb rather than allow gangrene to spread.

An alternative view is suggested by those who believe that the language used in these passages uses hyperbole, overstating the case in order to make the point more strongly. If I were to tell you that I listen to Radio 1 'all the time', nobody would think that I literally spend every second of the day hanging on every word of the world's best DJs and their favourite playlists – everybody would understand that it is just something I like to do a lot! In the same way, when in Deuteronomy and the book of Joshua God speaks phrases such as 'completely destroy them' and 'do not leave alive anything that breathes'[28] or even mentions 'women . . . young and old',[29] this could be an exaggerated expression for the total destruction of the city.[30] This seems a bit of a weaselly get-out, given the level of detail the Bible accounts go into, but in practice it is certainly likely that killing every single living thing would have been impossible.

In fact, historian Paul Copan even argues that the text 'does not

26 Malachi 2:16.
27 Genesis 1:26.
28 Deuteronomy 20:16.
29 Joshua 6:20–21.
30 Copan, P. (2011), *Is God a Moral Monster?*, Baker, p. 171.

require that "women" and "young and old" must have been in these cities'.[31] This gives us our sixth clue in considering this paradox. Copan ponders the possibility that the cities mentioned in the book of Joshua are actually more like garrisons or military installations – which would put a different perspective on the command to wipe out all signs of life. Mind you, the story of Jericho appears to challenge this view, because when Joshua sends two of his own spies into the Promised Land to reconnoitre the city of Jericho, Rahab, a Canaanite woman, hides them from the authorities. This implies a certain size and demographic makeup to the city. There were obviously few enough people for two spies to be noticed, but more people than just soldiers, as Copan suggests. Even in a military base, of course, there could have been civilians present who would have provided services for the troops. Rahab is described by different translations either as a prostitute or an innkeeper, both of which are credible occupations for a woman to be holding even in a military outpost. Perhaps it is easier, however, to consider the possibility that while these fortified towns would have held the only trained soldiers, these were likely very few in number, and knowing that the Israelites were coming, other men would have been roped in to fight while the majority of women and children would have been sent out to the country.

Additionally, Copan argues that 'the large numbers used in warfare accounts in the Old Testament are a little tricky; they may not be as high as our translations indicate. The Hebrew word "eleph" commonly rendered "thousand", can also mean "unit" or "squad" without specifying the exact number.' And so the numbers of people destroyed in these accounts could be significantly smaller than we would normally associate with genocide. Copan argues that 'Jericho

---

31 Ibid., p. 173.

was a small settlement, with probably 100 or fewer soldiers. This is why all of Israel could circle it seven times and then do battle against it on the same day!'[32]

In conclusion, faced with passages that seem to suggest God is not the loving deity we want him to be but rather is promoting wholesale ethnic cleansing, there are plenty of clues here to help us think more widely around the subject. Admittedly, there are no quick-fix certain resolutions, and this is not the last time we will struggle to resolve these biblical paradoxes. We will learn later from Habakkuk how to worship God when we face a dead end in our search for resolution. But at this juncture it is worth reflecting on two aspects of God's character that emerge through the horror of the Canaanite conquest. We have already seen that God both gives and takes away, and that he is both far and near, holy ('set apart') and loving; now we also have to reconcile how God can be both merciful and just.

The Joshua Paradox shows us a terribly compassionate God who displays incredible patience and mercy before bringing down judgement. For 400 years he waited to see if the Canaanites would repent. God gave them, and indeed gives all people, one chance after another to do the right thing and turn back to him, to turn away from evil and to seek him. Some take God's patience and his reserve in punishing evil as evidence that God doesn't care about sin. Nothing could be further from the case. The withholding of punishment is not forever. The apostle Peter tested Jesus' patience regularly, but later wrote in a letter to a young church:

The LORD is not slow in keeping his promise, as some understand slowness. Instead he is patient with you, not wanting

32 Ibid., p. 183.

anyone to perish, but everyone to come to repentance. But the day of the LORD will come like a thief. The heavens will disappear with a roar; the elements will be destroyed by fire, and the earth and everything done in it will be laid bare.[33]

The existence of evil in the world is at one and the same time – paradoxically, if you like – a sign of the mercy of God. He is withholding his judgement from the earth, giving every last chance for people to seek him. But God's patience does have a limit to its elasticity. He will also ultimately show himself as a God who is just. In one sense, the challenge here is the corollary to the paradox we considered in the previous chapter, as we pondered the location of God. When bad things happen, we want to know where God is and why he won't intervene. When he does intervene we question his right to execute judgement. We want judgement and justice, yet at the same time we don't want them. God is 'damned if he does and damned if he doesn't', to coin a phrase. Such is the contrariness of human nature. The Joshua Paradox can help us to learn to worship God aright. His patience is meaningless without his eventual judgement; his judgement is merciless without his extreme patience.

We have to somehow take seriously both the patience and moral purity of God. Jesus told a parable about the wheat and the tares (or weeds). A farmer sowed good seed in his field, but in the night an enemy deliberately sowed weeds among his wheat. When the wheat sprouted, so did the weeds. One of the farmer's workers asked if they should pull up the weeds. But the farmer warned against it, for fear of damaging the wheat. He said they should allow both wheat and weeds to grow together and only separate them out

---

33 2 Peter 3:9–10.

at the harvest, where the wheat would be gathered and the weeds would be burned.[34] This is a parable of great hope, and also a strong warning. This parable offers hope because God *will* finally intervene to root out evil from his world. It encourages us to hold on to our faith despite persecution, pain and suffering.

We see that these things have not caught God by surprise – it is not that he has no plan for dealing with them, but that he wants to give every chance for right to prevail at our hand rather than by his diktat. We see again the patience of God underlined as he gives every opportunity he can for more people to come into his kingdom.

But this parable is also a great warning to those who live as enemies of God. Just because God has not executed his judgement yet, it doesn't mean it isn't coming. Even when we have understood the 'texts of terror' in Joshua in their context, we still see it is a terrible thing to have to face the judgement of God. What we see in Joshua is a taste of things to come for those who refuse to accept the mercy of God. In fact, the very inclusion in the Bible of these stories, challenging as it is, may be a mercy in itself – like a warning shot across the bows to help remind a straying ship that God's patience is long, but it will not last forever.

When my wife and I moved back to the UK from Albania, we moved into an area of North West London where there just happened to be a large population of Kosovar Albanian asylum seekers. Our church became a hub for Albanian language and culture. One evening we hosted a large party with a fantastic array of Albanian music and food, including traditional dancing. I spoke to a young man at the event who said: 'I would never have dreamed of this. We are Muslims. We did not receive a welcome at the mosque

---

34 Matthew 13:24–30.

but here in the church we have been made to feel at home. We thought Christians wanted to kill us. But here we are, dancing in a hall that has the words "Jesus is Lord" on the wall.' For me, this was genuine worship, opening up the resources of our church family to give vulnerable people a taste of the peace of God and acting on our calling as the children of God to be peacemakers in our troubled world.[35] It was such a thrill to be able to offer this kind of loving hospitality to people who had suffered so much.

We shall see when we come to the paradox of the cross how the compassion and the judgement of God are intimately connected. It is important that we hold on to our faith firmly, and refuse to be bullied or lured into compromising on our beliefs. This was the risk the people of Israel faced, and it was to be their downfall in the centuries to come. Despite the apparent genocide they inflicted, there continued to be foreigners in their midst, and the Israelites were duly led astray. However, it is also important that we do not get our enemies confused: God has called us to bless the nations, and love our enemies. If we come to see those that are different from us as aliens, foreigners to be despised and even attacked, we need to take a long hard look at whether it is us rather than them that is at fault. The message of the whole Bible, as we shall see, is to love our neighbours into God's kingdom, not to exclude them from it for their imperfections.

---

35 Matthew 5:9.

Chapter 4

The Job Paradox
The God who is actively inactive

That stone-grey floor was a lot easier to look at than the heavy eyes of the shocked parents in the intensive-care ward. Only a few hours before, they had discovered that their baby boy, previously healthy, now had severe brain damage. Yesterday he had been bouncing around in our church's Mums and Tots group like every other toddler there, and now his life was going to be forever different. I had gone there to offer support and comfort and prayer, but found I had nothing to say. It was hard not to wonder how the good, loving and all-powerful God I had preached about the previous Sunday had let this happen. I wanted to pray for a miracle, a resurrection, but I didn't dare say it aloud and add more confusion to this distraught family. So I sat staring at the floor, secretly hoping it would swallow me up.

Eventually the boy's mother asked the question on everybody's minds – the one I was dreading: 'Why?' She was not looking for what we might call a 'functional' answer – she already knew that following the routine operation, during the recovery period, her son's brain had been starved of oxygen, resulting in severe neurological damage. She, like all of us, was asking: 'Why has this been allowed to happen? Why is this happening to my family? What is the purpose of this pain? Who is responsible?' And I didn't have an answer.

It was far from the first time I had been thus confronted with the need to wrestle with God's rationale for allowing suffering. I had suffered racist bullying from my peers at school. Why had God allowed them to get away it? I had put so much work into revising for exams. Why did my results not reflect that? Why did my health-conscious mother get cancer when the grouchy, agoraphobic elderly lady next door – who my mother selflessly supported – had chain-smoked her way through six decades with no health complications?

Whether we are forced to watch the suffering of others, or experiencing suffering in our own lives, we desperately want to know 'Why?' Why does God stand passively by when there is so much suffering going on all the time? Why does he criticize our tendency to walk on by on the other side of the road when we see people in need, when he himself sees all suffering and yet chooses to do nothing? Does God not care? Does God not understand? Or perhaps he is, after all, incapable of stepping in? God's deliberate policy of not fixing things when we are suffering highlights one of those universal paradoxes – we believe that God is active and powerful, so if he does not intervene, we are forced to conclude that this God is actively choosing to be passive.

The problem of suffering is one of the most enduring questions humanity has to grapple with, and from an anthropological point of view it is one of the main reasons humans have sought to explain the world we live in by reference to a God or gods. At the same time, in our culture particularly, it has become perhaps the main reason raised in objection against belief in God.

In times past this issue of suffering was precisely the thing that drove people to look for higher forces to whom they could appeal for help. Now, though, it has become an important extension to the

'Where is God?' question that exercised us in the Moses Paradox. As Philip Yancey put it in his first book, still a bestseller all these years later, *Where is God When it Hurts?*

Perhaps the most challenging articulation of this deeper question in recent times was raised by Elie Wiesel in his harrowing semi-autobiographical account of surviving internment in Auschwitz. In his profound and moving book *Night*, Wiesel's character had grown up a devout believer and even hoped to train to be a rabbi. But during the journey from his home to the ghetto, and then finally to Auschwitz, his faith died.

What was it that killed his faith? Was it the horror of being herded by the hundred into a railway carriage and given only tiny portions of bread and water for the ten-day journey that destroyed his trust in a benevolent God? Was it being forcibly separated from his mother and sister, never to see them again? It could have been witnessing hundreds of children's bodies being dumped from a lorry into an incinerator. But Wiesel is clear: none of these tolled the death knell for his faith. Instead, he paints a grizzly picture of the exact moment when his faith was annihilated. The entire camp was summoned to witness the execution of three thieves, one of whom was a popular young boy.

> Then came the march past the victims. The two men were no longer alive. Their tongues were hanging out, swollen and bluish. But the third rope was still moving: the child, too light, was still breathing . . . And so he remained for more than half an hour, lingering between life and death, writhing before our eyes. And we were forced to look at him at close range. He was still alive when I passed him. His tongue was still red, his eyes not yet extinguished.

Behind me, I heard the same man asking: 'For God's sake, where is God?'

And from within me, I heard a voice answer: 'Where is He? This is where – hanging here from this gallows.'[1]

This incident has clear echoes of Jesus' desperate cry to his Father from the cross, and later, when we consider the Cross Paradox, that may help us to round out our understanding further. For now, though, let me just say that I have been confronted with this same question over and over again by friends and family who have experienced tragedy in their lives. When life is at its toughest, we wonder where God is when we need him, or whether he even exists at all. The apparent absence of God at key moments both in world history and in our personal histories is what lies at the heart of many people's rejection of God.

The question of God's whereabouts in the midst of crisis haunts believers and non-believers alike, especially when we hear about another bloody revolution, another natural disaster or another school massacre. There will come times in our lives when we watch or experience suffering at close hand, when the apparent absence of God will challenge everything we have come to believe and make it impossible to worship him. That's why we must not shy away from the need to wrestle with this problem.

In fact it is a problem common to every faith and every system of thought. Let's take a brief look at the three most common ways of resolving the problem of the pain: Hinduism, Buddhism and Atheism, and compare them with the way Christians are encouraged to understand the paradox.

---

1 Wiesel, E. (1982), *Night*, Bantam Books, p. 62.

When the boy who had been left brain damaged after the routine operation was finally discharged from hospital, the family experienced a second wave of upset and grief. They had to get used to caring for their son at home, still not knowing if he would be permanently blind or deaf or both; trying to communicate in what was their second language, with carers who invaded their private space; trying to come to terms with the new 'normal' of life looking after a child with disabilities and an uncertain future. If that wasn't hard enough, they then had to deal with phone calls from family in India. Their Hindu relatives offered the only comfort they had been taught – that the reason this had happened was because they had committed awful sins in a previous life. In the midst of their turmoil the faltering family had to deal with this additional burden, as well as the fact that their relatives back home were now ashamed of them.

This is the heart of the idea of karma, where the good and bad deeds performed by human beings in the present determine the quality of their lives both now and in future births[2] – such that the suffering we experience now is seen as the punishment for bad things we have done in previous lives. This philosophy is present in various forms in Hinduism, Sikhism and Buddhism.[3] It is not a personal God that oversees this process, though, but rather an impersonal cosmic principle at work in the universe.

Most of my relatives are Hindu, but I have always struggled with this doctrine. Firstly, it is clearly impossible to prove who did what in a previous life. The doctrine is based not on any kind of evidence, either from personal testimony or historic reference, but rather on a set of stories that are acknowledged to be mythical, yet the unknown

---

2 Narayanan, V. (2004), *Understanding Hinduism*, DBP, p. 58.
3 See Wright, N. T. (2006), *Evil and the Justice of God*, SPCK, p. 16.

origins of which are deemed to be irrelevant to their veracity. Secondly, at the very heart of the karmic system there seems to be an injustice. We are punished, therefore, for things we have no recollection of doing. We are held accountable for our previous lives' crimes in our current lives, but when we die we cannot pass on the learning to our future reincarnated selves. There is no remedial benefit, therefore, in receiving the punishment. Furthermore, when others suffer, there is no reason to help them if we believe that they are being punished for past sins. Karmic thinking looks at the starving child in the Brazilian favela and thinks they could be Adolf Hitler or Joseph Mengele reincarnated, enduring punishment for those atrocities they perpetrated in a previous life. Who would want these amoral monsters to miss out a second time on receiving their just deserts? These are just some of the difficult implications of viewing suffering as a result of bad karma.

Buddhism offers its own approach to the problem. Buddhism's central teaching is all based around the problem of suffering. The Four Noble Truths are the truth of suffering (*Dukkha*), the truth of the origin of suffering (*Samudāya*), the truth of the cessation of suffering (*Nirodha*), and the truth of the path to the cessation of suffering (*Magga*).[4]

In short, suffering is the central human problem – so far, so good; and, for the Buddhist, it comes about only because there is a fundamental mismatch between what we desire and what we receive.[5] In other words, it is a problem of expectation due to the

---

4 Nhat Hanh, T. (1999), *The Heart of Buddha's Teaching: Transforming Suffering into Peace, Joy and Liberation*, Rider, p. 11.

5 The second Noble Truth argues that 'suffering arises from craving or "thirst"'. See Keown, D. (2000), *Buddhism: A Very Short Introduction*, Oxford University Press, p. 47.

difference between what we want in life and what we get. The solution is simple – we must get rid of desire, then there will be no mismatch and thus we will not experience suffering. If we do not desire our children to grow up healthy, for example, then if they are unhealthy we have lost nothing and therefore do not suffer. The implication is that if we can desensitize ourselves sufficiently, then nothing can hurt us.[6] Buddha taught that the way to get rid of desire is to liberate ourselves from attachment:

> This, O Monks, is the Truth of the Cessation of Suffering. It is the utter cessation of that craving (tanha), the withdrawal from it, the renouncing of it, the rejection of it, liberation from it, nonattachment to it.[7]

We will not suffer if we can detach ourselves from this world. If we can disengage then we won't feel loss, grief, pain, loneliness, or despair. For a Buddhist the ultimate aim of life is to reach Nirvana – which literally means extinguishment – the place where our desires are finally snuffed out. I don't know about you, but I find this approach fundamentally dissatisfying.

Firstly, I believe that the idea of extinguishing desire, while it may seem like an attractive solution for individuals to pursue, is impossible to propagate as a solution to a world full of needs. I cannot tell the billion people suffering because they go to bed hungry each night simply to turn off their desire and not feel hungry any more. I cannot tell grieving parents to stop thinking about what they have

---

6 'As a result of the cessation of consciousness, mental and physical phenomena cease . . . as a result of the cessation of again-becoming, decay, death, suffering cease.' Ibid., p. 257.
7 The third Noble Truth cited by Keown, ibid., p. 51.

lost and focus on what they already have, as though they had dropped a penny through a crack in the pavement. Along with my desire and my pain, I would have to also turn off my empathy, as though it were a faulty smoke alarm that needed to be discarded. Part of my reluctance to accept such a teaching is no doubt cultural – our Western culture is in large part predicated on the developing ideas of Christianity and the Enlightenment over the past several centuries, holding that the human condition can and must be improved – but even setting that aside, it seems to me to strike at the heart of the human desire to love and help one another, to be engaged in the life we have before us.

If bad karma and the badness of desire are inadequate solutions to the paradox of pain, how about a third option, as offered by the atheists – sheer bad luck? Richard Dawkins puts the atheistic position on the problem of pain most eloquently and most starkly:

> If the universe were just electrons and selfish genes, meaningless tragedies . . . are exactly what we should expect, along with equally meaningless good fortune. Such a universe would be neither evil nor good in intention . . . In a universe of blind physical forces and genetic replication, some people are going to get hurt, other people are going to get lucky, and you won't find any rhyme or reason in it, nor any justice. The universe we observe has precisely the properties we should expect if there is, at bottom, no design, no purpose, no evil and no good, nothing but blind pitiless indifference.[8]

8 Dawkins, R. (1995), *River Out of Eden: A Darwinian View of Life*, Basic Books, pp. 131–2.

According to Dawkins, it is just statistically unfortunate if bad things happen, and the only comfort we can offer is to say 'bad luck' and cross our fingers that it doesn't happen again. As philosopher Julian Baggini puts it, 'as evolved creatures, there should be no expectation that the world should be a good place'.[9] Once again these conclusions are difficult to live with. They do not explain why our first reaction to suffering is to question 'Why?' as though somebody somewhere ought to have an answer. Dawkins argues against any ultimate difference between good and evil, thus denying the moral sense. But at the same time he is very happy to apply moral criteria against God, as we saw in considering the Joshua Paradox.[10] Some atheists seem to want to have their cake and eat it – using a moral argument to denigrate God but then arguing there is no ultimate morality anyway. Which is it?

Look how C. S. Lewis grappled with this same inconsistency in his own atheism:

My argument against God was that the universe seemed so cruel and unjust. But how had I got this idea of 'just' and 'unjust'? What was I comparing this universe with when I called it unjust? Of course I could have given up my idea of justice by saying it was nothing but a private idea of my own. But if I did that, my argument against God collapsed too . . .[11]

Bad karma, bad desire and bad luck are all bad news for the suffering and bad solutions to the paradox of a world where some suffer more

---

9 Baggini, J. (2003), *Atheism: A Very Short Introduction*, Oxford University Press, p. 29.
10 When Dawkins called God 'morally repugnant'.
11 Lewis, C. S. (1960), *Mere Christianity*, Macmillan, p. 31.

than others, apparently without reason. So how do Christians seek to reconcile the existence of suffering and God's apparent passivity? Unlike atheists, we believe that the inevitable question 'Why?' is in fact crucial evidence that we intrinsically believe things don't happen by chance, that someone is in control and that things don't have to be this way. It seems counter-intuitive initially, but when we ask the question 'Why?' we actually reveal that we believe there *is* a God, and not just any God, but a God who could and should be powerful enough to make things different, and who might care enough to want to both answer our question and make things better. The question 'Why?' reveals that none of us can escape the paradox that we believe in a powerful and loving God, albeit we don't understand how we can reconcile this with a broken world replete with injustice and suffering.

The book of Job in the Bible addresses exactly this problem. The storyline is contained in only a few lines of its forty chapters.[12] The narrative zooms in on the life of a good, upright and prosperous man called Job, and his family. Job was a man of unblemished character and was revered in the region. Then the narrator peels back another layer of reality to reveal what is taking place in the spiritual realm. What we find is a form of heavenly courtroom where Satan is a kind of (un-)angelic prosecutor, laying down a challenge to God. Satan argues that Job's devotion to God is based purely on the fact that he has an easy life. In other words, Job doesn't really love God, he just loves the life God has given him. In response to this challenge a deal is struck: Job will be a test case. Despite the apparent challenge to his authority, God permits Satan to bring suffering into Job's life, saying, 'everything he has is in your hands,

---

12 Job 1–2 and 42.

but on the man himself do not lay a finger'.[13] The essential question that runs through the rest of the book is whether Job will still honour God when all of his prosperity is taken from him, or will he 'curse God to his face'?[14]

How will Job respond to a full-frontal attack? Satan goes off and destroys Job's wealth and his family in freak accidents. But Job, unaware of the behind-the-scenes action, responds despite his distress:

> Naked I came from my mother's womb,
> and naked I will depart.
> The LORD gave and the LORD has taken away;
> may the name of the LORD be praised.[15]

This is a deeply inspiring declaration of confidence and trust in God despite all that he has suffered, and a real challenge to us. This is not a Buddhist-style denial of the reality of suffering, or atheist defeatism in light of the balance of probabilities. Job's confession reveals a commitment to continue trusting God despite his circumstances. Job's perspective is that life itself is a gift, and so is everything that comes with it, and he will continue to love God for who he is, not for what he has given to Job. But this statement initiates phase two of the test of Job's worship. Satan is given permission to afflict Job physically – but he must 'spare his life'.[16] What follows in the rest of the book is a torturous dialogue between Job and his

---

13 Job 1:12.
14 Job 1:11.
15 Job 1:20–21.
16 Job 2:6.

friends as they wrestle with the question 'Why?' from their limited perspectives.

The Job Paradox gives us some useful – but rather unexpected – clues as to how we can wrestle with that same question, as we gain a rare insight into both the earthly and the heavenly perspectives. The introduction to the book of Job resolves some issues for us, but it also raises some very uncomfortable questions.

First, we are clearly told that God is in control. He is portrayed as the King of the universe, the rightful ruler of heaven and earth. Even Satan, who is literally the personification of evil, has to present himself before God and ask permission for his activities. In a book that addresses the problem of suffering there is no backing away from the fact that God is in control – there is no downplaying total divine sovereignty. We can be assured that the universe is not ultimately a cosmic lottery, filled with 'outrageous fortune' and terrible misfortune.

Second, we learn that not all suffering is deserved. Job is not being punished for things he has done – he stands out as being a most innocent and blameless person, yet he suffers. He is perhaps the archetype for this predicament, but this is far from the only time in the Bible when this question is addressed. In an encounter with a man born blind, Jesus's disciples asked the question everybody had been discussing – whether it was the fault of the parents or the man himself that led to his suffering. Jesus replied: 'Neither this man nor his parents sinned.'[17] The karmic equation found in Hinduism and many Eastern philosophies, proposing that current suffering is the direct result of previous personal sin, is not supported by the Bible's teaching. Our suffering, according to Jesus

---

17 John 9:3.

himself, is not the direct result of sin. It is true at a macro level that suffering in general is a result of sin – the very first sin in the Garden of Eden is the trigger for a chain reaction of suffering in the universe. But it does not apply at a micro level. The whole world has been damaged by sin, and its effects are not spread according to what each deserves: the innocent as much as the guilty are affected by the far-reaching consequences of sin.

Third, we see God specifically allowing suffering to happen to an innocent person. Satan is permitted to disrupt Job's life, which throws us back to the classic paradox: does suffering continue because God is not all-powerful, or because God is not all-loving? The book of Job clearly states that God is all-powerful; Satan can do nothing to Job without God's permission. So the question becomes whether God is all-loving. Can we truly continue to believe in a loving God when he allows such extreme suffering simply to win what appears to be nothing more than a divine wager? As the story unfolds, however, we will see that there is more at stake than a cruel test.

The book of Job challenges the premise of the paradox that God is either too weak to stop suffering or too mean to bother to do so. This book asserts that there are circumstances when an all-powerful and all-loving God might allow suffering to take place. Acknowledging this point is very difficult to grasp, most of the book of Job argues the opposite case. After the big set-up scenes involving the wager between God and Satan, followed by Job's life being reduced to dust, there comes a very long interlude. The bulk of the book of Job's forty chapters is filled with what will prove to be theological and philosophical nonsense. There is more than enough time for a good answer to emerge, but none will. Job receives a seemingly endless cycle of visits and lectures delivered by his so-called friends

Eliphaz, Bildad, Zophar and Elihu. They all assume more or less that 'if you sin, you will suffer' and equally, 'if you suffer, you have sinned'.[18] They spend hour after hour, page after page, repeating this line of reasoning. They behave like many a British tourist on holiday – apparently believing that if they just restate their case over and over they will eventually win the argument. More space is given to this debate than anything else in the book of Job and it is a substantial portion of the Bible as a whole. It is impossible, in the light of its extensive airing of the arguments, to maintain that the Bible simply ignores the issue of suffering.

Sometimes it feels that Job's counsellors might be just trying to wear him down with their many words. It makes the book difficult to read, let alone understand. Perhaps the exasperating experience of reading the book of Job is intentional, as we encounter the obtuse and yet insistent counsellors. Possibly the aim is to deliberately frustrate us as readers. Maybe finding Job's friends infuriating acts as a warning to us to avoid their mistakes. They are earnest and well-meaning, but they are almost completely wrong in what they assume about God, Job and the universe. Perhaps too we may be reminded of the need for genuine humility, the need to be slow to speak and quick to listen.[19] If we follow this advice we will be able to avoid causing some of the pastoral and emotional damage that Job's friends bring.

Before we look at how the Job Paradox plays out, we should consider the classic way Christians have sought to resolve the problem of suffering. This is known as the free-will defence. Simply

---

18 See Dillard, R. & Lonman III, T. (1995), *An Introduction to the Old Testament*, Apollos, p. 209.

19 James 1:19.

put, God desires genuine relationships with us as human beings, something which is only possible when there is free choice. Without freedom, genuine relationships are next to impossible: the idea of a wedding is a lot less romantic if the father of the bride has a shotgun trained on the groom to keep him in the room. So God gives human beings genuine choice as to whether they love and obey him, or ignore and disobey him. God gives us freedom of choice, and the exercise of that freedom is what has led to all the suffering in the world. Once we choose to rebel against God, there are consequences. Just as a crack on a windscreen cannot be contained in one corner but spreads throughout the whole pane, or like a drop of ink which contaminates a whole jug of water, so sin has infiltrated the whole of human existence – causing emotional pain, physical illnesses and natural disasters.

As humanity ignores and disobeys God, every one of us and indeed the whole of creation, experiences a mangled set of relationships, damaging not only our relationship with God, but also our relationships with other people, with our environment and with ourselves.[20] God is still in control, but as he has given us space for us to exercise our freedom, so we have to reap some of its consequences, and live in a world that is not as God originally intended, nor how it will eventually end up. The Bible teaches that one day God will call time, and eradicate evil and suffering. At that point it will be too late for us to turn to follow God – the end of suffering is also the end of opportunity to beg forgiveness and change our allegiance. And so God waits, waits for us to recognize him. As we saw in the Joshua Paradox, God's endless patience is not inactivity

---

20 See Meyers, B. (2013), *Walking with the Poor*, 2nd edn., Zondervan; Kandiah, K. (2005), *Destiny*, Monarch; and Newbigin, L. (1956), *Sin and Salvation*, SPCK.

but mercy, as he waits for more people to seek him and be reconciled with him.

This big-picture overview of the grand narrative of the Bible has been helpful to many people, myself included, as we wrestle with the reasons for suffering.[21] But what is fascinating about Job, a forty-chapter book entirely focused on the problem of suffering, is that this line of reasoning does not get a look-in. God never gives Job any explanation at all for what he has to go through.

Mind you, Job does ask for an audience with God – and gets one. Far from there being any censure on him doing this, Job's request, and the manner of its being answered, actually reveal important truths about the nature of God and our relationship with him. Throughout the book, Job does not resign himself to fatalism; he does not picture himself at the mercy of blind physical forces. (Nor does he seek escape from his suffering through transcendental chant or meditation!)

Job seeks an audience with God precisely because his suffering has not dampened his belief in a personal and powerful God, a God who can and should be called to account. Despite everything that has happened to him, which he knows is undeserved, his belief in an almighty God has not been diminished. Despite the circular arguments of his so-called wise counsellors, Job continues to deny that he has sinned sufficiently to deserve this suffering.[22] As one commentator puts it, 'Job was right, but not self-righteous, to insist on his own integrity.'[23] He asks for an audience with God so he

---

21 It is most succinctly expressed in Lewis, C. S. (1944), *The Problem of Pain*, HarperCollins.

22 Dumbrell, W. (1989), *Faith of Israel*, IVP, p. 220.

23 Andersen, F. I. (1976), *Job*, Tyndale Old Testament Commentaries, IVP, p. 69.

can state his side of the argument. The detailing of Job's request shows the degree to which the Bible encourages us to seek a genuine relationship with God, not to either dismiss him or to accept pat answers for our dilemmas. The Psalms are full of examples of people pouring out their doubt, grief, guilt and even anger at God,[24] and in the same way Job models what we ought to do when we have a case against God – bring it to him. We don't resolve a problem with God anywhere but with God himself:

> If only I knew where to find him;
> if only I could go to his dwelling!
> I would state my case before him
> and fill my mouth with arguments.[25]

Yet when Job finally gets his opportunity to address God, he does not raise his questions or make any arguments. God knows already what Job is thinking and feeling, of course; but the point is that when Job does come into God's presence, he finds himself rather more inclined to listen than speak. In fact he is completely silent as God asks Job a stream of questions:

> Who is this that obscures my plans
> with words without knowledge?
> Brace yourself like a man;
> I will question you,

---

24 Brueggemann, W. (2007), *Praying the Psalms: Engaging Scripture with the Life of the Spirit*, Cascade Books, pp. 1–15 explains why the psalms that wrestle with our dissonance between expectation and reality are a particular gift to us.

25 Job 23:3–4.

and you shall answer me.
Where were you when I laid the earth's foundation?
Tell me, if you understand.
Who marked off its dimensions? Surely you know!
Who stretched a measuring line across it?
On what were its footings set,
or who laid its cornerstone –
while the morning stars sang together
and all the angels shouted for joy?[26]

Job thought he was going to be the one asking God the questions, but instead God asks question after question of Job, about who is in control of the universe. What is the point of God asking all of these questions? Most of the questions seem hypothetical anyway – God knows the answers, and Job doesn't. Finally and crucially God asks Job, 'would you discredit my justice?'[27] Job's credentials for bringing a case before God are questioned by God himself.

This raises a question about how we handle any of these apparent paradoxes in thinking about God. Some argue that we should not presume to ask any questions of God, or dare to try and put God in the dock. Instead we should recognize our status as creatures in front of an inscrutable God and not expect answers. A friend of mine attended a lecture given by a theologian he greatly admired, and afterwards, my friend went to converse privately with the lecturer. He was grappling with huge doubts, and here was a man who had been introduced with the words, 'This man has a brain the size of a planet.' So my friend worked up the courage to open up to this

26 Job 38:2–7.
27 Job 40:8.

learned professor and, as carefully and accurately as he could, he formulated his questions. When he had finished speaking, the professor listed a number of books and asked if he had read them, to which the answer was no in all cases. The speaker then replied: 'You are the singularly most unread person I have met: I am not going to answer your question.' My friend went away with his doubts very much intact, and his admiration of his preaching hero in tatters.

What is going on here, then? Is God simply pulling rank? Is he intent on demeaning this man intellectually, having watched him go through mental and physical torment already? Is God simply refusing to address Job's burning questions, because he cannot match the knowledge or abilities of the maker of the universe? Perhaps in one sense the situation is even more serious than that my friend faced. His encounter with a Christian celebrity speaker was brief and discouraging, but at least this lecturer was not the cause of my friend's problems in the first place. God, meanwhile, appears to have toyed with Job, allowing him to undergo severe suffering – all for the sake of a bet with Satan. And now God won't explain his actions or his motives.

In fact, the constant barrage of questions from God is not designed to silence and belittle Job, but rather to help him to see something of the wonder of the world as God sees it – to experience a sense of awe. Job doesn't learn about God's perspective on his own suffering, but he does learn about God's perspective on the whole world. Job finds himself knowing God better: 'My ears had heard of you, but now my eyes have seen you.'[28] Job finds himself trusting God better: 'I know that you can do all things; no purpose of yours can be thwarted.'[29]

---

28 Job 42:2.
29 Job 42:2.

It is certainly possible to see here an echo of the Zen-like questions that Buddhists use to help their consciousness disconnect from the world – to grab a couple of the more popular examples of this type of thinking: 'If a tree falls in the forest and there is no one to hear it fall – does it make a sound?' or 'What is the sound of one hand clapping?' These unanswerable questions are supposed to set up an array of mental paradoxes to divert the thinker's thoughts away from the suffering around them, and towards an illusion of life. What is radically different about the series of questions that Job is asked is that they don't deny the reality of the world, or undermine the reality of suffering. Rather, God's questions to Job act like a mental version of a defibrillator, shocking the brain out of self-importance and introspection and forcing him – and us – to see our true place in the universe that God has created. God seeks to engage our brains not with confusing questions to distract us, but ones that force us to reflect upon and revel in the magnitude and complexity of God's world, and the mastery of God who knows its every detail. Job is never once reprimanded for feeling pain or lamenting loss. He is not told that his desires are wrong or ordered to mute his emotions. Rather, God asks Job to follow the clues that intrinsically draw together suffering and worship.

In her captivating book *Canon: The Beautiful Basics of Science*, Natalie Angier reflects on the scale of the universe as a cause for humility. Just like Job, reflecting on the vastness of the universe can be for us the contemporary equivalent of God's questions.[30] We too can revel in the awe we feel when we are confronted by a tropical storm, or a thirty-foot wave, or the faraway stars in the sky. Closer

---

30 In her captivating book Natalie Angier reflects on the scale of the universe as a cause for humility. Angier, N. (2007), *The Canon: The Beautiful Basics of Science*, p. 83.

to home, we can dwell on the birds and plants in a garden, or we can watch the hidden secrets of the planet in a television nature documentary. When we look at the images that have come back from the Hubble space telescope or the scans from a tunnelling electron-microscope, we are humbled by the scale of the universe, and this realization that we only have a partial grasp of its wonders is a spur to our better understanding of God. Just like a Sudoku puzzle in a newspaper improves our mental maths or a running machine improves our cardiovascular capacity, so reflecting on the wonders of the world is like a spiritual challenge, forcing us to reboot our conceptions of God. The Bible teaches us that 'the fear of God is the beginning of wisdom',[31] and when Job comes to God looking for answers, these questions that boldly ignore his own agonies and right concerns instil in him an awed appreciation of God's wisdom, power and majesty.

The only answer to the problem of suffering we will find in Job is the example of reflecting on the universe to observe the power, skill and wisdom of God demonstrated in nature. This is evidence enough to prove beyond question that if God is able to create and order the universe, then he is more than capable of overseeing the details of our lives. If God is powerful enough to create the constellations[32] and yet is attentive enough to watch while 'the doe bears her fawn',[33] then he is capable enough to work out the complexities of our lives.

From the tiny snapshot of experience that our lives provide us with, we cannot see the scale of what God is doing throughout eternity. We are like caterpillars crawling across a cinema screen, so close to the picture that we cannot come close to seeing the design

---

31 Psalm 1.
32 Job 38:31–32.
33 Job 38:1–2.

that God is working out on the grand canvas of history. By asking Job to reflect on his power, God is helping Job to develop confidence in his credibility and qualifications to rightly guide Job's life.

God's plan in allowing Job to suffer seems not dissimilar to the struggle Abraham had to go through. God had something he needed Abraham to experience, insights he wanted to give that could only be taught through suffering, and that would become a part of the bigger picture, although Abraham and Job would never guess just how far-reaching that influence would be. Through telling him to sacrifice his own son, God helped Abraham to a deep and early understanding of what Christ would do on behalf of all humanity, as well as drawing him into a deeper trust of the power of God. In the same way, God allows Job to prove in his own experience that he really does love God more than the gifts he has been given. Job is not just a pawn in a spiritual drama, he is drawing closer to the all-powerful God. But these lessons do not come cheaply. Unlike Abraham, Job really does lose everything he cherishes, including not just one but ten sons. Is this lesson really worth the pain of the tragedies involved? The book of Job includes this summary:

> After the LORD had said these things to Job, he said to Eliphaz the Temanite, 'I am angry with you and your two friends, because you have not spoken of me what is right, as my servant Job has. So now take seven bulls and seven rams and go to my servant Job and sacrifice a burnt offering for yourselves. My servant Job will pray for you, and I will accept his prayer and not deal with you according to your folly. You have not spoken of me what is right, as my servant Job has.'[34]

---

34 Job 42:7–8.

At the end of the story of Job, God silences the unhelpful friends and publicly affirms and vindicates Job. What his so-called counsellors said, although seemingly rational, is denounced as rubbish. As one commentator put it: 'the drama of the book of Job is a vigorous, artistic invitation in Israel to rethink in radical ways . . . explanations that over time were undoubtedly reduced to moralistic clichés'.[35] God stands by Job, and defends his cause. God commends Job and does not deem his questions inappropriate or out of place. In fact, throughout the book he has shown nothing but confidence in Job. He alone was not embarrassed or uncertain about Job's faith. God was willing to have his servant tested, putting his own reputation on the line. In fact the whole of his creation was at stake in Job. God created human beings as an overflow of his love, but was it all in vain? Could any humans actually love God for who he is, or is everyone simply driven by selfish desires, wanting not the Provider of all things but only the provision he gives?

The free-will defence of suffering puts God's desire for genuine human relationships at its centre. So, in the end, does the book of Job. Will anyone still choose to trust God even if they lose everything? The book of Job answers, yes. The pain of Job's tragedy and the steadfastness of his faith despite it proves that God's creation project has not been a waste of time. Job's story encourages us that when life is hard and perhaps God feels distant and passive, we can get through this with our faith intact.

At the end of the book, we are told that God restored Job's prosperity. In fact, he doubled it.[36] This provision does not eradicate

35 Birch, B. C., Brueggemann, W., Fretheim, T. E. & Petersen, D. L. (1999), *A Theological Introduction to the Old Testament*, Abingdon, p. 394.
36 Job 42:10.

the grief that Job experienced, but it does go some way towards restoring life as he knew it. This could perhaps be taken to argue that every human tragedy will have a happy ending, and that God will come to the rescue in every situation if we can only wait long enough. Some have even gone so far as arguing that God will always bring you material prosperity and bodily health if you have enough faith. We shall look at this folly in more detail when we explore the Corinthian Paradox. But even here there are clear signals that this is not how we are supposed to understand events.

> All his brothers and sisters and everyone who had known him before came and ate with him in his house. They comforted and consoled him over all the trouble the LORD had brought on him.[37]

This is an artistic, and a theologically fitting, end to the story. It is important that Job's vindication be not just a personal and hidden reconciliation with God in the secret place of his soul, but also visible, material, historical, in terms of his life as a man. It was already a kind of resurrection, as much as the Old Testament could know.

The book of Job points us to another time when an innocent suffered because God's honour demanded it. The paradoxes that trouble us in thinking about God's character coalesce around what we as Christians believe to be the most important events of human history – the life, death and resurrection of Jesus. On the cross we see the perfectly innocent and blameless Jesus suffering due to no fault of his own. What Job was asked to do involuntarily, Jesus

---

37 Job 42:11.

volunteered for. Satan was not allowed to touch Job's life – Jesus gave up his life.

For God, suffering is not a philosophical question. Suffering is not an illusion or a mistake. For God, suffering was a choice he made to buy our freedom. The same freedom that brought suffering into the world in the first place led to God in Jesus giving up his freedom and undergoing suffering himself, as described so poignantly by the prophet Isaiah, hundreds of years before the time:

> Surely he took up our pain
> and bore our suffering,
> yet we considered him punished by God,
> stricken by him, and afflicted.
> But he was pierced for our transgressions,
> he was crushed for our iniquities;
> the punishment that brought us peace was on him,
> and by his wounds we are healed.
> We all, like sheep, have gone astray,
> each of us has turned to our own way;
> and the LORD has laid on him
> the iniquity of us all.[38]

Ultimately, God has not been passive about the evil in the world: he has actively submitted himself to suffer on our behalf. As we shall see in the paradox of the cross, it is because of Jesus' death that the sin and suffering of the world will be finally resolved. This has two important implications, which help us with the paradox of pain. First, when we suffer we are not further away from but rather

38 Isaiah 53:4–6.

drawn closer to the one who suffered for us.[39] Second, when we reach out to relieve the suffering of others we are most like God, because God did everything that was necessary to deal with the evil and suffering in our world.

Let us go back for a moment to that young boy dying in a concentration camp, and the man watching as his faith dies: 'from within me, I heard a voice answer: "Where is He? This is where – hanging here from this gallows."'[40] Elie Wiesel looks at the torment of a young boy dying an unjust death and sees the death of God. But Wiesel spoke better than he knew. God had already died on the gallows, two thousand years earlier. But that death was not the end of God. Instead it was a final blow to the problem that separated us from God's presence.

When we see suffering we cannot dismiss it as bad luck, bad desire or bad karma. All suffering is connected to the bad choices the human race made when God gave us the good gift of freedom. Nothing now is as it should be. Nothing now is as bad as it could be, for sure – but nothing is as good as it should be either. The Job Paradox tells us to take the long view. God staked his reputation on Job's response to suffering. He won the wager with Satan, as Job stayed faithful despite the suffering he went through. Job stands out as the model of a believer who will trust God not just because of what he is given but in spite of what is taken away from him, not because he detaches emotionally, but because he struggles emotionally.

We who live this side of the cross of Jesus have even more reason than Job to trust that even when God seems to be holding out on

---

39 Hebrews 2:18, for example.

40 Wiesel, E. (1982), *Night*, Bantam Books, p. 62.

us, in fact he is actively working out what is best for his universe. We worship a God who acted decisively to deal with suffering, and a God skilful, reliable and wise enough to be trusted in the darkest times.

Chapter 5

The Hosea Paradox
The God who is faithful to the unfaithful

Frankly, there doesn't seem to be a lot I can do about them. They cost me a lot of money and cause me a lot of anguish. Rain or shine, win or lose, they delight or embarrass me by turns. People even laugh at me when they find out. The weird thing is, these people don't even know I exist. I managed a handshake with one of them once but for the most part, no matter how hard I scream at them, they don't pay the slightest bit of attention to anything I do or say. I am talking about Liverpool football club. I have moved house fifteen times, moved job six times, even moved country twice, but I have never switched my allegiance to the team. I am more faithful to my club than the players themselves: they are paid hundreds of thousands of pounds a week to play, while I pay them for the privilege of being an avid supporter. I am sure that most of the team would be happy to go and play for our opposition if the right deal came along, while I will continue supporting them in sickness and in health, for richer or poorer, until death do us part.

Apparently the choice to follow a football team is one of the most enduring commitments that men make in their lives. Some have even suggested that men are more likely to be faithful to an unsuccessful football team than to their faithful, loving wife. It seems incongruous that we are more likely to be faithful to a name, a badge and a temporary group of players who couldn't pick us out of a crowd than we are to the wives we have known and loved and with whom we have exchanged solemn vows.

In an increasingly consumerist culture, where everything seems to be easier to replace than fix, faithfulness in marriage is becoming rarer.[1] Yet it is a defining theme in Scripture, as the Bible uses the metaphor of a committed marriage to describe our relationship with God. In many ways it is a strange metaphor to use. God's love for his people is not romantic, sexual or mutually beneficial in the same way human marriage is, so in what sense does God 'marry' his people? And why would an all-sufficient God commit himself in such a permanent way to fallible, fickle, inconsequential, temporary beings such as us? Why should God remain faithful to us, when we are more often than not unfaithful to him?

The story of the little-known prophet Hosea, who has his own relatively short book in the Bible tucked away towards the end of the Old Testament, is perhaps the Bible's best illustration of the paradox of the God who demands faithfulness yet carries on being faithful even to his unfaithful people. For reasons we shall see, this was no mere intellectual conundrum for Hosea; this was an all-encompassing struggle of heart, mind and soul, both an intensely private problem and an extremely public challenge. During a time

---

1 The desire to be married still persists in Western culture. Indeed, in times of economic downturn it seems that weddings are on the increase, even though (according to the Office for National Statistics) in the UK 42 per cent of marriages currently end in divorce. http://www.ons.gov.uk/ons/rel/vsob1/divorces-in-england-and-wales/2011/sty-what-percentage-of-marriages-end-in-divorce.html

of relative peace and prosperity[2] in Israel's history, around 700 BC, the prophet Hosea has a message to address to the northern kingdom of Israel (confusingly referred to either as Israel, as opposed to Judah, the southern kingdom, or as Ephraim, after one of the twelve tribes of Israel that settled in the north).

But Hosea doesn't just have to pass along a message: he has to live it. Through the painful example of Hosea marrying an unfaithful woman, and then taking her back when she's strayed, God challenges his people about their unfaithfulness to him, and illustrates the extent of his own faithfulness. God promises judgement on Israel, but still offers a hope of restoration if they will heed his message.[3]

For some of us the subject of faithfulness stirs up painful memories because we have been betrayed in our past. Whether it is by a friend, a work colleague, a parent or a spouse, the betrayal of a trusted relationship feels like a stab in the back, leaving scars that never fade.

My youngest daughter is beginning to understand more clearly that she is adopted, and my constant prayer is that the love we have shown her will reassure her that we accept her unconditionally and unreservedly as our daughter, and always will. No paternity test will prove my fatherly love for her, but I pray that she will always know that I love her equally with my biological children. Sometimes, no matter how loving their adopted families, the pain adopted children feel at being relinquished by their own flesh and blood,

2 Evans, M., 'Hosea', in Vanhoozer, K. (ed.) (2005), *Dictionary of the Theological Interpretation of Scripture*, SPCK, p. 308 – although Hosea warns the people of impending doom from the Assyrian power and of the coming restoration if Israel responds to God's message.

3 'It is important to understand that the promise sections do not hold out hope for an avoidance of divine wrath.' Stuart, D. (2002), *Hosea–Jonah*, Word Biblical Commentary, Word, p. 8.

whatever the circumstances, proves difficult to heal. For those who are old enough to remember neglect, abandonment, betrayal and abuse, it is harder still. Many children believe it was their fault that they were relinquished – they were, they think, too naughty, too ugly or too much trouble. This self-blame can lead to a disintegration of their self-image and a reticence to trust even those who have not betrayed them. The same symptoms – scars of suspicion, self-blame and shame – are commonly found in the wake of any betrayal; and the closer the relationship was to begin with, the harder it is for us to find healing.

We have already looked at how God seems to betray the trust of Abraham, Moses and Job, appearing cruel, distant or passive respectively. But in the book of Hosea, God himself is the one who has been abandoned. Even the perfectly compassionate, eternally gracious and morally pure God has experienced betrayal, the pain of being the innocent party in a marriage failure. He was faithful to his people but he describes his beloved Israel as being an unfaithful wife who 'went after her loves and forgot me'.[4] When Israel worshipped other gods[5] instead of Yahweh, the true God, they were committing spiritual adultery.[6] In using this language, God shows us how serious right worship is. When we turn away from God he experiences this

---

4 Hosea 2:13; cf. 13:6.

5 Baal worship is referred to seven times (Hosea 2:8, 13, 16, 17; 9:10; 11:2; 13:1), but this may be an allusion to any kind of worship that is not of the true God rather than to specific worship of a god called Baal in Israel. See Boda, M. & McConville, J. G. (2012), *Dictionary of the Old Testament Prophets*, IVP, p. 341.

6 There is some debate about whether the language of sexual infidelity – 'harlotry' and 'adultery' – is used because there was actual sexual practice involved in the worship of Baal. See Boda, M. & McConville, J. G. (2012), *Dictionary of the Old Testament Prophets*, IVP, pp. 342–3.

with the same level of betrayal and jealousy as an innocent spouse who has been abandoned for a lover. God understands exactly what it is to be rejected by those that he has loved faultlessly. In the middle of the excruciating pain of our abandonment, God can be a comfort because he can empathize with this experience.

Perhaps you can relate to the sense of betrayal that God evokes when he inspires Hosea to write:

> Rebuke your mother, rebuke her,
> for she is not my wife,
> and I am not her husband.
> Let her remove the adulterous look from her face
> and the unfaithfulness from between her breasts.
> Otherwise I will strip her naked
> and make her as bare as on the day she was born;
> I will make her like a desert,
> turn her into a parched land,
> and slay her with thirst.
> I will not show my love to her children,
> because they are the children of adultery.
> Their mother has been unfaithful
> and has conceived them in disgrace.
> She said, 'I will go after my lovers,
> who give me my food and my water,
> my wool and my linen, my olive oil and my drink.'[7]

God is explicit about the pain, anguish and turmoil that he experiences because of Israel's unfaithfulness. He is deliberately using the

---

7 Hosea 2:2–5.

language of a break in the most sacred of relationships to impress on us the depth to which he experiences false worship. In contrast to the Job Paradox – where God is seemingly emotionally unaffected while Job suffers – here God lets us in way past his defences as he offers us a glimpse of the pain he is going through. For some, perhaps, the idea that God has emotions is difficult to imagine. Indeed, the doctrine of 'divine impassability',[8] as advanced by a few Christian thinkers, states that because God is a self-sufficient, all-powerful being, he cannot be harmed or negatively influenced by his creatures, because this would show weakness in God's nature, making his divine perfection contingent upon our actions towards him. God therefore stands as a detached observer watching the plight of human pain and suffering, but ultimately unmoved by it. The story of Hosea shows this view is mistaken. God allows even the people that have betrayed him to know how deeply he feels about them. God's emotional life is not something that he apologizes for or is ashamed of. We have a heavenly Father who really can empathize with our pain.[9]

Perhaps, on the other hand, you can relate to Hosea's story because you have abandoned or betrayed someone. This story has two edges to it – God wants us to know how much he hurts because he wants us to know the terrible emotional impact our unfaithfulness can

---

8 A more orthodox understanding of divine impassability is that God cannot involuntarily be hurt by his creation. 'The Christian mainstream has construed impassibility as meaning not that God is a stranger to joy and delight, but rather that his joy is permanent, clouded by no involuntary pain.' Packer, J. I. (2000) 'God' in Ferguson, Sinclair B. and J. I. Packer (eds.) (2000), *New Dictionary of Theology*, IVP, p. 277.

9 Indeed, when we come to the New Testament we see that the whole Trinity is able to sympathize with us. Jesus is described as a great high priest who can empathize (Hebrews 4:15) and the Spirit groans on our behalf when we don't know how to pray (Romans 8:26).

have. This is not just intended to heap guilt and despair on us, however. God wants us to feel the impact our betrayal causes others, so that we might know the astonishing generosity of his offer of undeserved and unmerited reconciliation. There is a way back to God, no matter how deeply we have wounded both God and the people in our lives.

Perhaps you have looked on at the sadly familiar scenario of the wife who allows her serial-cheating husband back into the family home, or that of the parent who pays off a son's gambling debts for the umpteenth time. While we may admire their persistence to some extent, the question is also raised as to whether their actions are foolhardy. What a few may praise as a strength, the majority will criticize as a weakness. Surely just going along with the way things are is not the answer? This is the problem we face with the Hosea Paradox: if God just lets his people come back with no consequences, is he failing to fulfil his responsibilities?

Is God naïve – continuing to believe the best in the face of all the evidence?

Is God foolish – unable to learn from his mistakes?

Is God weak – manipulated by his betrayer?

Is God gullible – does he really believe those empty promises that it will be better next time?

The dramatic life story of Hosea the prophet can help us get to the bottom of these questions, because his failed marriage was designed to serve as a worked example – a visual aid made flesh – specifically constructed to help the people of Israel understand the heart of their God. The story is the flipside of where we left off with the Joshua Paradox. The people of God had conquered the land and attempted to cleanse it of the people who had worshipped other gods, and they had clearly heard the warning of God not to copy their ways and defile themselves. But that is exactly what Israel had subsequently gone and done, despite knowing full well the terrible punishment that God would mete out – because their ancestors had delivered exactly that punishment to the people living in the land before them. But rather than expel his people from the land, or destroy them, God gives them one last chance, by asking a prophet to do something very strange.

God's command to Hosea is reminiscent of God's call to Abraham to sacrifice his own son. It seems at first glance that God is toying with Hosea, asking him to do something that will bring unimaginable pain into his life, vilification from those closest to him and humiliation in the eyes of the general public. The plotline of the book of Hosea is established in two sentences. Hosea finds Gomer, a woman that Hosea is told will be unfaithful to him; they marry and they have children. God calls Hosea to find a promiscuous woman – quite possibly a prostitute, in fact – and marry her, or, in other words, to go choose a wife that he knows will be unfaithful to him.[10] How could God ask this of Hosea?

Despite the message – widely preached in some circles – that becoming a Christian will make you happier, your wallet heavier and your family healthier, there is in fact no such guarantee in the

---

10 Hosea 1:2–3. There is debate about whether Hosea actually was asked to marry an unfaithful woman or whether this is purely symbolic and parabolic language. Stuart is right to comment that the main point of the book of Hosea is not to provide a biography of a prophet. However, I concur with Dillard and Longman that 'it needs to be re-emphasized that a straightforward reading of the text leads most naturally to the conclusion that Hosea was ordered by God to marry a promiscuous woman'. Dillard, R. B. & Longman, T. L. (1995), *An Introduction to the Old Testament*, Apollos, p. 357.

Bible. For Abraham, Moses and Job, certainly, the call of God made their lives more painful and complicated, and now God calls Hosea to deliberately enter into a marriage that will end badly. All of these stories strike us as paradoxical, because there is such a mismatch between what God asks of his followers in the stories and what we humanly expect God might do for us. When God appears not to be operating with our best interests at heart, we are sure something must be wrong.

The fact that God is not doing what we want is, paradoxically, a good sign. When you're in a relationship and everything is going smoothly, obviously you take that as a good sign. However, on the flipside it might actually indicate that you are seeing not the real person but your own projection of them. Ira Levin describes in her 1972 novel *Stepford Wives* a Connecticut town where all the wives are both incredibly beautiful and at the same time docile and perfectly submissive to their husbands. The men claim marital bliss but as the novel unfolds we find out that the men have replaced their wives with androids.[11] This thriller, which has been turned into two Hollywood films, offered a critique of gender stereotypes and patriarchy – more broadly, though, it helps us to see how real relationships do and don't work. Perfect relationships are a myth. When two people marry it will lead to conflict along the way – any two people must and will clash from time to time.

If this is true at a human level, how much more will it be true in a relationship with a perfect God? If we never experience conflict in our relationship with God, the chances are we have replaced the real God with a substitute god made in our own image. Hitting up

---

11 Levin, I. (1972), *Stepford Wives*, Random House. The book was later made into two separate Hollywood movies, both of which made the woman-replacement plotline more explicit.

hard against the paradoxes in Scripture is a good sign that we are in a relationship with the true God and not just a projection we have created to suit ourselves.

Much of our problem with these paradoxical passages, though, stems from the fact that we have had our egos massaged by a culture that has conditioned us to believe we can have what we want when we want and how we want it. We apply this kind of thinking to marriage as much as any other part of our lives. Many people have a very clear picture of the kind of person they want to marry, a dream of a fairy-tale wedding ceremony and then an idealized picture of what life together will look like. Things become difficult when reality doesn't measure up to expectations. Christians are far from immune to this cultural trend – if anything, we approach marriage in a remarkably similar way to the wider culture, but with the added bonus that God is the divine matchmaker. We want to believe that when we meet the life-partner God has hand-picked for us, we will live out the fairy-tale ending: 'They got married and lived happily ever after.'

So to read that God deliberately matches Hosea with a promiscuous and unfaithful wife crosses a line. Who is God to mess around with someone's private life? Life, we naturally assume, should be easier for Christians, seeing as we are in tune with God's will – so when it is not easier, we are the ones who feel betrayed by God. But here is another occasion when a difficult passage can reveal the true nature of God, and the true nature of worship.

We know that the culture we live in can easily shape the way we see God as just another product or service which will make our lives work better. God becomes just another lifestyle accessory to help us have the kind of life we really want. With our tightly defined consumer rights, we have become experts at expecting good treatment, and boy, do we know how to complain when something doesn't measure up. It becomes natural for us to approach God and worship of him in the same way.[12] And our affections are constantly being courted by alternatives to Yahweh. Even secular authors understand the power of other gods in everyday life. Listen to how American novelist D. F. Wallace puts it:

> in the day-to-day trenches of adult life, there is no such thing as atheism. There is no such thing as not worshipping. Everybody worships. The only choice we get is what to worship. And an outstanding reason for choosing some sort of God to worship . . . is that pretty much everything else you worship will eat you alive. If you worship money and things.[13]

Ironically, in a culture of consumerism, where we prioritize feeding our appetites, we are unwittingly serving gods that end up consuming us; the consumer becomes consumed. Slowly, imperceptibly we assimilate into the customs and values of our host culture. This is not dissimilar to the way the people in Hosea's day had adapted to the worship and lifestyle of the Canaanites. The prophet Hosea presents this process of assimilation not as a necessary cultural adaptation but rather as a seduction. God describes how Israel

---

12 In a fascinating snapshot of modern life, author James K. A. Smith describes how the daily worship of the wider population is developing affections and habits in us that shape our approach to life in general, through an exposition of a trip to the shopping mall. Smith, J. K. A. (2012), *Desiring the Kingdom: Worship, Worldview and Cultural Formation*, Baker, pp. 19ff.

13 From Wallace, D. F. (2005), Commencement Address to Kenyon College, available online at http://moreintelligentlife.co.uk/story/david-foster-wallace-in-his-own-words (also cited in Keller, T. (2013), *Centre Church*, Zondervan, p. 127).

chased after her lovers because she thought they had given her what she needed to live:

> She said, 'I will go after my lovers,
> who give me my food and my water,
> my wool and my linen, my olive oil and my drink.'[14]

In fact it was God who had provided everything that Israel's lovers had tried to seduce her with. Ironically, the punishment for Israel's adultery was insatiable appetite.[15] God's challenge to Hosea, as an Israelite, was to experience in his own person the same series of experiences that God said were in store for his unfaithful wife Israel: commitment, betrayal and then compassion and grace.

Following God's commands will often involve taking a difficult route. God doesn't ask Hosea if he would like to marry an immoral wife, he just tells him to do it – and he does. The emphasis of the account is not on the heart-wrenching nature of such a command, but on the immediate obedience of Hosea. Hosea is faithful despite the apparently bizarre nature of God's command, and the personal sacrifice involved. Just like Abraham, he trusted God's word even when it seemed out of character. Hosea believes God to be trust-worthy; he trusts that in the end God does know and want what is best, if not for him so much, then for his people as a whole – even though it might not be what Hosea wanted or thought he needed.

---

14 Hosea 2:5.

15 'They will eat but not have enough; they will engage in prostitution but not flourish, because they have deserted the LORD to give themselves to prostitution; old wine and new wine . . .' (Hosea 4:10–11).

Unlike fairy tales that *end* with a marriage made in heaven as the couple ride off into the sunset, or drift off in their boat towards the horizon, or skip through meadows into the distance, this story *begins* with a marriage literally made in heaven, but we know there will be no happy ending. The book of Hosea starts where most of those romantic fantasies finish.

After Hosea and Gomer marry, they have children. The very names God tells Hosea to give his children are indicators that things are not going to end well. There are three sons – three omens of doom. Hosea names his first son 'Jezreel', after a massacre; it would be equivalent to calling a child Hungerford, Columbine or Ground Zero. God is reminding his people of the place where judgement came to King Ahab and Queen Jezebel for killing Naboth and stealing his vineyard. Through this eldest son, God predicts the bloody end of Israel. The second son was 'Lo-Ruhamah', whose name literally means 'Not loved'. The third was called 'Lo-Ammi', which translates as 'Not my people'. Everyone he knew must have thought Hosea was mentally ill. Can you imagine if a modern-day preacher called his children 'Faithless', 'Hopeless' and 'Joyless'?

Perhaps some people might have had some sympathy with Gomer when she left Hosea for another man – he doesn't sound like an easy man to get along with – but she got herself not just into an adulterous relationship but into financial difficulties.[16] Hosea could have pressed charges – the law prescribed capital punishment for adultery committed by a married woman. But instead Hosea chooses to pay up – the price of her freedom from debt and the death sentence was thirty shekels, which, as an indication of the value of

---

16 Hosea 3:2–3, where Hosea has to buy her out of debt or slavery.

women in those days, was the same compensation you would pay to someone for a lost slave.[17]

The reason Hosea is prepared to bear the cost, emotionally and financially, to win back his cheating wife, is because of God's call, and his explanation for that call. God says: 'Go, marry a promiscuous woman and have children with her, for like an adulterous wife this land is guilty of unfaithfulness to the LORD.' Hosea is going to receive a God's-eye view of God's relationship with Israel. He is being called to experience the same emotions that God experiences with respect to his people. And as a prophet – of actions, not just words – all his dirty linen would be washed in public to help others too grasp God's emotional response to his people's unfaithfulness.

When someone I knew told me he had bought a bride in Thailand, I was worried. As they walked down the street everyone could guess the back-story. He was old and she was young. She was attractive and he was – less so. He was needy and she was desperate. He wanted sex and company, she wanted a way out and a visa. There was little connection emotionally, little chemistry, little conversation between them. This was a marriage of convenience. Everybody knew it and they commented behind their backs, belittling them for settling for less than they had dreamed. We can just imagine the gossip about Gomer's history, which would have been common knowledge. In the small communities of ancient Palestine, news travelled fast. Hosea's reputation must have been torn to shreds. Why would someone claiming to speak for the Holy God keep such company, let alone marry her? What on earth did he see in her?

---

17 Thirty shekels. This amount is equal to the amount due as compensation for the loss of a slave in Exodus 21:32. Matthews, V. H., Chavalas, M. W. & Walton, J. H. (2000), *The IVP Bible Background Commentary: Old Testament* (electronic edn.), IVP, Hosea 3:2.

Didn't he realize he could have done so much better? How could anyone take him seriously again?

The very same questions could be asked of God. Why did God pick such a lousy nation as Israel to be his people? Why choose a country which would not be a credit to him? Just as Judas' betrayal will raise questions about Jesus as a judge of character, so the choice of Israel as God's people casts aspersions on God's wisdom. Rewinding through Israel's history, in fact, we see that God was in a habit of choosing the wrong people. Abraham was old, impatient[18] and a liar.[19] Jacob lied, stole and cheated his way into his inheritance.[20] During Moses' leadership the Israelites seemed to spend most of their time complaining and grumbling, and point-blank refused to trust that God would help them conquer their enemies. The list goes on and on. God's people have a hopeless record when it comes to faithfulness – hasn't God learned yet?

By earthly standards, God risks diminishing himself by being associated with us. But that is exactly the point made by Hosea's story: God isn't ignoring this risk. No, his constant choosing of people who would let him down is no jinx or accident – it is his deliberate policy. This is what he writes in Deuteronomy:

> The LORD did not set his affection on you and choose you
> because you were more numerous than other peoples, for you
> were the fewest of all peoples. But it was because the LORD

---

18 Abraham fathers Ishmael with his wife's Egyptian maidservant rather than waiting for God's provision of a son. Genesis 16:1ff.

19 Genesis 20:2. Abraham lies that Sarah is his sister; either that, or he breaks the Mosaic law that says he shouldn't have sexual relations with his sister or half-sister.

20 Genesis 27.

loved you and kept the oath he swore to your ancestors that he brought you out with a mighty hand and redeemed you from the land of slavery, from the power of Pharaoh king of Egypt. Know therefore that the LORD your God is God; he is the faithful God, keeping his covenant of love to a thousand generations of those who love him and keep his commandments.[21]

There was nothing about Israel that would mean they warranted or deserved to be loved by God; they were no more numerous, intelligent or righteous than the other nations. Less, even! In fact, when God chose Abraham and Sarai they were just two childless pensioners – a long way from being a nation. And God knew that his people would let him down. But God chose them anyway. He loved them, because he loved them. God does not care if it seems humiliating to love the unlovely; rather, he makes clear that it demonstrates and highlights the magnitude of his love.

The same strategy appears to be at work in Jesus' choice of disciples. These social misfits and spiritual dropouts seem to be about as competent as any of the teams put together on *The Apprentice*: not very. So what's the logic here? 'In for a penny, in for a pound'? The apostle Paul reflects the same train of thought as Deuteronomy in his first letter to the Corinthian church. God sees a greater principle at work when he deliberately picks those who, in the world's eyes, seem like losers:

Brothers and sisters, think of what you were when you were called. Not many of you were wise by human standards; not many were influential; not many were of noble birth. But God

---

21 Deuteronomy 7:7–9.

chose the foolish things of the world to shame the wise; God chose the weak things of the world to shame the strong. God chose the lowly things of this world and the despised things – and the things that are not – to nullify the things that are, so that no one may boast before him.[22]

This was written by a man who himself was the most unlikely of converts – a former persecutor of the church and a self-confessed murderer. But Paul reminds this church in northern Greece that they too were unlikely converts – at least by human standards. They were not part of the A-list glitterati, the social elites, the movers and shakers. In fact, we hear elsewhere in the letter that some at least were 'sexually immoral, idolaters, adulterers, male prostitutes, homosexual offenders, thieves, the greedy and drunkards and slanderers'.[23] But God chose even them to be part of his new creation, his chosen people, his family. He chose them deliberately to turn the system on its head, to challenge the norms, to bring a revolution, to teach the world about how his grace operates and how far his love extends. This New Testament church, like the Old Testament story of Hosea and Gomer, provides a worked example to show that we are not measured by what we are, but by what we can become through God's transforming love.

It's a bit like the advertisements for anti-dandruff shampoos. It must be one of the worst jobs in television to be a model for those products. As the camera zooms in, first on the face, and then on the hair, it shows the world that they have (at least on one side of their head) a significant amount of dandruff. Of course the other

---

22 1 Corinthians 1:26–30.
23 1 Corinthians 6:9–11.

half – which has been washed in the new improved leading brand shampoo – is blissfully clear of the white flakes. The commercial only works if the model has a serious and obvious 'itchy, flaky scalp'. The worse the problem, the better the advert!

In a similar way (though without the TV fakery) the transforming nature of God's faithfulness is most clearly displayed in the lives of people who are broken, failing and damaged. God shows his grace to us, and in doing so shows his grace through us, so that others might be drawn to seek out and experience God's love for themselves. Ironically, many people rule themselves out of receiving grace from God because they consider themselves too bad, too broken, too sinful. Yet Israel's history, and the life and ministry of Jesus, show a reversed logic at work. It is those who know they have fallen short who are first to receive grace from God. The religious elites had little time for Jesus, because they thought they had little need of him. Whereas the outcasts, the sinners, and the social misfits flooded to Jesus, because they were painfully aware of how much they needed a Saviour, and Jesus loved spending time with them and watching them being transformed.

But what if the model for the anti-dandruff shampoo didn't show much sign of improvement, even after using the product for years and years? Why, if Israel is so unfaithful and uncooperative even after receiving the fruit of generations of loving faithfulness from God, doesn't he give up on them and start again – with the Babylonians, say, or the Amalekites or the Assyrians? Frankly, it seems like God's transforming grace isn't working very well. There's not very much transforming going on at all. We may see why God might initially be faithful even to the faithless, but why does God continue being faithful to such a resolutely unfaithful people?

This, then, is the Hosea Paradox. It was bad enough at the start that he chose to marry a woman with a terrible reputation, but now she has cheated on him, and he has chased after her, paid her debts and welcomed her home again. Has he no self-respect? (This is exactly the same charge levelled against Jesus by the Pharisees because of the company he kept.) God's extravagant, taboo-breaking love is one thing, but add to that his willingness to face the humiliation of pursuing his adulterous people. Late on in the book of Hosea we are given an insight into God's heart and mind – listen to him make his appeal:

> When Israel was a child, I loved him,
> and out of Egypt I called my son.
> But the more they were called,
> the more they went away from me.
> They sacrificed to the Baals
> and they burned incense to images.
> It was I who taught Ephraim to walk,
> taking them by the arms;
> but they did not realise
> it was I who healed them.
> I led them with cords of human kindness,
> with ties of love.
> To them I was like one who lifts
> a little child to the cheek,
> and I bent down to feed them . . .[24]

These are not the words of a distant, uncaring deity. This is not divine impassability. Here is a God who has been committed to his

---

24 Hosea 11:1–4.

people since they were like a child. God taught them how to walk and held out his hands to them until they were strong. When they fell down, he picked them up. When they did not know which way to go, he showed them the way. When they were tired, he bent down to lift them up. When they were hungry, he fed them. For God, these people are not a pet project, an advert for the change he can bring about, or a means to an end. We see in Hosea a picture of a God who loves his people with a deep affection. He delights in them. And so he calls out to them again and again to come home, to repent and ask for forgiveness, to recognize him as their God:

> Return, Israel, to the LORD your God.
> Your sins have been your downfall!
> Take words with you
> and return to the LORD.
> Say to him:
> 'Forgive all our sins
> and receive us graciously,
> that we may offer the fruit of our lips.
> Assyria cannot save us;
> we will not mount warhorses.
> We will never again say "Our gods"
> to what our own hands have made,
> for in you the fatherless find compassion.'[25]

Despite his longsuffering faithfulness, despite his pleading, his cries, his emotional vulnerability, God's call was ignored. There was no national outpouring of grief at the offence they had given to God;

---

25 Hosea 14:1–3.

there would be no signs of repentance. The Israelites were ejected from the Promised Land and taken into exile, as God had warned, and Israel as a nation never existed in the same way again.

Just as we saw in the Joshua Paradox, where God gave the Amalekites 400 years to change their ways, God's patience is very long. However, if they are sufficiently determined, God will eventually accept his people's rejection of him. God's faithfulness to us includes being faithful to our freedom of choice, and being consistent in following through on the warning of eventual punishment. If we want life without God, then we will receive it. If we want to reject his mercy, then he will allow us to do so.

God's extreme love and commitment to his people is what lies behind the strong words of Hosea. He tries every way he can to show the Israelites what they are doing to him, and what they are ultimately doing to themselves. He challenges the abuse of his love, he warns them of another massacre at Jezreel and he promises judgement on his own beloved people. Eventually we learn that the faithfulness of God does have its limits.

God's patience and generosity seem to expose him to criticism that he is weak or desperate or emotionally dependent, or just a bad judge of character. Maybe we feel like we don't want a God who seeks out the lowest common denominator – we want a God who recognizes achievement, ambition, a God who has standards. But in fact, God is strong, consistent and just. The Hosea Paradox exposes our sloppy thinking: we struggle with a God who accepts the unlovely, but we also struggle with thinking about God coming to a point where there are no more chances – we don't want to experience the full extent of his judgement.

Essentially, we want to play fast and loose with God. We want God's faithfulness to extend as far as we need, but we want God's judgement to come into play when other people are unjust to us. These two elements will rub up against each other once more when we consider the Jonah Paradox.

The book of Hosea reminds us to take stock. Like Israel, we must be careful in times of stability and peace in our lives not to forget that our lives depend on God. Just as the problem of pain can cause us to doubt God's goodness, so the problem of prosperity is that it can cause us to take it for granted. By remembering God's mercy and patience and love for us in the past, we can go some way to developing an attitude of gratitude in our relationship with God. That gratitude will help protect us against insulting God by giving other things in our lives the place in our affections that only he deserves. When things are going well in life, we need to consider whether our job, our bank balance, our home, our family or even our football team has become more precious to us than honouring the God who created us, rescued us and sustains us through every step of our lives.

We don't know what happens next in the story of Hosea and Gomer – there is a happy-ish ending, in the sense that they are reunited and Hosea continues to show her love. But for those of us who have experienced or watched others try to live with reconciliation after an affair, we know it is by no means an easy road. Hosea himself hints at the length of time it would take to heal – the 'many days' he mentions parallels the following verse where the same phrase refers to the time it will take for the Israelites to repent:

> Then I told her, 'You are to live with me many days; you must not be a prostitute or be intimate with any man, and I will behave the same way toward you.'
> For the Israelites will live many days without king or prince, without sacrifice or sacred stones, without ephod or household

gods. Afterward the Israelites will return and seek the Lord their God and David their king. They will come trembling to the Lord and to his blessings in the last days.[26]

Through this difficult love story, God speaks to us with Hosea's voice – he will be faithful to us, but he asks for faithfulness from us as well. For those of us who live in the 'last days', we are closer than ever to the time when God's patience will finally be at an end. It is now that we should return to God with wholehearted worship. We are called to honour the faithful God with lives of obedience, trusting that despite our unfaithfulness, he is longing to forgive us and welcome us home.

Hosea's prophecy ends on a challenge that is worthy of reflection:

> Who is wise? Let them realise these things.
> Who is discerning? Let them understand.
> The ways of the Lord are right;
> the righteous walk in them,
> but the rebellious stumble in them.[27]

---

26 Hosea 3:2–5.
27 Hosea 14:9.

Chapter 6

The Habakkuk Paradox
The God who is consistently unpredictable

In the middle of the night, on the deserted streets of Cologne, the sound of ringing came from a telephone box. Ringing and ringing, but no one was there to pick up. That phone box was empty, unlike the one I was standing in on the similarly cold, dark streets of Leamington Spa. I punched the long string of numbers in again, from memory now, as I had dialled it over and over for the past twenty minutes. No answer again. This was attempt number twenty-two. I asked myself: How many attempts is considered polite? How many attempts before it's considered nagging, or even worse, stalking? Everyone had told me long-distance relationships were tough – but I didn't think it would be like this. The last time I phoned, the call had not gone so well, and I had run out of coins before I had time to fix things. Maybe she was deliberately avoiding me? Or maybe she had found herself a German boyfriend she could chat to for free? Maybe this was her way of telling me our relationship was over? Or maybe it was nothing – maybe she was just delayed? This was in the dark ages, way back before mobile phones, emails and instant messaging. The only way I could arrange to talk to her again was to send an airmail letter suggesting a new 'phone-box date'. That would take days. I dialled again.

What do we do when people we are relying on don't do what we hope or expect? How do we go on trusting when nobody picks up the phone? And what about when it's God we're trying to get hold of? The Sunday School answer would be that God never lets us down, that he is utterly reliable and consistent and a rock for us to rely on. But in any closer reading of the Bible, this isn't always the experience of his people. As we have seen already, God is more likely to do the more unlikely things. So how do we trust a God whose most reliable quality is his unpredictability?

Now, the Sunday School answer isn't wrong. The Bible does teach that God is immutable[1] – that is, unchanging in his nature, character and purposes.[2] He is described as being the same 'yesterday, today and forever'[3] and does not 'change like shifting shadows'.[4] He is our faithful rock[5] – our Alpha and Omega, beginning and end.[6] He does not change his mind;[7] his love endures forever.[8]

And yet God constantly surprises us. He doesn't do what we

---

1 The early church theologian Irenaeus asserted, 'Let them learn that God alone, who is Lord of all, is without beginning and without end, being truly and for ever the same, and always remaining the same unchangeable Being.' Irenaeus, *Against Heresies*, 2.34.2 cited in Montgomery Hitchcock, F. R. (1981), *Irenaeus of Lugdunum: A Study of His Teaching*, Cambridge University Press, p. 81.

2 Grudem helpfully argues, 'God is unchanging in his being, perfections, purposes, and promises, yet God does act and feel emotions, and he acts and feels differently in response to different situations.' Grudem, W. (1994), *Systematic Theology*, IVP, p. 163.

3 Hebrews 13:8.

4 James 1:17.

5 Deuteronomy 32:4.

6 Revelation 22:13.

7 Numbers 23:19.

8 Psalm 136.

expect, and what he does do is often exactly what we would never dream of. We ask him for one thing and he gives us another. How can we trust in a God who seems to continually confound our expectations? How do we live with a God who could ask you one day to sacrifice your only son, marry a prostitute or destroy a city? How do we worship a God who is most consistent at being unpredictable?

The importance of wrestling with this paradox hit home to me one day when I was filming with a sports celebrity. As we waited for the next shot there was plenty of time to chat about where he was with his faith. This particular celebrity had travelled extensively as an evangelist. He spent many years sharing his powerful testimony of how God had saved him and helped him in the world of sports, and encouraging young people to strive to fulfil their God-given potential. Now, though, while he admits to believing in God in some form or another, he is far away from the church – in fact, he said that as far as his faith was concerned, his former self was almost unrecognizable to him. So what changed? As a young convert he was nurtured by a brand of Christianity that came as a complete package with political views, cultural markers and black-and-white theological positions on every subject under the sun, all fully formed and cast in stone. This was fine for a time, but when he began to question the political views he was being schooled in, or the church's position on the roles of men and women, he began to wonder whether he had been wrong – not just to hold these particular theological positions, but wrong about everything he had been taught. When he became destabilized in one area of his faith, the whole edifice came crashing down.

His tragic story forced me to consider whether we are really helping each other to develop a faith resilient enough to cope with surprises. What do we do when God doesn't fit into the boxes we've made for him – culturally, politically, personally? When he surprises us by challenging a theological assumption or a personal expectation? What will happen to us when God steps in and shocks us – our emotions, our intellect, or our behaviour?

We have already seen how God surprised Abraham, Moses, Joshua, Job and Hosea – this theme thoroughly permeates the Bible. No one seemed ready for the birth of Jesus, the Messiah, whose coming the Jews had been eagerly anticipating for centuries. Nobody expected his death; nobody expected his resurrection.[9] Through Jesus, God was continually challenging people's expectations and rewiring their imaginations about what the Christ should be like. Nobody expected the Messiah to talk to women and children, eat with sinners, challenge Israel's leaders and offer kindness to Romans, and then get rejected by his own people. Who would have thought that twelve so unlikely disciples would be chosen by the Messiah and then succeed in spreading the gospel to the ends of the earth? Even today, we are told to expect the unexpected; the end of the world will come like a thief in the night, as unpredictable as the arrival of a baby. And in an ever-changing world, we are constantly having to work out fresh ways of being faithful and fruitful in our worship of an unchanging God.

Here's the paradox of this paradox. If God is consistently unpredictable, how are we supposed to live lives of worshipful trust in him? There are lots of injunctions in Scripture to cast our anxieties and worries onto God; or else to not let our hearts be afraid and to trust God. But we have already seen the kind of disruptive events God authors in the lives of those he loves. In fact, the fact that we

9 Wright, N. T. (2005), *The Resurrection of the Son of God*, SPCK, p. 85.

are given such reassurances is itself an indicator of just how likely it is that we will need them to get us through! Many of us spend our lives attempting to smooth out as many of the unpredictabilities of life as possible – we develop routines, save money, take out insurance policies and construct other safety nets to guard against all manner of surprises. What we do in church tends to take on the same flavour. We routinize our worship so that there is little room for God to intervene. We develop clear boundaries as to what God is allowed to say or do to us. It is easy to worship a God who never surprises us. But the God of the Bible is described as the Lion of Judah. To pick up on C. S. Lewis's famous allegorical depiction of Aslan the Lion, ruler of Narnia: "'Course he isn't safe. But he's good. He's the King, I tell you.'[10] How can we even begin to worship a God like this?

The economist Nassim Taleb describes how governments and economists face a similar problem as they have to make decisions in the face of potentially huge fluctuations in the stock markets. Taleb calls these paradigm-shifting occurrences 'Black Swan'[11] events, because no one believed black swans could exist – until they were found in Australia. These game-changing incidents

---

10 In a wonderful soliloquy in *The Horse and His Boy*, Aslan explains himself to Shasta, a young runaway slave who has been chased through the night by a lion. 'I was the lion who forced you to join with Aravis. I was the cat who comforted you among the houses of the dead. I was the lion who drove the jackals from you as you slept. I was the lion who gave the Horses the new strength of fear for the last mile so that you should reach King Lune in time. And I was the lion you do not remember who pushed the boat in which you lay, a child near death, so that it came to shore where a man sat, wakeful at midnight, to receive you.' Lewis, C. S. (1976), *The Horse and His Boy*, Puffin, p. 139.

11 Taleb, N. N. (2008), *Black Swan: The Impact of the Highly Improbable*, Penguin.

– such as the 9/11 tragedy, the social impact of the worldwide web, or the recent global economic crisis – are usually unpredicted and unpredictable. It is only after they have occurred that we realize with hindsight that perhaps we should have seen them coming. But if such major disruptive events cannot be predicted, how then are governments to plan? Taleb later coined the phrase 'anti-fragile'[12] to encapsulate a way of building resilience and security into our economic systems so that they can withstand unforeseeable events. This seems like a good theory to apply to faith-building when we are dealing with a God who constantly surprises.

Habakkuk was someone who wrestled with this paradoxical trait in God's character. He learned the hard way how to build an anti-fragile faith. He lived in dangerous times. The once-great Assyrian empire had swept away the northern kingdom of Israel, but was finally decreasing in power and influence. But as it declined, neighbouring Babylon, a wannabe imperial superpower, was on the rise.[13] Nebuchadnezzar was the upstart new king and he was picking off former Assyrian strongholds. Judah, the southern kingdom, had survived thus far, but this was all a bit too close for comfort.

Things were not going well in the Promised Land. There was trouble in this perceived paradise. Despite many prophetic warnings, God's chosen people had chosen to ignore God, and injustice and wrongdoing were rife. In despair, the prophet Habakkuk raises his voice heavenwards and opens his heart to God.

---

12 Taleb, N. N. (2013), *Antifragile: Things that Gain from Disorder*, Penguin.
13 Dillard, R. B. & Longman, T. (1995), *An Introduction to the Old Testament*, IVP, p. 410.

The prophecy that Habakkuk the prophet received.
How long, LORD, must I call for help,
but you do not listen?
Or cry out to you, 'Violence!'
but you do not save?
Why do you make me look at injustice?
Why do you tolerate wrongdoing?
Destruction and violence are before me;
there is strife, and conflict abounds.
Therefore the law is paralysed,
and justice never prevails.
The wicked hem in the righteous,
so that justice is perverted.[14]

This is not what we normally read about the Old Testament prophets. We are used to them saying to the people what God has already said to them. We imagine prophets as 'professional' believers, archbishop-types perhaps, with their spiritual life in order and well fitted to express grand pronouncements with great gravitas. But this prophet is pouring out his heart *to* God; his book in the Bible kicks off with an unedited moan about the state of the world. Instead of being a mouthpiece from God to his people, he is mouthing off to God. This prayer is not one full of saccharine lines like on a Hallmark greetings card. It's not full of profound, long sentences pregnant with theological profundity and filled with clauses and sub-clauses. This is not the kind of prayer you want to turn into a poster with a litter of playful kittens in the background. No T-shirt designers are queuing up to put these words into next year's collection.

---

14 Habakkuk 1:1–3.

This is a prayer of protest. A prayer of impatience. A prayer of honesty and raw emotion. Like Job, Habakkuk teaches us that when we have a problem with God, the best place to take that problem is back to God, wearing our hearts on our sleeves. The intellectual and emotional challenges God and his nature present us with are best – in fact, will only be – unravelled in conversation and confrontation with him. Most of us feel awkward about this; in an attempt to avoid conflict at all costs, because it doesn't seem very 'Christian', we will often allow our questions and doubts to build a wall between us and God, until so many objections have been raised that we lose sight of him altogether. Habakkuk shows us that instead of sweeping our issues under the carpet, storing up our intellectual objections, or silently seething over our unanswered prayers, it is in dialogue with God that we are most likely to find answers to our questions – ways to worship him through the paradoxes.

We might tend to think that a prophet ought to know better – he should have it more together. People are depending on him to hear from God and pass the message on: what's he doing getting bogged down fighting God? In fact, though, Scripture models to us total transparency in relationship with God. Here, this fight is exactly the point. Rather than burying our doubts and fears and pretending they don't exist, Scripture gives us example after example of honest and robust conversation, even argument, between God and even his most cherished leaders. Abraham, Moses, David, Job, Hosea and now Habakkuk all model a tempestuous and plain-speaking relationship with God. Abraham pleads the case of Sodom,[15] Jacob literally fights with God[16] and Moses pleads with God not to destroy

---

15 Genesis 18.
16 Genesis 32.

rebellious Israel.[17] All these significant leaders in the history of Israel speak candidly with God; they argue their case as they struggle with the Almighty's precepts. Their questions, challenges and doubts have not been airbrushed out, as you might expect, but preserved as part of the infallible, unchanging, eternal word of God. The struggle of faith is cemented into the foundation of biblical Christianity.

It is too easy to settle for a pre-packaged, disengaged faith that happily goes along with the flow and avoids any tricky questions. But this is not the faith of the Bible's heroes. Their lives were messier than we like to dwell on, and each one's relationship with God has its ups and downs too. In an increasingly unpredictable and chaotic world, boil-in-the-bag religion will not build a faith that is mature enough to survive the intellectual or emotional turmoil that life is all too good at throwing at us. A resilient faith that can handle the unpredictability of life in God's world must also be an honest faith with room to express doubt.

The prophecy of Habakkuk is set up as a dialogue, dividing neatly into sections. It begins with what is known as Habakkuk's first complaint. Then comes God's reply. The end of chapter 1 is Habakkuk's second complaint, followed by God's second reply in chapter 2. The final chapter records Habakkuk's prayer, as he meditates on all he had said to God and heard from God. The to and fro structure of the book is a wonderful picture of God engaging in real conversation. He is willing to respond to the questions, complaints and doubts of his people.

Habakkuk prays to God about the contradictions, the paradoxes that he sees about him in his world. There is corruption within the

---

17 Exodus 32.

very legal system[18] that is supposed to protect people from corruption. The righteous, who are supposed to define the country, are being set about by the wicked and their impact is nullified. But the main problem for Habakkuk is the seeming inactivity of God in the face of unrelenting evil.[19]

Why does God put up with it? Why does God make his faithful people put up with it? Why *does* God let evildoers thrive and good people get put upon? Life as Habakkuk experiences it does not match with what he reads in the law about life in the Promised Land. He wants God to intervene, so that justice will prevail, and his people can be saved. God assures Habakkuk that he is going to do something – but what he proposes would have been totally shocking to the prophet:

> Look at the nations and watch –
> and be utterly amazed.
> For I am going to do something in your days
> that you would not believe,
> even if you were told.
> I am raising up the Babylonians,
> that ruthless and impetuous people,
> who sweep across the whole earth
> to seize dwellings not their own.
> They are a feared and dreaded people;
> they are a law to themselves
> and promote their own honour.[20]

---

18 Habakkuk 1:3–4.

19 Smith, R. L. (1998), *Micah–Malachi*, Word Biblical Commentary, Word, p. 96.

20 Habakkuk 1:5–7.

God is entirely up-front about the unexpectedness of what he is about to do. Nobody could have seen this coming. No one would have guessed it. No one could have prepared themselves for it. For the faithful Jews, what he is about to do is going to be literally incredible.

In some circles this first sentence of God's answer is one of the most quoted lines from the book of Habakkuk, often used when there is an expectancy of revival. This is a seriously egregious example of a verse used out of context. The unexpected, unbelievable, unpredictable 'something' that God is about to do is not to usher in a time of great blessing, but rather to visit a terrible judgement on his people through that nasty neighbouring pagan superpower, Babylon.

Imagine praying against a spirit of complacency in your church, and then finding out God's answer to your prayers was allowing the mosque next door to close down your building so they could knock it down and build an extension over it. That is the kind of shock that Habakkuk would have experienced when God revealed to him how he was going to respond to the injustice of his chosen people. I expect there have been times in your life when God has done things that run contrary to everything you imagine or pray for. Perhaps you felt led to apply for a new job, only to get turned down and get in trouble at your current workplace for thinking about leaving. Perhaps you felt God prompt you to propose to your girlfriend or boyfriend, only to find out they didn't share your convictions about making a lifelong romantic commitment to each other. Perhaps you have prayed for friends who are ill, but they have got worse. It is very hard to pray or worship when life is so unpredictable. Sometimes these disappointments are so shocking that they become disruptive to everything – your faith, your life, your very identity – just like they did for that sports celebrity mentioned earlier.

Old Testament scholar Walter Brueggeman describes a three-stage process in the life of faith. At first it is securely oriented, but then God shocks us with some unexpected turn of events, and our faith becomes painfully disoriented. Thirdly, though, he says that faith can be reoriented, often in surprising ways.[21]

Many Christians spend most of their lives in the first phase. 'Securely oriented in their faith', they have a way of understanding how Christianity fits into their lives, or how their lives fit into their Christian faith. They don't dig too deep into what they believe or why. They can just go along with what their favourite author, preacher or Christian friend says – everything is all OK. But then they experience a disruptive 'Black-Swan' event, something they never saw coming: personal suffering, the fall from grace of their favourite preacher, a toxic experience of church, or simply a question that wobbles their understanding of one particular doctrine. They now experience exactly that 'painful disorientation'. This unexpected and disconcerting experience can and does lead some to drop out of church altogether. It seems their faith is broken and there is no way or no will to fix it. But we have seen in Abraham, Moses, Job and Hosea that the disruptive events God initiated in their lives did not demolish or debilitate their faith but actually deepened it. This is the third phase – a 'surprising reorientation'.

Building an 'anti-fragile' faith does not mean finding a way to avoid or navigate around the challenges that will come our way; but rather finding a way to see through them to something greater on the other side. God deliberately destabilizes and unsettles us, his children, not out of spite but with the intention of helping us to reach a new level of integrity, intimacy and humility through the

---

21 Brueggemann, W. (2007), *Praying the Psalms*, 2nd edn., Paternoster, p. 2.

process. The book of Habakkuk offers us yet another example of someone who faces a deeply disruptive episode but ends up stronger as a result.

There are three big clues in the story of Habakkuk to help us not only reconcile the paradox of how to follow a God who is consistently unpredictable, but more than that, to develop an anti-fragile faith that is able to boldly face up to, rather than shy away from, the disruptive experiences that God sends into our lives. One has to do with the future, one with the past, and one with the present. Let's take a closer look to see how it works.

First, it is only because of our limited time-bound vantage-point that God appears to be unpredictable, when in fact his actions are entirely consistent with his character. We only see a glimpse of what God is doing. Our lives are like a screen-grab from a movie. We can only comprehend a tiny fragment of the total picture, so it is hard for us to understand what God is doing. Imagine that you had never seen the classic Disney Pixar movie *Finding Nemo*, and you were given a single frame of the film and asked to guess the storyline. In this single image is a tiny orange clown fish talking to a huge shark. You can marvel at the colours, at the amazing graphic skill the digital artists have achieved, and the strange posture of a hunter communicating with his prey. But you couldn't know whether this is the end of the film or the beginning. You couldn't tell whether the shark is about to eat the clown fish, or if the clown fish has managed to talk down his aggressor. There is certainly no way of telling that the shark is a jolly aspiring vegetarian who is deeply moved by the clown fish's story of loss and determination. One picture cannot possibly give enough background information to guess what happens next.

Compared to the eternal purposes of God, even a decade of our lives is like that freeze frame in a movie. Of course, God can zoom in and know every miniscule detail of our daily lives, but we are incapable of zooming out to see our lives with the advantage of distance, bigger context or retrospect. Even if we apply ourselves to try and get a sense of the height and breadth of all that is going on in the world, from our personal relational history to the grand sweep of international politics, it is still very difficult for us make full sense of God's grand design for the universe. So, frankly, we should not be surprised that God surprises us. We are so limited in our understanding of the context of what God is doing that, although we may jump to all sorts of conclusions, unless he tells us his purposes we are really just working blind. Without knowing the future, we must be slow to judge based on the limited information before us.

So what should we do when God's actions (or his inaction) seem unpredictable or irrational? God's response to Habakkuk is to tell him to . . . wait for it . . . yes, to wait for it.[22] When we get to the end of the story, we will be able to understand all the twists and turns that had our minds working overtime to try to guess the outcomes as we went along. Our questions will be answered – in the future. This is not just the crazy positivity of a hopeless optimist – like that of Sonny, a young hotelier in the recent British comedy film *The Best Exotic Marigold Hotel*,[23] who promises his guests that 'Everything will be all right in the end . . . If it's not all right then it's not yet the end.' There is only one being in the universe who can make good on that promise. God does not offer a rosy maxim to his troubled prophet Habakkuk, but he does encourage him to wait and see how he will work all things out for good.

---

22 Habakkuk 2:10.
23 Madden, J. (director) (2011), *The Best Exotic Marigold Hotel*.

Waiting is a difficult thing to practise. We live in a culture of immediacy. Apparently the most used button in a lift – the one which is most likely to be rubbed smooth – is the 'close door' button.[24] (Check it out the next time you are in one.) I am one of the cynics who are inclined to believe the rumour that most such lift buttons are not actually wired in – they are just there as a stress reliever so that we feel like we are doing something to speed things up. If waiting for a lift door to close is stressful enough, how much more so waiting for the bullies at work to get their comeuppance, or waiting for the last chemotherapy treatment to wipe out every last cancer cell? We want justice now. We want results now. But God tells Habakkuk to wait. To play the long game. It might look like he's being unwise, unjust, or unfair, but in the long run we will see why God has set things up the way he has.

In the short term, God knows that Habakkuk will find his tactics – that is, commandeering pagans to teach his people a lesson – unpalatable. But God promises that one day he will see why it had to be that way. He also promises that the bombastic and barbaric Babylonians will be held to account for what they do. They may be free to plunder and kill now, but one day there will be a reckoning – just you wait and see!

Waiting is difficult, though, because we like to feel we are doing something. But the waiting that God asks for is not tedious passivity – he encourages us to wait actively, giving ourselves to God's purposes in the world. Waiting involves continually living by the values of the coming kingdom, knowing that one day they will be vindicated by God himself.[25] Waiting is also difficult for us because

---

24 Gleick, R. (2000), *Faster: The Acceleration of Almost Everything*, Vintage.
25 See the parable of the wise virgins, Matthew 25:1–13.

the more we have to do it, the more we are inclined to give up hope. But waiting can be a powerful testimony of our true allegiance, as the following story indicates.

One of my Kosovar Albanian friends, who had been forced to leave his homeland because of acts of the most brutal cruelty against his innocent neighbours, once showed me his front-door keys. He had left with great panic and only the minimum of possessions, but nevertheless he had grabbed those keys in the belief that one day, he would be able to return to his home. The keys he held on to so expectantly through the following weeks and years were a sign that he believed in the future. They were the keys, not just to his front door, but to hope. In some ways taking care of those keys was an act of protest against the current order of things, a declaration of confidence that this time of despair would pass and a new day would come. Eventually that refugee with a key took his family back to the home he had held in his heart. And it is a powerful testimony for all of us – we too are refugees with keys, waiting for our eternal home.

For Habakkuk, to wait would mean watching the destruction of his nation, the devastation of the temple and the exile of his people into Babylon. But as he waited he would hold on to the key of his faith while God, the Lord of time, did what no one would ever have guessed.

In summary, when faced with the Habakkuk Paradox of a God whose only constant is his unpredictability, the first clue is to look to the future. Wait and see. Waiting shows us where our hope is and where our trust is. In the twenty minutes I spent calling that telephone box in Cologne, each ring seemed to take an eternity. But, in the end, it was only twenty minutes! To write off a relationship because someone missed a phone date would have been short-sighted. (I would also have missed out on all the intervening years with my lovely wife!) God calls his people to patient endurance, to trust that his apparent unpredictability will be seen to be utter consistency in the long run.

Our second clue has to do with the past. God can often appear unpredictable because we do not fully understand the history or the context of every event. In the same way that trusting that he will bring his justice, his kingdom and the restoration of all things in the future helps us to faithfully wait through the rollercoaster ride of life, so being more familiar with the past may help us to become more accustomed to God's ways of doing things. Unlike the future, the past offers us quite a bit more information. In his final prayer, Habakkuk says: 'LORD, I have heard of your fame; I stand in awe of your deeds, LORD.'[26] And then he goes on to list the things he remembers about how God has acted in Israel's history. Like Job confronted with God's wondrous creation, Habakkuk came to see – and in the end was satisfied by – what he saw of God's interaction with his world.

Looking back reminds us of God's character and his power. We see Habakkuk spending time reviewing this as he recounts God's rescue of his people from Egyptian tyranny. He remembers the details of how the soldiers, with their horses, arrows and chariots, were defeated in the waters of the Red Sea.[27] He remembers how God came from Mount Paran[28] to rescue his people.[29] We get a description of how God's arrival at that time must have appeared to bystanders – his splendour was like the rising sun. Habakkuk remembers a pillar of fire[30] going ahead of his people. He remembers the

---

26 Habakkuk 3:2.
27 Habakkuk 3:8.
28 Habakkuk 3:3.
29 Deuteronomy 33:2.
30 Habakkuk 3:4.

ten plagues,[31] which preceded God's rescue like motorcycle outriders preceding a royal cavalcade. He focuses on the stories where God took control of the natural world to defeat a seemingly invincible enemy, and this gives him confidence in the God who holds the future in his hands. Looking back into history helps Habakkuk trust in God. If God did not turn a deaf ear to his people then, he can be relied upon now. Although the world around him is changing, Habakkuk remembers that God's compassion and power and impeccable character and timing have been the same for centuries past, and he has no reason to change now.

Looking back also reminds us of God's standard *modus operandi*. The way God held the future of the Egyptians, the Canaanites and the Israelites in his hands leaves Habakkuk in no doubt that he has power over the Babylonians too.[32] God used the flawed and failing Israelites as his instrument to judge the Egyptians, and now that God's chosen people are in need of discipline he chooses the flawed and failing Babylonians to judge them. There is a consistency to God's actions, when looked at from this perspective of history.

When we are facing difficult circumstances, our minds sometimes play tricks on us. Twenty minutes in a Warwickshire phone box felt like a lifetime: in just a third of an hour I had managed to convince myself, based on no other evidence than a missed phone call, that a relationship must be over. I had to rein myself in and review everything I knew for sure about the character of the girl in Cologne. I knew she was not the type to forget a date, or avoid a difficult conversation, or play with my emotions. Remembering our history together helped me trust her, despite her apparent no-show. In a

31 Habakkuk 3:5.
32 Habakkuk 3:11–15.

similar way, we too have to force ourselves to recollect the past occasions when God has been faithful and consistent, when he has shown his power and grace and compassion, as these will help us not to get blown around by our doubts and fears when we don't understand what he is up to. We do this not simply by bringing to mind our personal experience of the blessing of God but also by becoming more literate in the biblical story. For Christians both the Old and the New Testaments are our family history. The more conversant we are with it, the less historically myopic we become, and the better equipped to wait faithfully for the end towards which God is working everything.

Our third clue from the Habakkuk story on how to build an anti-fragile faith in a consistently unpredictable God has to do with how we see the present and whether we are in fact judging God ourselves, based on whether or not he is currently delivering what we want. Sometimes life feels like a zero-sum game because there seem to be winners and losers in so many life situations. Habakkuk definitely felt like he was on the losing team. First of all, his fellow citizens were making life miserable for those few who were determined to remain upright. And second, because of their refusal to turn back to God, the entire nation would be punished. On the other hand, the Babylonians felt like they were on a winning streak – their gods were delivering yet another crushing military victory for them. If our love for God is dependent on being on the winning side all the time, then God is going to disappoint us a lot. The Bible never promises that we will never be on the losing side. True worship is about living in the ups and downs of the present, knowing that God is in control whichever way things go.

Habakkuk knew this – in his final prayer he models a type of worship which runs absolutely counter to the consumer mentality that infects us all. In one of the darkest points in Israel's history, in the middle of disaster, unsure of what will happen in the future, Habakkuk composes an inspirational song of praise that expresses his intention to hold on to an unshakable faith, whatever surprises and shocks God may have in store for him. Habakkuk's prayer is a model of anti-fragility – he is determined that his faith will be robust and resilient, no matter what happens. If you and I can pray like this, we will have learned how to worship a God who is consistently unpredictable:

> Though the fig tree does not bud
> and there are no grapes on the vines,
> though the olive crop fails
> and the fields produce no food,
> though there are no sheep in the pen
> and no cattle in the stalls,
> yet I will rejoice in the LORD,
> I will be joyful in God my Saviour.
> The Sovereign LORD is my strength;
> he makes my feet like the feet of a deer,
> he enables me to tread on the heights.[33]

---

33 Habakkuk 3:17–19.

Chapter 7

The Jonah Paradox
The God who is indiscriminately selective

When I walked into Sunday School, the very first thing I noticed was that my skin colour did not match that of all the other children in the room. It wasn't long before I realized that it was not only my Asian heritage that made me stand out, but also the fact that I was not being raised in a Christian home. When people asked me how it was that I had come to be part of the small church, it seemed like I was reeling off a random series of events. A brass band parade. A sunny morning with nothing in the calendar. An eight-year-old's curiosity. A chatty mother. Some years later, through the kindness of an elderly Sunday School teacher, the courage of a school friend, and the persistence of a firefighter turned youth-worker, I came to understand enough about Jesus to know that I needed to commit to follow him for the rest of my days. I had not set out to discover God for myself; rather, I became a Christian due to a number of unlikely events, unrelated people and seemingly unconnected coincidences.

Looking back, I can certainly see how God sought me out and I am eternally grateful for it. But whenever I celebrate God's amazing plan that brought me to faith, there is this nagging question in the back of my mind: Why me, here in the UK, and not my cousins on the other side of the world? I think about our grandfather, who grew up in a rural part of Jaffna in northern Sri Lanka. He was born into a Hindu family, as were his ancestors as far back as anyone can remember. As a young man he moved to Malaysia where he married and raised a strong family, working hard on the railways to provide for his six children. He spoke very little English and on the couple of occasions when I travelled halfway around the planet to visit him, I remember having plenty of hugs but very few conversations. As a teenager I noticed how the years were taking their toll on his health, and one summer I realized this would probably be the last time I would see him. I prayed hard and often that God would somehow get the good news about Jesus to him, and yet as far as I know, he died as he was born – a Hindu.

Why did God arrange so many details in my life to help me hear the good news, but not get the message through to my devoted grandfather? Why did God choose me and not him? Why does God seem to offer grace to some but not everyone? How can it be true that God loves the whole world and yet only draws some people to himself? How is it that God can be indiscriminate in his love and yet selective in those he chooses?[1]

The paradox is that the God who loves the whole world appears to be indiscriminately selective. In the Bible, God makes it very clear that he is no tribal deity. He is not limited by geography or political boundaries. He rules over all the earth and loves all people, irrespective of their class, culture, gender or race. But the Bible

---

1 Commenting on John 3:16, Bruce Milne argues, 'John's readers would have been familiar with the thought of God's special love for Israel, but in truth his love is (and always was) indiscriminate, embracing every man, woman and child.' Milne, B. (1993), *The Message of John: Here is your King! (With Study Guide)*, The Bible Speaks Today, IVP, p. 77.

also reveals that God chose one single nation out of all the nations on the earth to call his chosen people. Most of the Bible concerns itself with this one nation of Israel, and God's promise to the Israelites that they will be his people and he will be their God. In the New Testament, John tells us that God so loved the whole world that he sent his Son, but Jesus talked about the narrow road that few would find,[2] the many who were called but the few who were chosen,[3] the value of the one rescued sheep[4] – as well as sending his disciples out into all the world.

The Bible seems to teach both that God is indiscriminate in his love, and that he is selective in his choices. Like so many of these paradoxes, this one strikes to the heart of our relationship with God, raising questions about how we understand, love, worship and defend him. Does God love the whole world – or just Israel? Perhaps he has favourites? Even worse, perhaps God is racist? Why does he cherry-pick some people to be on his team, leaving others behind? Are we supposed to see God as Israel's mascot? Is there some sort of pecking order even amongst God's followers? How can we worship a God who, judging by his apparent indifference to their ignorance of him, seems not to love our families and friends as much as we do? What does it mean that God, with all his grace and compassion and wisdom, does not help everyone to come to faith in Jesus, the way he helped me?

This was exactly the problem faced by the rather strange and very famous Old Testament prophet known as Jonah. Every Sunday School child (possibly excepting latecomers like me) knows about

---

2 Matthew 7:14.

3 Matthew 22:14; 20:16.

4 Luke 15.

Jonah and the whale, but the clue to the significance of Jonah and the key to this paradox has more to do with the story of Jonah and the worm, which comes at the end of the book.

Jonah is simultaneously the best and the worst prophet in Israelite history. He was the worst prophet, because he did just about everything wrong, as we shall see. But he also has to be acclaimed as the most successful prophet of his day, because the message he brought led to an astonishing full-scale revival, and in a pagan city to boot. This peculiar story is full of contradictions and paradoxes.

Just like the prophecy of Hosea, and indeed almost all of the Old Testament prophetic books, the book of Jonah begins with the statement that 'The word of the LORD came to [fill in prophet's name here]'. So far, so normal. But unlike Hosea – who, as we saw, immediately obeyed the call to go and marry an unfaithful wife – Jonah, who was simply given a message to deliver to the great city of Nineveh, ran in the opposite direction.

The message Jonah was unwilling to deliver was that God knew about Nineveh's wickedness. But Jonah decided he would rather be anywhere else than Nineveh, so he boarded a ship heading for a different destination altogether. This is an atypical reaction from God's chosen prophet. Mostly we are told that the prophets simply obeyed whatever surprising instructions they were given. We have observed already the radical obedience of Abraham and Hosea. But Jonah's reaction is even more unusual, given the nature of the message. Being asked to 'preach against'[5] an enemy of God's chosen people surely ought to be the dream job for a prophet. What school-child doesn't fantasize about being the one chosen to publicly banish the school bully and send him to the head-teacher's office? God is

---

5 Jonah 1:2.

commissioning Jonah to go up against the biggest military bully in the region – a colossal near-neighbour nation with enough fire-power to wipe out Israel. In our day this commission would be the equivalent to God calling someone from Chechnya to go and preach against Russia, or someone from Cuba to go and preach against America. But with God behind him, surely Jonah should have risen to the challenge? Instead, rather than take up this literally God-given opportunity, he ran away.

The foolishness of Jonah's attempt to 'flee from the LORD'[6] is starkly illuminated during the severe gale that hits the ship on its way to Tarshish. The storm that God sends is so powerful that we are told that even the hardened sailors are fearful for their lives. Jonah, apparently untroubled by either his conscience or the motion of the fierce pounding waves, is asleep in the boat as the sailors desperately attempt to lighten the load and keep the vessel afloat. Ironically, it is the pagan captain of the ship who has to awaken the Hebrew prophet to tell him to pray. The sailors try to discern who is responsible for the calamitous storm that has come to them, and yes, the lot falls to Jonah.

The fugitive prophet, running away from his missionary responsibilities, is faced with a sea of confused faces and he is forced to admit that he is a worshipper of 'the LORD, the God of heaven, who made the sea and the land'.[7] The terrified sailors obviously believe him, and ask what they must do to be saved. Jonah explains

---

6 Jonah 1:3. Perhaps we might discern an echo of Adam and Eve hiding from God in the Garden of Eden, or again the words of David, who asked, 'Where can I go from your Spirit? Where can I flee from your presence? . . . if I settle on the far side of the sea, even there your hand will guide me, your right hand will hold me fast' (Psalm 139:7, 9–10).

7 Jonah 1:9.

how he was trying to run away from God, and commands them to throw him into the sea. After exhausting all other possibilities they eventually relent and pray to this new-found God not to hold them accountable 'for killing this innocent man'.[8] As Jonah sinks beneath the waves, the storm is stilled and these pagan men grow in their respect and awe for the Lord God of the Hebrews. Somehow, even in his disobedience, Jonah the reluctant prophet makes an impact on these fearful sailors. But it is these pious pagans who come across as the most honourable people in this story. Unlike Jonah, who ignored and disobeyed God, the sailors seek God, find God, obey God, pray to God, confess to God and worship God, despite being from an unnamed and thus indubitably a non-chosen nation. This is a clue for what is to come and one of the keys to help us unlock the Jonah Paradox.

Already strange things are happening in this story, and the God who, as we saw in the previous chapter, is consistently unpredictable now surprises us with another twist in the tale. The same God that sent a storm on the ship to remove Jonah, now sends a large fish to rescue him. God arranges both the crisis and the solution. In the belly of the whale Jonah prepares a song of repentance and praise,[9] and when he is finally vomited out, he finds himself in Nineveh. He didn't want to go to Nineveh, but God's pet fish, more obedient than the prophet, took him there anyway.

Already in this short narrative we have seen some clues as to the

---

8 Jonah 1:14.

9 There is debate as to whether the story of Jonah is a parable or a literal historical event. Either way, the story sheds light on God's indiscriminate selectivity. See Dillard, R. B. & Longman, T. (1995), *An Introduction to the Old Testament*, IVP, p. 392, who point out other anomalies to a historical account: even the king of Nineveh has no name, and even the animals repent.

nature – and the possible resolution – of the Jonah Paradox. Jonah was certainly not chosen because of his trustworthiness, faithfulness or courage. We will see as the story progresses that he is grumpy and resentful, as well as cowardly and faithless. And just as the prophet has not been chosen to speak on behalf of God because of any moral superiority, so this serves as a reminder to Israel that their call as God's chosen people is not due to any kind of superiority. Jonah is no hero in this story. He slept while the brave sailors prayed and toiled. While the rogue prophet ran away and hid, God did everything possible – even fixing the weather, the drawing of lots and a freak of nature – to make sure that his message got through to the Ninevites. We cannot understand it yet, but it is somehow very important that God's message is delivered to a moral failure of a foreign city by a failure of a Jewish prophet. This story cuts through the sense of national superiority that Jews tended to feel towards other nations. Indeed, as we have already considered, God made the following clear when his chosen people were travelling from Egypt to the Promised Land:

> The LORD your God has chosen you out of all the peoples on the face of the earth to be his people, his treasured possession. The LORD did not set his affection on you and choose you because you were more numerous than other peoples, for you were the fewest of all peoples.[10]

The same logic applies in the New Testament. It is not because of any moral superiority or intellectual ability that God chooses anyone to be included in his family. The doctrine of grace – the unmerited

---

10 Deuteronomy 7:6–8.

favour of God towards us – precludes any sense of entitlement from our perspective or belittling of other people.[11] This is a foundational belief and recurs over and over throughout the whole of the Scriptures. For example, Paul writing to a church leader in Crete states unequivocally that 'when the kindness and love of God our Saviour appeared, he saved us, not because of righteous things we had done, but because of his mercy'.[12]

The Jonah story proves beyond all reasonable doubt that God cares for all the other nations just as he does Israel. After being vomited from the belly of the great fish, Jonah finds himself on terra firma again – Jonah is recommissioned by God[13] and this time the reluctant prophet obeys. Nineveh was a vast city of the ancient world and it took Jonah days to adequately proclaim the message of the coming judgement of God throughout its streets. Eventually the pagan king of Nineveh got wind of this strange prophet of doom, and immediately responded by putting on sackcloth and ashes, the outward signs of deep sorrow and mourning. The king got down from his throne and sat in the dust, from which position he ordered a nationwide fast, that included even the livestock. This total and public act of contrition was not with the intention of manipulating God into submission. No, he humbly offered up a fast in the hope that: 'Who knows? God may yet relent and with compassion turn from his fierce anger so we will not perish.'[14] There seems to be a genuine repentance here, and a real understanding of God's supremacy, power and justice, which stands

---

11 Ephesians 2:8–9.

12 Titus 3:4–5.

13 Jonah 3:1.

14 Jonah 3.

in contrast to the Jewish prophet's rather small picture of a God from whom he could run and hide in disobedience.

God responded to the penitence of the king and his country and did not bring his threatened destruction,[15] which means that in one (non-)fell swoop Jonah the Jewish, jump-ship, jelly-fish, job-shy prophet becomes the most successful prophet in Israel's history. No other Old Testament prophet who was given similar messages of warning about the coming destruction ever saw a nation heed those warnings in the way that Nineveh did. Hosea faithfully prophesied to the northern kingdom of Israel, imploring them and illustrating to them their unfaithfulness in his own family life, but God's chosen people remained hard-hearted and didn't change, and so wound up facing the promised destruction. Jeremiah was given a stinging message to Israel about living as God's enemies. He became known as the weeping prophet because he witnessed not the turning of Israel but the burning of Jerusalem as his warnings too went unheeded. Similarly, when the word of God comes to his chosen people through such mighty prophets as Ezekiel and Isaiah, they fail to repent. But when the word of God comes to the pagan nation of Assyria in the city of Nineveh through such a useless prophet as Jonah, the whole nation repents, right down to their livestock.[16]

This is repentance on a pretty grand scale. What is grander still is that it actually has repercussions for the whole of human history. Jesus picks up this theme when he tells Israel:

The men of Nineveh will stand up at the judgement with this

---

15 Jonah 3:10.

16 Contra Lawson, S. L. (2001), *Bibliotheca Sacra*, Vol 158, pp. 345–56.

generation and condemn it; for they repented at the preaching of Jonah, and now something greater than Jonah is here.[17]

God offers grace to the pagan city of Nineveh; he holds out his forgiveness to the enemies of his people. He is not partisan or prejudiced. In the end we are not judged on the basis of our ancestry or genetics. We will be held accountable for how we have responded to God. When God challenges us about our sinfulness, whoever we are, whatever our background, he speaks to provoke a response in us. God wants us to know the extent of the mess we are in so we might receive his mercy. He exposes our sin so that we might know that we need his grace. My grandfather was not disqualified from God's mercy because of his race, nationality or history. If he truly responded to God's offer of grace and mercy in Jesus, then he would have been as acceptable as anyone else on the planet. But was he given that opportunity? Did God send a missionary to him – a missionary who decided to go in the opposite direction, regardless of God's call, perhaps to the USA instead? Is God fed up with having to reroute his reluctant missionaries? How *is* God's forgiveness offered to all people? Perhaps the rest of the Jonah story will shed some light.

The response of Nineveh was so widespread and so authentic that it changed God's heart towards the people[18] – but it hardened Jonah's heart against God. Jonah went off to sulk in his corner, and we discover the real reason why he did not want to bring the message to the Ninevites in the first place: he was angry, because he knew how the story was going to end.

---

17 Matthew 12:41.

18 'When God saw what they did and how they turned from their evil ways, he relented and did not bring on them the destruction he had threatened' (Jonah 3:10).

He prayed to the LORD, 'Isn't this what I said, LORD, when I was still at home? That is what I tried to forestall by fleeing to Tarshish. I knew that you are a gracious and compassionate God, slow to anger and abounding in love, a God who relents from sending calamity. Now, LORD, take away my life, for it is better for me to die than to live.'[19]

Jonah's desertion from his call as a prophet had been prompted, not (as we might have thought) by fear of what the Ninevites might do to him, but because he knew what God would do for the Ninevites. Jonah may have had a message of doom and destruction, but he knew his Old Testament history, he knew how Moses, when he became the first person to see God's glory, had talked about him as 'a gracious and compassionate God, slow to anger and abounding in love'.[20] Jonah knew that his mission wasn't really about ushering in God's vengeance on the city, but about enabling them to receive God's mercy.

In our time there are two equal and opposite dangers when bringing bad news to those who don't know God. Some Christians seem to take some sort of sadistic delight in explaining just how angry God is at people's sin. They seem to enjoy delivering the bad news of God's judgement more than they enjoy explaining the good news of God's grace. These preachers overstate their case, explaining how much God hates everything about people who don't know him. Sometimes preachers picket funerals or hold up billboards denouncing a group of people that God apparently abhors. These alleged Christians deliberately burn the holy books of other faiths.

---

19 Jonah 4:2–3.
20 Exodus 34:4–7.

This doesn't sound like the Jesus we read about in the New Testament, who was known as a friend of sinners. But it doesn't sound like the God of the Old Testament either – the God who speaks so highly of the faith of pagan people in contrast to the actions and attitudes of his own rebellious prophet.

Equally, another group of Christians repackage the message of Christianity so that it has no bad news at all. Christianity becomes a feel-good religion which helps us to feel better about ourselves and raises our self-esteem. This doesn't sound like the Jesus of the New Testament, who speaks more about hell and judgement than anyone else in Scripture. Just as we cannot withhold God's grace from others, so too we cannot unilaterally offer grace to people who imagine they somehow deserve it in their own right. This second option shows no confidence in God, if we have to edit the message down to make it more palatable to our friends and family. We learn from Jonah that the bad news God asks us to deliver is neither to be ignored, nor over-egged. We have to offer bad news out of a sense of true concern, just as a neighbour may wake you up in the middle of the night because he has seen smoke coming from your kitchen window. The bad news that God asked Jonah to deliver to the city of Nineveh was offered because of his concern for this and for all the nations.

Nineveh was the capital city of Assyria, a long-term enemy of Israel, and Jonah was afraid that God would be gracious to the Assyrians. He had good reason to be. It was scary, living in the shadow of an evil super-power. It would have been much nicer for the Israelites to see them obliterated from the map, but God had other plans.

If God had simply intended to bring judgement on the Ninevites, he could have launched a pre-emptive strike – taking out the city in one go, perhaps with a lightning bolt, a volley of fire and brimstone or a squadron of angels. God didn't need to have 'people on the ground' in order to bring judgement to Nineveh. He had every possible strike option available to him. Jonah understood that perfectly well – he knew that God was giving the Assyrians yet another chance to repent, and he wanted that kind of mercy to be reserved for Israel alone. Jonah did not like the fact that God was indiscriminate with his love and forgiveness. He was not alone. All through Israel's history, God had to remind them that they are to bless the outsiders, the neighbours, the foreigners. But they failed. And we too, although we are sent to be salt and light to the whole world, find it very difficult to love our enemies and share what we know of God's grace with our neighbours.

As Jonah sat outside the city, still hoping that God would surprise him again and annihilate its inhabitants, he was fuming.[21] It was a hot day, which had exacerbated Jonah's bad temper further. But he still had a lesson to learn from the God who had sent a storm and a large fish to make sure that the Ninevites heard Jonah's message. God sent him some shade, courtesy of a vine – something which made Jonah inordinately happy. Then God sent a worm to eat the vine, at which Jonah threatened to commit suicide. Jonah's attitude, compared to that of Habakkuk, makes for a stark contrast: Habakkuk was willing to trust and praise God even though 'the fig tree does not bud and there are no grapes on the vines'.[22] Habakkuk knew that God was doing what was best for everybody, even when the whole nation's crops failed. Here was self-absorbed Jonah, on the other hand, willing to curse God when his own personal organic parasol withered.

---

21 Jonah 4:1.
22 Habakkuk 3:17–18.

Do you remember the very first time you received an email explaining that you had inherited a multi-million-pound inheritance, or that someone in Nigeria needed your help to process a huge payment – all completely legal, of course? It makes you feel good that you are the lucky long-lost relative who is next in line for a huge pay-out; until you discover that everybody else you know has received an identical email, and the pleasure begins to subside. Eventually it dawns on you that this is an internet scam, where the only real winner is the con artist who is more than happy to take your bank account details and wipe them clean. You are left feeling cheated instead of rewarded. Jonah probably felt exactly the same way as he sat on the hillside watching the Ninevites basking in God's mercy while he got sunstroke.

How does it work for God to hand-pick a nation for his very own, and yet still love all the other nations too? Jonah can't work it out: he never resolves this paradox. The book ends with him on the hillside continuing to wrestle with it, as God challenges him about why he was so emotionally connected with a short-lived vine, and whether he should not be more concerned about a city of 120,000 men, women and children (not to mention the animals)?[23] It's a paradox we are left confused about too, especially since we spend more time, money and energy worrying about the roof over our heads than about the hundreds of thousands of people who have never heard the good news of Jesus. Let's rewind a little and look back through Scripture to help us navigate this paradox so that we can learn how to worship God precisely *because* he is absolutely indiscriminate yet individually selective.

Up until Genesis 12, the Bible records the story of the origins

---

23 Jonah 4:10–11.

of the whole universe – all that was created and all the peoples of the earth. But just like at the beginning of a feature film, when the camera has panned across some huge landscape, it then zooms in to one couple, one family and then one nation. In Genesis 12 one man, Abraham, is promised a son – not just for his benefit, but for the benefit of the whole world:

> I will make you into a great nation,
> and I will bless you;
> I will make your name great,
> and you will be a blessing.
> I will bless those who bless you,
> and whoever curses you I will curse;
> and all peoples on earth
> will be blessed through you.[24]

God simultaneously focuses on one nation, and on the whole world. He may have selected Abraham, but he is thinking of everybody. He chooses the one for the sake of the many. God is deliberately selective, because he wants everybody to get the good news that God's love is both universal and particular, which missionary theologian Lesslie Newbigin called 'the logic of election'.[25] God's love is universal, in that he loves everybody in his universe – his love does not respect political boundaries or ethnic divisions; he is not racist or xenophobic. But God's love is also particular – he chooses a particular elderly barren couple and a particular ethnic group and

---

24 Genesis 12:2–3.

25 See the chapter 'The Logic of Election' in Newbigin, L. (1989), *The Gospel in a Pluralist Society*, SPCK, pp. 80ff.

loves them against all odds with a compassionate, jealous, faithful love. His extravagant love is not exhausted on this one group – he has plenty more to go around. God always intended a mission for his people. Even before the first child of the promise was born, God told Abraham that the chosen nation he would father was blessed in order to bless.

So why does God work in this way? If I want to show love to my family, I do not single out one of my five children to treat, and then hope they would one day decide for themselves to treat another sibling. I might hide a card under *each* of their pillows, or drop some goodies in all five schoolbags, or arrange for a day out that we would all enjoy. How can we understand God's different perspective of how to draw the whole world to himself?

Imagine I wanted to set up a female friend of mine with a date. I hear about an eligible young bachelor teacher with a passion for God who also happens to enjoy wrestling with theological paradoxes. I want him to have a copy of my new book. So I could just package up my book, along with my other friend's personal profile and contact details, and post it to him. Then I would have to wait and see if he responded about the book or pursued the date. Alternatively I could ask my friend if she wouldn't mind, on her way back from work, delivering a copy of my new book to a young teacher I happened to know. I would still have to wait and see what transpired, but I would at least know that there had been a face-to-face encounter between the two people I was matchmaking with.

So it is with us and God: rather than giving everyone a blanket revelation of the standard truths about himself, God wants us to realize the importance, not just of himself, but of the people he's put around us. God chose one nation to be the means through which his grace is passed on, and this means that two things get accomplished at the same time. Men and women find out the truth about God, as they encounter the God of Israel themselves, but they are also brought into relationship with God's people. What Jesus called the two greatest commands are brought together in the logic of election. God calls us to 'Love the Lord your God with all your heart and with all your soul and with all your mind' and to 'Love your neighbour as yourself.'[26] There is a vertical and a horizontal reconciliation going on simultaneously. We come to know God through the mission of his people, and through the mission of God we also come to know the people he has put around us to be his witnesses.

This same principle – now no longer restricted to the ethnic or political nation of Israel – is in play when the church in Jesus' name seeks to demonstrate and deliver the truth and power of the word of God in our neighbourhoods, communities, towns and cities. God delivers the message of reconciliation though his people so that those who believe are brought into fellowship both with God and with his people at the same time. God's love is universal but his mission is particular; that is how he accomplishes his purpose of not just drawing individual souls that connect to him, but creating a community made up of people from every nation that love him and love each other.

The book of Jonah is valuable because it reminded the Israelites to share God's compassion for the whole world and pass on what they had received. It shines a light on the paradox that by trying to hold on to their 'special' identity as God's people, they were actually losing that 'special' identity. By failing to reflect God's desire to love and bless their Ninevite neighbours for God's sake, they were acting less like God's chosen people. The more protective

---

26 Matthew 22:37, 39.

Israel were about their God, the less like Israel's God they were, and the less they were truly behaving as God's Israel.

Jabur Hissan was a modern-day Jonah.[27] The thirty-two-year-old Royal Mail postman felt unable to keep up the demanding postal route he had been given, so took an unusual approach to solving his problem. He put on his washed and ironed uniform and his polished shoes, jumped into his shiny red van, and dumped some of the letters into a canal. Then he burned around 400 more, and the other 29,000 items of mail he couldn't be bothered to deliver he buried in his garden. He may have looked every inch a postman, but as he refused to deliver the letters he had been given, his actions denied that identity as a postman. Similarly, if Jonah was not willing to pass on to others the grace and mercy he had himself received from God, then he was certainly not God's prophet. And if we do not follow and reflect Jesus Christ, then logically we cannot call ourselves Christians.

In Jesus, we see the mirror image of Jonah. Jonah was an unwilling missionary sent by God to Nineveh, whereas Jesus was a willing missionary sent by God to earth. Jonah's life and words, as recorded in the Bible, betray his underlying feelings of rebellion and resentment, whereas Jesus' life and words reveal God's love, grace and compassion for the world. Jonah slept on a boat in a raging storm, was woken by seasoned sailors scared for their lives, and stilled the storm by throwing himself into the sea. Jesus too slept on a boat in a raging storm, was woken by seasoned sailors scared for their lives, and stilled the storm – simply by speaking to the storm and telling it to stop. Jonah was in the belly of the whale for three days

27 'Postman jailed for burying 30,000 letters in garden', *Daily Telegraph*, 18 February 2013.

and three nights; Jesus was in the grave three days and three nights.[28] Jonah preached about judgement to pagans; Jesus preached about judgement to Israel. Jonah cried because judgement didn't come, Jesus cried for Jerusalem because judgement was coming.[29] Jonah was angry at God's mercy; Jesus showed us mercy by taking on God's anger. Jonah didn't want God's grace to be shown to other nations; Jesus sent his Spirit to fill his disciples and to send us to all the nations.[30]

Through the paradoxes of Jonah and the parallels of his story with that of Jesus, we are given a clear picture of how God expected Israel to bless the nations around them, and we see also how God expects us to understand his universal, particular love.

If Israel had done their job properly, perhaps the Indian subcontinent would have had clearer, earlier, access to the gospel, and my grandfather would have had more chance of hearing the good news of Jesus. Or perhaps if I had done my job properly, I could have prioritized the learning of Tamil as a youngster and read the Bible with him in his native language. But God, who is powerful enough to override Jonah's decision to go to Tarshish, is also powerful enough to overcome our shortcomings. What should we do about those we love who seem so far away from knowing God? Perhaps if he could just intervene in their lives as he did in our own with various experiences, people and events, then they would come to faith in Christ too? What about those who have never heard? Why does God leave so many people without access to faith, or will he save them all in the end anyway?

The book of Jonah offers us some pointers.

---

28 This connection is made by Jesus himself – Matthew 12:38–42.

29 Matthew 23:37–38.

30 Matthew 28:18–20.

Some people believe that good pagans will be saved through their own religions; that by being faithful to the gods that they have come to believe in, there can be salvation through sincerity. This is a very attractive solution to me – I would love to believe that my Hindu relatives could find God through their temples and rituals. But Scripture doesn't seem to leave room for such a solution.

First, both the pagan sailors and the people of Nineveh seem to be spiritually sincere – the former are praying to their gods before they meet Jonah, and the latter have an effective method of expressing guilt with sackcloth and ashes. Nevertheless, God still sends Jonah with his message from Yahweh. If there was hope of salvation through the gods they had been worshipping, then Jonah's mission was a waste of time. Similarly, the missionary commissions in the New Testament would be irrelevant too: why would Jesus commission his friends to 'go and make disciples of all nations', if sincerity to indigenous religions was enough?

Throughout the Bible we see references to God's global mission, whether it is to Amorites, Ninevites, Babylonians, Samaritans – or everybody else, like us, otherwise known as 'the ends of the earth'. These days talk of the church having a global mission fills many Christians with fear or embarrassment, because we worry that if we cannot respect the sincere beliefs of people from other faiths as a means of salvation, then we must try to convert them – but that feels like imposing our cultural superiority.

Now, there are many embarrassing and indeed ungodly things that have been done in the history of the church's mission to the world. But there are some wonderful and incredible things too. Not least the fact that the faith of all of us in the Western world is the fruit of missionary endeavours. If we have received grace from God through the mission of God's church, how can we withhold it from anyone? Colonialism and imperialism may be an embarrassing recurring element in the history of the church,[31] but that is our fault, not God's – he does not intend or instruct us to evangelize with any sense of superiority. Indeed, in the book of Jonah, great respect and honour is given to pagan people, since the whole point of the book is to highlight how their piety outstrips even that of God's own prophet, indicating that God's mission is not at all about preaching down to people. Rather, we show respect if we boldly and humbly speak and demonstrate the message we have been given.

Second, there is consistency all the way through Scripture about how God intends people to come to faith. All along, God promises that the whole world would be blessed by Israel. Abraham and his descendants were to illustrate this in their unique national commitment to God's law, and their open-door policy towards others who wanted to worship God with them.[32] When Jesus was born, he showed that it was through him that *all* people, throughout the world – whose known borders were just at that time expanding rapidly – could find God. Throughout the accounts of his death and resurrection and the work of his Spirit, Jesus' story keeps on including non-Jews to be involved in his mission.

Third, if we hold to the traditional view of the exclusivity of salvation through Jesus, the apparent unfairness of the system is a major problem. Where and when my grandfather was born made it a lot more difficult for him to come to faith in Jesus, so how can it be fair for him to face the consequences of eternity without God's

---

31 See Smith, D. (2013), *The Kindness of God*, IVP; and Stanley, B. (1990), *The Bible and the Flag: Protestant Mission and British Imperialism in the 19th and 20th Centuries*, IVP.

32 Not just the Ninevites here but Rahab the Canaanite, Ruth the Moabitess, Naaman etc.

love and compassion? Is it all just a lottery of time and place of birth? Does the faith you are born into effectively dictate your eternal future? Jonah shows us that there is no advantage in being born into God's chosen nation. First, the Ninevites prove themselves more receptive than the Israelites, so being born in the right tribe or nation does not guarantee a relationship with God. On the flip-side we saw that a whole generation of Israelites died in the desert because of unbelief, and God used the Assyrians to punish the Jews, as we read in Habakkuk. So being born Jewish did not come with automatic entry to eternal life, just as being born into a Christian family is no guarantee of remaining in the faith either – we still have to decide.[33] Everyone, regardless of their ethnicity, needs to seek God's forgiveness and mercy. The important point is that God is not passively waiting for all the nations to come to him. He is sending his people to the four corners of the world to demonstrate his love in deeds and words. God pursued Jonah because he wanted the message to get to Nineveh through him. This divine concern for and commitment to the nations is evident throughout Scripture.[34]

As we saw at the beginning of this chapter, there is an interesting reference to the Ninevites in the New Testament. Matthew's Gospel records Jesus declaring that the people of Nineveh will have the right to judge the unbelieving Israelites of his day who were rejecting his teaching. According to Jesus, the pagan Ninevites were responsive to the preaching of a minor-league prophet like Jonah, so how much more then should God's chosen people respond to God's word 'now something greater than Jonah is here'.[35] Jesus hints at

---

33 John 1:12–18.

34 For an overview see Wright, C. (2006), *The Mission of God: Unlocking the Bible's Grand Narrative*, IVP.

35 Matthew 12:41.

the idea that different groups of people may be more culpable than others. There seems to be a differentiation in exposure to judgement based on what we have heard and how we have responded to it. Similarly, Jesus challenges two towns in Israel for failing to respond to the teaching and the wonders they had seen:

> Woe to you, Chorazin! Woe to you, Bethsaida! For if the miracles that were performed in you had been performed in Tyre and Sidon, they would have repented long ago, sitting in sackcloth and ashes.[36]

Some see in these verses a philosophical concept known as 'middle knowledge'[37] – the idea that God doesn't just judge us on what we actually do, but on what we would have done under different circumstances. I am not convinced that this particular and individual passage can carry the weight of theological evidence necessary to support such a view. It seems to be more a turn of phrase than a precise philosophical statement. Nevertheless, I am convinced that as a perfectly just judge, God is able to take every extenuating circumstance into consideration. We do not know his conclusions; what matters is our response, both personally and in sharing his message.

The Jonah Paradox teaches that God is both highly selective and simultaneously indiscriminate with his love. In his desire that everyone is given opportunity to come to him, to love him and to

---

36 Matthew 11:21.

37 William Lane Craig argues that since God 'knows what any free creature would do in any situation, he can, by creating the appropriate situations, bring it about that creatures will achieve his ends and purposes and that they will do so *freely* . . . In his infinite intelligence, God is able to plan a world in which his designs are achieved by creatures acting freely.' Craig, W. L. (1987), *The Only Wise God*, Baker, p. 135.

love his people, God set up a chain reaction – one that falters or stutters at times, but carries on regardless, all down the centuries. Starting with Israel, he sent his people into the world to be a blessing. God continues to send his people into the world to share in word and deed the good news of his grace and forgiveness, the gift of his Holy Spirit and the challenge of his coming kingdom. Sadly, time and again the chain is broken because of our indifference, hoarding of grace, fear or laziness. When we hold back we betray our God-given identity as ambassadors, prophets, light, salt, stewards, trustees, and co-workers with Christ. But as we have seen from Jonah, God is not held captive by our unwillingness to join in his mission. We are to have confidence in a God who will not be ultimately frustrated from offering his grace to a dying world by the inactivity of us, his church. But we will have lost the opportunity to join God's family business of bringing reconciliation.

As the book of Jonah comes to a close Jonah is left outside of the city of Nineveh in the heat of the day, sulking, angry that God was compassionate and gracious, patient and loving towards everyone when, in Jonah's view, he should have smitten them with his judgement. I am reminded of the older brother in the prodigal son parable, who also ends the story skulking outside the place where the action is – the place where God is having a party – precisely because of the extravagance of God's grace. Jonah is an easy target of ridicule, because the flaws in his character, his foolish actions, are so obvious.

But what about our own shortcomings? When it comes to our worship of an all-compassionate, gracious, patient and loving God, how often do we know what he wants and choose to do the opposite? How often do we express keenness to have a relationship with God, but remain unconcerned about offering the same privilege to others?

How often do we express a passion for God but show very little concern for the people who God loves? How often do we try to hoard, rather than share, God's blessings? The Jonah Paradox requires us to wrestle with God's purposes for the nations, to work out before him our responsibility to share his good news, wherever that takes us – over the road or halfway round the world – and on the one hand to be sure we are not keeping our light under a bushel, and on the other to trust God to know what he's doing when the time does finally come for the judgement.

Chapter: 8

The Esther Paradox
The God who speaks silently

One of my earliest memories is of holding my mother's hand on my first day of school. I was so nervous I wouldn't let go as I entered the classroom. I can still remember the smoothness of her palms and the warmth of her fingers reassuring me, my fast-beating heart pounding away in my chest. Her hand was my lifeline and my security when I was scared and alone.

I was reminded of that day a few years ago as I sat again, holding my mother's hand in a darkened room. The silence was deafening as I strained to hear the muted words coming out of the mouth of a woman whose body had been ravaged by cancer. This time my mother held on to my hand, seeking reassurance from its warmth in her time of distress. The comforter had become the comforted.

Those were heart-breaking days. One moment I was praying for a miraculous recovery, and the next for the end to come quickly. Sometimes I gave in to uncontrollable tears and sometimes I was just weighed down by a cold numbness. But I was also haunted by another paradox – the deafening silence was exacerbated by God's conspicuous absence. What I would have given during those long, languishing hours for that still, small voice of calm!

I know I am not alone in that experience of the silence of God. I have spoken to so many people – to a girl devastated at the breakdown of a relationship, a parent trying to come to terms with her child's disability, a couple desperate to conceive, a wife distraught at her husband's infidelity, a woman whose son was still imprisoned despite evidence that pointed to his innocence. All of these people, confident in their faith as mature Christians, spoke of the doubts that crowded in on top of the struggles they were facing. Why is it that just at the times when we need God by us the most, he is often the most silent?

When we read the Old Testament, time and time again what we see is a God who speaks to his people. The God the Israelites worship stands in stark contrast to the gods of other nations. The prophet Habakkuk taunts those who practise idolatry, asking:

> Of what value is an idol carved by a craftsman?
> Or an image that teaches lies?
> For the one who makes it trusts in his own creation;
> he makes idols that cannot speak.
> Woe to him who says to wood, 'Come to life!'
> Or to lifeless stone, 'Wake up!'
> Can it give guidance?
> It is covered with gold and silver;
> there is no breath in it.
>
> The LORD is in his holy temple;
> let all the earth be silent before him.[1]

---

1 Habakkuk 2:18–20.

Our God is not like idols made of wood and stone, who are mute and silent. Habakkuk declares that all the earth must be silent and listen to the true God. These idols are dead – but even if they were alive, they would have to be silent before the Lord. However, his taunt to the idol-worshippers also picks at the defences of those of us who have experienced the silence of God when we have been straining to hear just a word of comfort or challenge when we need it most. We are tempted to wonder whether our God, too, is just a man-made invention. This is the paradox of the God who is silent yet still speaks. Many people speak about God drawing closer to them in times of distress, as he certainly often does, but there are also times when the opposite is true. Where do we go when we seem to need God's comfort most desperately, but he withholds his voice from us?

C. S. Lewis put it like this in his powerful memoir, *A Grief Observed*:

Meanwhile, where is God? This is one of the most disquieting symptoms. When you are happy, so happy that you have no sense of needing Him, so happy that you are tempted to feel His claims upon you as an interruption, if you remember yourself and turn to Him with gratitude and praise, you will be – or so it feels – welcomed with open arms. But go to Him when your need is desperate, when all other help is vain, and what do you find? A door slammed in your face, and sound of bolting and double-bolting on the inside. After that, silence . . . Why is He so present a commander in our time of prosperity and so very absent a help in time of trouble?[2]

---

2 Lewis, C. S. (1961), *A Grief Observed*, HarperCollins, pp. 4–5.

Knowing that the experience of God's silence is common may be reassuring. It may even be somewhat inspirational. In the middle of the horrific genocide of World War II, apparently a Jew in hiding scrawled on his cellar wall the following words: 'I believe in the sun, even when it isn't shining. I believe in love, even when I do not feel it. I believe in God, even when he is silent.'[3] This is a great sound-bite. It has inspired many people down the years. But in truth, how can faith survive, starved of the oxygen of God's voice? The story of another Jew, facing a similar threat of genocide, but thousands of years previously, may prove a helpful starting point.

Esther is one of two women in the Bible to have their own book named after them. Her story is strange. The book is full of sexual exploitation, personal vendettas and the threat of anti-Semitic ethnic cleansing. But as I was reading it during the last few weeks of my mother's life, I noticed then that nowhere in the story does anyone mention God.[4] Not once. No one refers to the Scriptures and no one explicitly prays. God is on mute while murder is plotted, mass rape is legislated for and lives are ruined. Yet this book made it into the canon of Scripture and, despite his silence, God's sovereignty rings out loud and clear.

Let us join the action mere days away from the planned genocide. One of the king's henchmen, Haman, had taken a personal dislike to Mordecai, a Jewish man who was living in exile in Susa, the

---

3 Apparently these words were scratched on the walls of a cellar in Cologne, Germany, by a Jew hiding from Nazi persecution.

4 Fuerst suggests that this may have contributed to why there were no Christian commentaries on the book for 700 years. Fuerst, W. J. (1971), *The Books of Ruth, Esther, Ecclesiastes, The Song of Songs and Lamentations*, The Cambridge Bible Commentary, CUP, p. 41.

capital of the mighty Persian Empire. Haman's hatred was so strong that rather than looking for a way to kill just Mordecai, he decided to try and wipe out his entire race.[5] Haman erected an oversized gallows over seventy-five feet tall on which to execute Mordecai, and had the king pass a law for the extermination of all the Jews in the kingdom. But a young Jewish girl was working undercover to frustrate Haman's plans.

Orphaned and then brought up by her uncle, Esther did not have the easiest of childhoods. Because of her great beauty, she was forced to become another member of King Xerxes' harem. Xerxes had been upstaged by his wife Vashti at a banquet he threw for his citizens, as recorded in the first chapter of the book. He was humiliated by his wife's refusal to be gawped at by a drunken crowd. As a result, Xerxes banished Vashti and replaced her with Esther, the winner of his beauty contest. But Esther was Mordecai's natural niece and adopted daughter, and for her safety in the palace, her Jewish ancestry had been kept secret. On discovering the plot against her people, Queen Esther had to come front of stage, and risk being discovered as a Jew, in order to make an eleventh-hour attempt to save her people. She assembled all the key players in this ethnic-cleansing crisis for a series of banquets. The king, perhaps typically for the time, was a fickle husband and had since turned his affections away from Esther. Simply going to see him uninvited could have resulted in a death sentence; inviting him to a banquet at which she intended to challenge him was an incredibly dangerous manoeuvre.

---

5 We are specifically told that Haman was an Agagite. His people were longstanding enemies of Israel. 'Haman's reaction is unmistakably motivated by racial hatred so callous and senseless . . .' Bush, F. W. (1998), *Ruth, Esther*, Word Biblical Commentary, Word, p. 385.

We will see shortly that the Esther Paradox revolves around a God who speaks even in silence, but it is interesting to consider here that Esther herself knows the pain of this dilemma – to speak or not to speak? She is placed in an impossible position – should she remain silent while her people are condemned to the gallows, or should she speak out for them, knowing that her words will more than likely get her killed? It was the words of her foster father Mordecai[6] that helped her make her mind up – perhaps the reason that she was made queen was 'for such a time as this'.[7] Perhaps this dilemma was exactly what she was born to deal with.

By the end of the first banquet, the king was once more charmed by Esther's beauty and agreed to attend a second banquet. But the night before, he was unable to get to sleep and he ordered someone to read him a bedtime story – and, given the strange self-absorbed quality of an ancient king, what reading material could be better than the archives of his reign? There the king discovered that a few years before, one of his loyal subjects had uncovered an assassination plot against him, but had received no reward or honour. The king eventually did drop off, but he awoke the next morning wondering just what he should do to reward such a loyal subject. In a plotline worthy of a Shakespearean comedy, Haman just happened to turn up wanting to chat to the king about executing Mordecai on the 75-foot gallows. Before Haman had a chance to make his request, the king engaged him in a hypothetical conversation, asking his advice on how to honour a loyal subject. Haman, assuming that the king had him in mind for this accolade, dreamed

---

6 See Kandiah, K. (2013), *Home for Good: Making a Difference for Vulnerable Children*, Hodder & Stoughton.

7 Esther 4:14.

up the most lavish reward he could think of. We can only imagine the horror on Haman's face when Xerxes revealed that it was Mordecai, not him, who deserved this special treatment – and Haman who was to execute it.

When the king turned up to dinner he was on tenterhooks, intrigued to discover his queen's intentions. Haman was there too, having had a very bad afternoon parading his mortal enemy around the city, not knowing just how much worse it was about to get for him.

Esther's petition was simple. At the end of the banquet she asked the king to

> grant me my life . . . and spare my people – this is my request. For I and my people have been sold for destruction and slaughter and annihilation. If we had merely been sold as male and female slaves, I would have kept quiet, because no such distress would justify disturbing the king.[8]

This beautiful Jewish girl, with great tact, made the request for a cancellation of the genocide seem so straightforward. There is a pantomime humour in her words – almost as if she might be saying, 'If we had merely been sold into slavery I wouldn't have bothered you, but for genocide I thought it was OK to disturb the king.' By the time the outraged king had demanded that Esther reveal the villain behind the plot, we can just imagine an animated audience at the pantomime shouting at King Xerxes, 'He's behind you!' – while Haman tried to hide. Queen Esther calmly identified Haman as the war criminal intending to wipe out her people.

---

8 Esther 7:3–4.

The king flew out of the room in a rage to get some air in the garden, only to return at the very moment when Haman had thrown himself on Esther to beg for mercy. That wasn't how it looked to the king, who couldn't believe that his own right-hand man was not only using his high position to plan genocide, but molesting his queen right under his very nose. By now everybody has guessed the ending – the oversized gallows would not be used on Mordecai but instead, with poetic justice and appropriate symmetry, it was Haman himself who was hanged, on the very day that he had ordered the Jewish execution.

We have come to the end of the story, but there is something missing. Where was God?[9] He utters not a single word. There is no prophecy. No reading of the Scriptures. There is no visible intervention. No class-A miracles like a flood, lightning strike, plague of frogs or earthquake, none of the good stuff that could have stopped the genocide attempt earlier. God is silent and unseen throughout this relatively short book. Yet, paradoxically, God does speak, even through the silence.

Reading Esther is like watching a film at the cinema. There are plot twists, suspense, setups and setbacks, crises, dilemmas and a perfect grand finale. There are heroes and villains, supporting actors, bit parts and extras. But every good film needs a good director, the person who shapes every scene and controls every character. The placing of each prop, the lining up of each camera angle and the positioning of all the incidental characters is deliberately and strategically worked out from start to finish by the

---

9 'Instead of giving up on a theological quest, we find ourselves searching more earnestly for a God whose non-appearance seems to enhance his presence.' Reid, D. (2008), *Esther: An Introduction and Commentary*, Tyndale Old Testament Commentaries, IVP, p. 20.

director. It is the most important role, yet in (virtually) every film I have seen the director remains silent and invisible throughout. For most of Esther's story it is hard to see how the threads are going to weave their way towards a happy ending, but in the final scene we can discern God's direction loud and clear as he brings things to a satisfying resolution. In the end we see how God weaves the plot elements together: a sleepless king, a huge gallows, a beauty pageant and several banquets come together into a storyline that not only sees God's people rescued, but brings him glory.

The film director illustration helps us, to some degree, to understand God's absence and God's role as our lives play out. Another way that Esther's story will help us is to indicate the timescales involved. It is only with the benefit of historical hindsight that we can understand that the years of exile, Esther's loss of her parents as a young child, her forced marriage and confined life eventually culminated much later with the rescue of God's people. Perhaps Esther felt God was silent during these traumatic years of her life. But somehow even in these dire circumstances, God was there, providing for her and protecting her, and building in her a trust that was deep enough to enable her to risk her life for the sake of her people.

Just as plants deprived of water put down deeper roots, so the struggle to keep trusting God during his silence and our tragedy proves not necessarily the vulnerability of our faith, but the vitality of our faith. It is the same in our experience of human relationships. It is when things are falling apart that the struggle – to hold them together, to rebuild trust, respect and routes of communication – proves the commitment and acknowledges the intrinsic value of those relationships. Perhaps if God's silence bothers us, it is an indicator of our love and need for him.

Maybe, for some of us, the silence we experience in our relationship with God during times of crisis provokes us to the realization that we actually stopped listening for God a long time ago. Maybe the silence is in fact a mercy from God – to help us realize where we are in relation to him before it is too late. Paradoxically, the silence of the God who speaks offers us a chance to resolve anew that we will deliberately make time and space in our lives to listen to him. C. S. Lewis famously explained, 'God whispers to us in our pleasures but shouts to us in our suffering. Suffering is God's megaphone to rouse a deaf world.'[10] Could it be that God's silence is a way of breaking through our deafness to his voice?

I once spoke to veteran evangelist and activist Tony Campolo about the struggle to hear God's voice. Raised a Pentecostal, Campolo explained to me how extrovert his praying had been in the past, and how prone he was to telling God things he (God) already knew. And so he had to work hard to incorporate listening into his daily disciplines:

I pray several different ways in the course of the day. In the morning I do what St Ignatius or Thomas Keating would call 'centring prayer'. I get up before I have to and I centre on Jesus. I drive everything else out of my mind and focus on Jesus alone. In the quiet and stillness of the morning I don't ask God for anything, I simply surrender to an infilling of the Spirit. I just yield. The greatest comment on prayer comes from the Bible when Jesus said, 'If you want to pray publicly, that has its own rewards. But if you really want to pray, go into the closet and close the door.' Sometimes I spend time

---

10 Lewis, C. S. (1962), *The Problem of Pain*, Macmillan, p. 93.

doing this and nothing happens. But about one out of every five times there is a sense of the filling of the Spirit.[11]

There is a school of thought that says that when we experience the silence of the speaking God, it is due to a lack of faith, or some unconfessed sin in our lives. Consequently we do not hear from God or get what we pray for. But Joseph, Job and Paul are just three examples from the Bible that break the rule. It was not Joseph's lack of faith that led to his imprisonment, nor was it Job's sin that led him to lose everything and almost everyone that was precious to him. Paul was inspired by God to retell his story of unanswered prayer when he explained, 'Three times I pleaded with the Lord to take [the "thorn"] away from me. But he said to me, "My grace is sufficient for you, for my power is made perfect in weakness."'[12] We must confront with Scripture the kind of teaching that heaps guilt on top of our suffering – that says it is because of our lack of faith that our prayers haven't been answered.

Ziya Meral, a Turkish friend working in the Middle East, wrote these powerful words:

Where is God when millions of his children are being persecuted in the most brutal ways? Why does he keep silent in the middle of persecution but speak loudly in the middle of conferences with famous speakers and worship bands? I have prayed many times like Luther: 'Bless us, Lord, even curse us! But don't remain silent!'[13]

---

11 From an interview in *Christianity* magazine, November 2010.

12 2 Corinthians 12:8–9.

13 Meral, Z. (2008), 'Bearing the Silence of God', in *Christianity Today* magazine, March 2008, Vol. 52, No.3, p. 41.

Meral's struggle with this question brought him ultimately to Jesus' own experience of the silence of God:

> The greatest glory Jesus brought to God was not when he walked on the water or prayed for long hours, but when he cried in agony in the garden of Gethsemane and still continued to follow God's will, even though it meant isolation, darkness, and the silence of God. Thus, we know that when everything around us fails, when we are destroyed and abandoned, our tears, blood, and dead corpses are the greatest worship songs we have ever sung.[14]

Similarly, Pete Greig in his book *God on Mute* focuses in on Holy Week as the place where we can find solace and make some sense out of the misery and mystery of suffering and silence: 'Even Jesus experienced the silence of God and unanswered prayers, but these became the occasion for the greatest miracles of all time.'[15]

Greig identifies three separate prayers, all apparently unanswered:

> On Maundy Thursday, Jesus prayed for the unity of the Church. But that week saw his friends and disciples scattering and hiding, whilst his enemies Herod and Pontius Pilate were united; sadly this pattern of the wicked being unified and the faithful suffering continues to happen far too often to this day. The promise remains, however, that God will return for his bride, the one worldwide Church.
>
> Later on Maundy Thursday, Christ prayed for the 'cup of

14 Ibid.

15 Greig, P. (2007), *God on Mute: Engaging the Silence of Unanswered Prayer*, Kingsway Books, p. 239.

suffering' of the cross to be taken away from him. It wasn't, but through his death the miracle of eternal life is offered to us all.

Finally, on Good Friday Jesus prayed to God, quoting Psalm 22: 'My God, my God, why have you forsaken me?' but there was no answer from heaven. Through Jesus' rejection on the cross, we have been accepted as sons and daughters into God's family.[16]

It is fascinating that the Bible, God's word written down for us, contains this incredible mixture of poured-out suffering: Jesus' anguished prayers in Gethsemane, the Psalmists' expressions of doubt, despair and depression, books such as Job, Ecclesiastes and Lamentations, Habakkuk's complaints and John the Baptist's questions from prison.[17] The Bible doesn't hide the difficulties of reconciling the three realities of the experience of suffering, belief in the goodness of God and the silence of heaven. Even biblical authors did not find resolution to their struggles but lived in the tension point, hanging on to their faith in the face of famine, destruction and bereavement. These dark passages don't get much attention in our pulpits, although it may be that these less confident passages of Scripture can offer us a refuge during times of suffering.

Some people I have met have found solace in the liturgical churches, where the richness and depth of ancient creeds and a strong tradition of the public reading of Scripture offer an antidote to the shallowness of some forms of contemporary worship. Pete Greig speaks about the importance of reading Scripture when God

---

16 Ibid.
17 Luke 7:19.

seems silent. His advice stems from his own agonizing experience of watching his wife suffer from a brain tumour:

> One of the things I had to learn was that silence and absence are different. There are definitely times when God chooses to become silent and it's tempting to assume he's absent. But St John of the Cross taught us that seasons of silence can actually be times of spiritual growth. When God's word gets muted, a living faith can be reduced to a sort of bloody-minded resignation to things we once knew for sure. But although Bible verses may seem dry, it doesn't make them less true. They still convey Christ, the word of God, to us. If sailors can still navigate by the light of stars that no longer exist, we too can stay true to the things we once knew to be true. My advice is this: believe your beliefs, doubt your doubts and don't get isolated by disappointment and pain. My heart was breaking and my ears were ringing in the silence, but the love of friends still remained 'the hope of glory' (Colossians 1:27).[18]

The Esther paradox shows us that God speaks through the silence; he speaks through his sovereignty as the unseen director; he speaks over our selfishness, sometimes shouting, sometimes whispering; he speaks through his own suffering, ultimately shown during Jesus' passion week; and finally he speaks through Scripture.

When I was a young boy, I didn't know how to pray. It was my mother who gave me words, kneeling by my bedside with her arm around me. She taught me that our recitation of a simple prayer together before I went to sleep helped me to connect each day with

---

18 Personal interview.

Almighty God. In the agonizing days before she died, when we were both lost for words, we turned together to the Psalms. It was in reading God's word together that we found God's voice in the silence. He is there, even when words have lost their meaning.

Interlude at the Border

Well done. You have made it through some of the big paradoxes spread across the Old Testament. For many of us the true meat of the Old Testament is undiscovered country, a closed book, and so my hope is that by tackling head on some of the paradoxes that may have kept you from reading it, you may perhaps be inspired to go on and discover it further.[19] Mind you, it would not be surprising if, as some questions are answered, others have flooded in to take their place. The old saying attributed to Aristotle goes, 'The more you know, the more you know you don't know.'

It is my hope that you may have acquired a thirst for discovery, and a little more insight into the way in which we can trust this God of ours – and are thus able to escape from our normal default of sweeping questions under the carpet.

As we cross the border into the New Testament, you may think you are on safer territory – what with all those great stories about Jesus. You may feel like you have the Home Team advantage. I feel I ought to give you a health warning: we are going to need to take

---

19 Some resources you may enjoy in rediscovering the Old Testament: Kandiah, K. (2011), *Route 66*, Monarch; Newbigin, L. (2001), *A Walk Through the Bible*, SPCK.

a good hard look at questions that you may have asked yourself many years ago and have allowed to fade from your attention. This may prove unsettling. You may find yourself thinking it is best, after all, to let sleeping dogs lie.

If that's the case, turn away now and let this book, like all those unanswered questions, gather dust on a shelf somewhere. Our quest has been to learn to follow and worship God better by trusting him enough to look at the hard parts of our understanding of him, so that our relationship with him grows deeper, richer and more authentic. We seek to face up to the difficult questions, so that our faith is resilient and able to cope with the things that life throws at us.

Perhaps a little reflection on a real-life story may help. This story even had the bereavement counsellor[20] in uncontrollable tears, as it was one of the saddest cases she had ever heard. It was an ordinary day, although Dad had left for a flight to America that morning, while Mum and the kids were safely at home getting ready for school, tidying up from breakfast, hanging up the utensils on the rack on the wall. A little while later a neighbour heard crying. She ignored it at first but when it persisted and she heard the four-year-old say to his five-year-old brother, 'Let's put a pillow under her head', she knew something must be wrong. Their mother, aged only thirty-four, had been electrocuted when a screw from the kitchen rack connected with a live wire laid too near the surface of the wall. The family had routinely been getting mild electric shocks but sorting the problem out had been on the list of things to do. No one had any idea how dangerous the situation was until it was too late.

---

20 As told to Emily Cunningham, *Guardian* newspaper, 26 October 2012: http://www.theguardian.com/lifeandstyle/2012/oct/26/experience-my-wife-was-electrocuted

If only those two young boys, found so carefully putting a pillow under their mother's head, had not had to watch her die on the kitchen floor. If only they could have gone to school as normal that day. If only somebody had fixed that dodgy wiring. I imagine the father, rushing back from the airport, trying to comfort his sons and replaying over and over those conversations that began by discussing who would call the electrician, but got overtaken by the doorbell, the washing up, the lost lunchbox, or any of the other million and one mundane jobs that needed doing. It was not a deliberate decision not to sort out the electrics, it just slipped off the to-do list.

All of us know how the important things get lost in the business of life. As I reflect on this family's tragedy I find myself carefully scanning through the list in my head to see if there is anything I have been putting off – that noise in the car, that rash that won't go away, the loose plank by the back gate.

This desperately sad story acts as a call for us to check our priorities. Not just with regard to the DIY jobs around the house, but also the everyday dangers to faith. There are nagging doubts that we put off investigating, or niggling questions that have been bugging us, but we have been trying to ignore. We know we need to get round to sorting them out, but life is busy. We know that without proper attention these questions will destabilize our faith, and gradually erode the foundations of our trust in God. Every now and again our faith may get a jolt: we hear of a good friend diagnosed with early-onset Parkinson's Disease, we catch a colleague at work cheating on her husband; or we stumble into a difficult part of the Bible that seems to make no sense, or get asked a difficult question by a neighbour. None of these are deal-breakers, faith-defeaters, paradigm-shifters in themselves. But the cumulative effect of them makes us more hesitant in trusting or worshipping God. These nagging doubts are warning shocks that, if left unattended, can become much worse. Will our faith hold strong when we need it most? When the tragedies and travesties of life hit us, will we know where to find God?

The tragic story we have looked at hints at another problem too. This woman was not a spectator at the IndyCar 500 with racing cars rushing past at 200 miles an hour. She wasn't shark diving off the coast of Cape Town or reporting for the BBC in a war zone. She was safe at home. But it was her home that was the death-trap. I don't know what your favourite bits of the Bible are – maybe it's the Old Testament stories, maybe it's the Psalms or, really pushing the boat out, perhaps Isaiah. But I'm pretty certain there are more no-go areas than safe ones as you read; Numbers and Deuteronomy and the minor prophets are all easier to skip than pay proper attention to. There are tough issues and challenging paradoxes there, to be sure.

It sometimes feels with the Bible that the New Testament is where we feel most 'at home'. In fact, it actually contains just as many dangers as the Old. Take the Christmas story, for example. Christmas is the time when most people feel safest being at church, as they celebrate a wonderful story of a baby born to save the world. But even in the Christmas story we can't escape the questions: systematic execution of babies; astrology experts worshipping God; most shocking of all, a baby who is supposed to be God. There are plenty of things here that can jolt us, and yet for many of us they have become a part of the furniture of our minds, unnoticed and ignored. The familiarity is dangerous, but of course there is a paradox! The dangerous questions of the New Testament can be the most helpful to our faith and our worship, as I hope we will see as we navigate the second half of this book.

The Bible scholar J. B. Phillips was a clergyman who ran youth clubs in the East End of London during World War II and wrote his own translation of the Bible so the boys he knew might actually be able to read and understand it. He described his job of crafting a modern translation of the Bible as being 'like an electrician wiring an ancient house without being able to turn the mains off'.[21] The awkward passages in the Bible are like exposed live wires. We ignore the risk they pose at our peril.

21 Philips, J. B. (1947), *Letters to Young Churches*, Macmillan, p. xii.

Chapter 9

The Jesus Paradox
The God who is divinely human

It is hard to escape Jesus, wherever you go in the world. I remember being with hundreds of others in a vibrant church service that took place in the Mausoleum of Enver Hoxha, the Albanian communist dictator who banned religion of any kind from his country. It seemed ironic that those gathered were praising a living Jesus in a pyramid built to commemorate a dead dictator. He would have turned in his grave had he known. I remember travelling to a remote village in the middle of Burkina Faso, one of Africa's poorest countries, where, apart from people's modest housing, the only building was a Pentecostal church. Under the simple cross on its roof a community gathered to worship Jesus with songs and preaching, as well as promoting the educational empowerment of young women with a school.

Around the world the person of Jesus is changing millions of lives every week.[1] He is the most famous person on the planet, despite having spent his whole life within a few days' walk of his birthplace. The only time we see Jesus writing is when he doodles in the dirt to

---

1 According to the International Bulletin of Missionary Research there are on average 80,000 new Christians per day. Cited in Wiegel, G. (2011), *Christian Number-Crunching*, http://www.firstthings.com/onthesquare/2011/02/christian-number-crunching

see how a bloodthirsty mob will respond to his call for mercy for a victimized woman; yet more books have been written about him than anyone else in history. He is almost universally admired, with Gandhi, the Hindu civil rights activist, commenting: 'To me, he was one of the greatest teachers humanity has ever had.'[2] Islam describes Jesus as the perfect prophet. Jesus carries the respect of people from almost every ideology. Yet at the same time, his name is one of the most common swearwords, and in that name some of the most terrible crimes against humanity have been committed. So when we begin to think about Jesus, we are faced with a whole barrage of paradoxes.

Napoleon Bonaparte famously commented about him:

I know men and I tell you that Jesus Christ is no mere man. Between him and every other person in the world there is no possible term of comparison. Alexander, Caesar, Charlemagne, and I founded empires. But on what did we rest the creations of our genius? Upon force. Jesus Christ founded His empire upon love; and at this hour millions of people would die for Him . . . Everything in Christ astonishes me. His spirit over-awes me, and His will confounds me . . . I search in vain in history to find the similar to Jesus Christ, or anything that can approach the gospel.[3]

Here is an empire-building general who plunged Europe into war for twenty years, yet he admires Jesus for his uniquely unworldly power.

2 *The Modern Review*, October 1941, republished on mahatma.org.in/

3 Napoleon Bonaparte, cited in Miller, D. (2004), *Searching for God Knows What*, Thomas Nelson, p. 138; also cited in Josh McDowell, *Evidence that Demands a Verdict*, Scripture Press, 1990, p. 106.

Yet this is also the problem – this iconic 'Jesus' is admired, but the impact of what he said and did is widely ignored. Napoleon did not stop his warmongering because of his declared respect for Jesus. In fact, far too often the name of Jesus seems to be easily co-opted into whatever system, campaign, cause or crisis that needs a mascot or a justification or a swearword. Just as the image of Father Christmas is used during December to sell everything from food to furniture, Coca Cola to consoles, so Jesus is co-opted by both Republicans and Democrats, capitalists and socialists. Ascetics and gluttons appeal to him as one of their own. Soldiers pray to him and pacifists appeal to his example. Jesus' radical commands about sharing possessions have been grist to the mill for communist revolutionaries; at the same time his birthday is used as the engine for consumer capitalism's biggest sales opportunity.

Everyone has taken a turn at adapting Jesus to their needs. Take for example the bloody and dismal history of the Crusaders who marched through Europe to the Holy Land, slaying all who came up against them there and fighting with the symbol of the cross on their shields. Chilean theologian Pablo Richard estimates that between 1492 and 1570 the indigenous population of South America plummeted from 100 million to around 12 million due to the Conquistadors invasion. These Spanish invaders who came from Spain to conquer the 90 million or so indigenous people of South America, brought missionaries with them on every boat.[4] And yet it was also in the name of Jesus that a Spanish missionary called Las Casas opposed the slaughter and fought against it.[5] Jesus has

---

4 Richard, P. (1990), '1492: The Violence of God and the Future of Christianity' in Bodd, L. & Elizondo, V. (eds.) (1990), *1492–1991 The Voice of the Victims*, SCM, cited in Smith, D. (2013), *The Kindness of God*, IVP, p. 99.
5 Ibid., p. 100.

been used across the centuries by many conflicting ideologies, denominations and creeds to justify their existence.

It is hard to resist recruiting someone as influential as Jesus to our team, or conscripting him to our cause. We love to think that Jesus takes care of us, watches our back, and wills us to succeed, and when we are wronged, we want him to vindicate us and sort out the culprits. But in our fragmented world Jesus can't really be on everybody's team. He is not in fact a benevolent mascot to be used and abused by all and sundry. Our appropriation of him to pet causes, while ostensibly showing a high regard for him and his powerful name, in fact too often disguises a cynical assumption that we can safely use his name for our own means without any negative consequences. Rather than rebrand him to suit ourselves, we should endeavour to find out more about who he really was, what he actually did and what, exactly, he claimed. Instead of signing him up to our personal projects, we should perhaps pay more attention to what we have signed up for as Jesus' followers.

After all, as Jesus said in the parable of the talents, when the time comes to assess people's success with what they've been given in life, those who have used their gifts well will be told: 'Well done, good and faithful servant';[6] equally, at another time he said that people who have seemed to do everything right will in the end be told: 'I never knew you. Away from me, you evildoer!'[7] Jesus does not slip easily into our existing lives; he is not an undiscerning supporter of personal causes. Nor is he a turbo-powered marketing tool. In these teachings Jesus warns that when he comes again, some of us will be in for a terrible surprise.

---

6 Matthew 25:21.

7 Matthew 7:23.

Everyone loves to think about Jesus as a good guy, a great role model and a wonderful example of selflessness in the face of adversity. We love to think that if he were physically present with us today, he would counsel us, encourage us, heal us and give us a boost to get through life. For Jesus the man there is widespread respect and admiration. But when we start talking about Jesus as God, the conversation changes. People are suddenly offended – they can't accept that Jesus would claim to be the one and only God, who has turned up on our little planet by becoming human to call us to repentance.

Jesus may be the most popular man in history, but claiming to be the God-Man is the most controversial claim in history. It is also one of the most difficult paradoxes to get our heads around. Is Jesus fully God or fully man? If he was 100 per cent man, then surely there's no room for him to be 100 per cent God too? Trying to reconcile the two natures of Jesus leads to paradox after paradox. If Jesus is God, does that mean God died on a cross? Wouldn't that make God mortal? If Jesus is God, then who was running the universe while he was on the earth? If God is omniscient and omnipresent – how come Jesus wasn't? If Jesus is God, could he have sinned? If Jesus could have sinned, then surely God's morally spotless character is called into question? If Jesus couldn't have sinned, then were the temptations real? Does he really understand what it is like to be human?[8]

The identity of Jesus is so central to the Christian faith, we cannot simply go through life avoiding these paradoxes. We need to find answers both to who Jesus was during his time on earth, and who Jesus is now. Otherwise, how can we know him, trust him, follow him and worship him today?

---

8 Hebrews 4:14–16.

As we explore some of these paradoxes, we will be guided by one of Jesus' closest friends. Someone who spent three years on the road travelling with Jesus, observing his life in all manner of situations. A friend who would stand by Jesus' family during his final hours, and take responsibility for caring for Jesus' mother as though she was his own. John was the disciple who was with Jesus when he turned the tables over in the temple, when he was being hounded by the religious elites, when he encountered God up the mountain, and when he was tired, thirsty, lonely and under such stress that he began sweating blood. When he'd observed all this – and more – and eventually came to write down all he'd seen, John began the introduction to his biography of Jesus with these words:

> In the beginning was the Word, and the Word was with God, and the Word was God. He was with God in the beginning. Through him all things were made; without him nothing was made that has been made. In him was life, and that life was the light of all mankind. The light shines in the darkness, and the darkness has not overcome it.[9]

John carefully and poetically[10] chooses each word and clause. In order to help puzzled people understand the identity of Jesus, he sets up a series of paradoxes for us to consider – Jesus *was* God, yet at the same time he was *with* God. He was with God in the beginning, yet he was born as a man on earth at one particular

---

9 John 1:1–3.

10 Some scholars are nervous of calling the prologue to the Gospel poetry, preferring the term 'rhythmical prose'. Carson, D. A. (1991), *The Gospel According to John*, The Pillar New Testament Commentary, IVP, p. 112.

moment. He was the life – or did he bring the life? Darkness usually banishes light, so how was Jesus a light that banished darkness? In these paradoxes John makes a number of allusions to ancient Jewish ideas, and drops in three big – but enigmatic – clues as to who Jesus is.

First, John uses words that would immediately remind Jewish readers of the first line of the Old Testament: 'In the beginning . . .' Now, a biographer might introduce their work with an account of the lives of a few generations of people before the birth of their central character. This helps their account to be framed within a historical context. But John takes biography writing to another level completely by starting his account of Jesus' life with the beginning of time itself. John is showing us that Jesus' life is not just of local significance; instead it is of universal import because history itself cannot be understood without Jesus. Of course, the phrase 'in the beginning' itself has a note of paradox to it. What exactly is 'the beginning'? The words used for 'beginning' both in Genesis and here in John's introduction carry the quality of an absolute *start* or 'origin'.[11] There was something before the beginning of the universe, and that something had no beginning. God has always existed. Jesus is eternal.

The concept that God is an eternal, uncreated Creator who has existed for an infinite amount of time is difficult to imagine. In fact, our human minds always struggle to cope when we think about infinite things. For example, try to imagine a hotel[12] with an infinite number of rooms. Imagine it is full. What will happen

---

11 Ibid., p. 114.

12 This illustration is adapted from that of the mathematician David Hilbert from the 1920s. See Crilly, T. (2011), *The Big Questions: Mathematics*, Quercus, pp. 58–9.

when there is a knock on the door and a passing traveller asks to have a room for the night? The accommodating hotel manager could ask each of the guests to move along a room, to give the tired guest Room Number 1. How many times could this scenario occur and the hotel still have space for more? The answer is, an infinite number of times. Imagine half the guests leave because they get upset at changing room every ten minutes – would there still be an infinite number of people in the hotel? Or whatever half of infinite works out to? The mathematical answer is that with an infinite number of guests, if half were to leave, there would still be an infinite number of guests in the hotel. This kind of puzzle is known as a 'veridical' paradox, where a valid argument leads to seemingly absurd conclusions.[13] Infinity always causes us mind-bending problems, so in the same way, when we think of a God who has existed in all eternity, our minds begin to crash – we just can't do it.

Just as schoolchildren are told very simply and matter-of-factly that a number line goes on to infinity, so too John states in his first sentence that before anything else was – God was. This concept of an eternal God is portrayed clearly throughout the whole of Scripture and is often used to encourage trust in God – he is faithful, and his love endures forever.[14] Just as he cannot lie, so he cannot die. He will not break down or fade away or cease to exist in any other way either. The claim that Jesus also pre-existed – before he was born in Bethlehem, and before even the universe was born – points to his identity as God himself. John the Baptist, who was

---

13 Sorenson, R. (2003), *A Brief History of the Paradox: Philosophy and the Labyrinths of the Mind*, OUP p. 351.
14 Deuteronomy 37:27; Psalm 90:1–4.

Jesus' older cousin, knew this. He declared, 'He who comes after me has surpassed me because he was before me.'[15] It is also expressed when Jesus poignantly states, 'Truly, truly, I say to you, before Abraham was, I am.'[16]

The second powerful way that John shows his readers that Jesus is the eternal God is by calling him the 'Word'. Jewish readers would have noticed immediately the deviation from the original script. The Old Testament starts with the words, 'In the beginning God . . .' With a flick of his pen, John rewrites this sentence to read, 'In the beginning was the Word', simultaneously introducing Jesus as divine, as eternal, as communicative and as authoritative.

Just as the words spoken in a church on my wedding day pronounced and introduced the creation of a new family unit, or the words spoken by a judge irrevocably declared the little girl in our arms to be forever our legal daughter, so God's words are authoritative – bringing the whole universe into being.[17] They communicate – the foundation for any relationship – and they are eternal. Isaiah the prophet put it this way: 'the grass withers and the flowers fall, but the word of the LORD endures forever'.[18] Equating Jesus with the God who spoke the planets, stars and galaxies into existence, and with the authoritative, eternal Word that will never pass away, clearly demonstrates John's insistence on the absolute divinity and power of Jesus.

---

15 John 1:15.

16 John 8:58.

17 Kevin Vanhoozer uses adoption as a case study of God creating a status through declaration; this is a fascinating way to resolve the debate about imputed righteousness. Vanhoozer, K. (2011), 'Wrighting the wrongs of the Reformation', in Perrin, N. & Hays, R. B. (eds.) (2011), *Jesus, Paul and the People of God: A Theological Dialogue with N. T. Wright*, SPCK p. 254.

18 Isaiah 40:8; 1 Peter 1:25; Matthew 5:18.

The poetry is not lost on his Greek readers either. By using the term *Logos*, John connects the ancient Jewish Scriptures with Greek philosophy.[19] Greek thinkers such as Heraclitus understood the *Logos* to be 'the omnipresent wisdom by which all things are steered'.[20] John draws on this line of thinking by introducing Jesus as the 'Word of God', as it is through his word that God rules, sustains and organizes his universe. Throughout John's Gospel the idea of the '*Logos* of God' is used to show that the Word is the means through which God gets things done, including – as D. G. Johnson outlines in his essay 'Logos' – 'creation, judgement, redemption and renewal'.[21]

John's message is unmissable for both his Jewish and his Greek readers, and yet the idea is so revolutionary, it can initially only be taken in as a mysterious paradox that awaits resolution. How will John, through the biography, show that Jesus was both God, and with God?

John also pays homage to the opening lines of the Bible by borrowing the images of light and darkness,[22] moving seamlessly on through his rebooted version of the creation account by talking about Jesus as the light of all mankind. But once again he reshapes the wording, taking the original phrase from Genesis 1 – 'God said, let there be light – and there was light' – and morphing it into 'In him

---

19 'Anaxagoras saw it as the principle of intelligence in the universe . . .' See Geisler, N. L. (1999), *Baker Encyclopedia of Christian Apologetics*, Baker, p. 430.

20 Beasley-Murray, G. R. (2002), *Vol. 36: John*, Word Biblical Commentary, Word, p. 6 (an idea not a million miles away from the Jewish idea of the wisdom of God being present at creation: see Proverbs 8).

21 Johnson, D. G. (1992), 'Logos', in Green, J. B., McKnight, S. & Marshall, I. H. (eds.) (1992), *Dictionary of Jesus and the Gospels*, IVP, p. 484.

22 Genesis 1:3.

was life, and that life was the light of all people.'[23] The Word of God is not only powerful on the scale of the creation of the universe, but also in its impact on people's lives. God's Word both switches the light on for people to understand who God is, and also brings life out of the darkness. God speaks, and his words both communicate and create life. But there is also something tragic afoot in this illuminating description. The light will shine but the darkness will continue. There will be conflict. This biography of Jesus is being framed as a tragedy, not a fairy story. How will it all play out?

For most of John's readers, the punch-line of the prologue comes in verse 14 when the divine Word is incontrovertibly identified as Jesus the man:

> The Word became flesh and made his dwelling among us. We have seen his glory, the glory of the one and only Son, who came from the Father, full of grace and truth.

John makes sure that in his biography about his human friend Jesus, there can be no missing the fact of his divinity. These themes of the introduction permeate the whole of John's Gospel, like melodies repeat and echo throughout a symphony.

John reiterates Jesus' claim to divinity by identifying Jesus as the one who existed before Abraham was born,[24] the one who is the true light of the world, the one who will bring about the resurrection at the end of time, the one who can forgive sins, the one who will judge the living and the dead, the one who is worthy of worship, and the one who is the way, the truth and the life.

---

23 John 1:4.
24 John 8:58–59.

And to top it off, seven times in his book John applies to Jesus the unique and special name of God that was revealed to Moses: Yahweh – that is, 'I AM'.[25]

In Jesus' day there was no doubt about the claim that he was making. In fact, even Jesus' enemies understood that he was 'making himself equal with God'[26] – it was this that got him crucified. From its earliest inception Christianity has been built on the fundamental claim that Jesus is God in flesh. C. S. Lewis famously put it this way:

> I am trying here to prevent anyone saying the really foolish thing that people often say about him: 'I'm ready to accept Jesus as a great moral teacher, but I don't accept his claim to be God.' That is the one thing we must not say. A man who said the sort of things Jesus said would not be a great moral teacher. He would either be a lunatic – on a level with the man who says he is a poached egg – or else he would be the Devil of Hell. You must make your choice. Either this man was, and is, the Son of God, or else a madman or something worse. You can shut him up for a fool, you can spit at him and kill him as a demon, or you can fall at his feet and call him Lord and God. But let us not come with any patronizing nonsense about his being a great human teacher. He has not left that open to us. He did not intend to.[27]

The popular, attractive Jesus who is a great moral teacher but, in the end, just a man, is the one option that, as Lewis makes clear,

---

25 Exodus 3:14–16.

26 John 5:18.

27 Lewis, C. S. (1952), *Mere Christianity*, Macmillan, p. 105.

the witness of the New Testament does not leave open to us. Jesus ticks every box that Jewish people would have attributed solely to God. He claims to be the eternal creator,[28] the revealer, the judge,[29] the resurrection[30] – even to be worthy of being worshipped.[31]

Centuries of theological debate have raged over the seemingly insignificant detail of whether Jesus had one nature or two. Whether he was really divine, and pretending to be human, or human, appearing to be divine. All of the battles were fought to defend the idea that Jesus was both fully divine and fully human – because this is the duality that the Scriptures affirm. The battles are not insignificant, because what is at stake is Jesus' ability to represent both God and humanity when dealing with our sins on the cross.[32] We will come to this aspect of Jesus' mission in the chapter on the Cross Paradox.

Unsurprisingly, people who do not claim to be Christian have a problem recognizing that Jesus is God. The fuse that connected the explosive description of the 'Word' of God to Jesus the man is the statement, 'the Word became flesh'. This is John's shorthand way of claiming that God in Jesus became authentically one of us; fully human. It is not just that Jesus looked human,[33] or limited himself

---

28 John 1:1–3.

29 John 5:22.

30 John 11:23–25.

31 John 5:23.

32 Athanasius, the third-century Egyptian bishop, famously argued that salvation was at stake, as he believed that only if Jesus was fully human could he atone for human sin, and only if he was fully divine could he have the power to save us. See Athanasius, *On the Incarnation*.

33 Ebonitism is the heresy taught by an early Jewish sect that purported that Jesus was exclusively human.

to humanness.[34] It is not that Jesus had a human body and a divine soul,[35] or that God morphed into a human being. God remained truly God, and yet he added humanity to himself.

On the other hand, many Christians struggle with the concept of Jesus being truly human.[36] We reason like this: Jesus was not able to sin, and he had God with him all the time, so when he was tempted, it was much easier for him to resist than it is for us. We rob ourselves of the challenge of Jesus by denying or ignoring his humanity. We somehow convince ourselves that Jesus isn't a realistic model for a life without sin that we could actually follow; instead, perhaps he just inspires us that we could maybe do a little better than we are currently doing. Or alternatively, we find no comfort in the fact that Jesus was, say, single. If he knew he was only going to be physically present on earth for a short time and had God the Father for company, then maybe it was easier for him than for those of us who plan to live until our teeth fall out and maybe even longer. Or again we think: it was easier for Jesus to live without possessions, partly because he lived in the first century, when nobody had much anyway, and also because he knew he had a backup mansion in heaven. We find ways to excuse ourselves from the challenge that Jesus' perfect humanity sets for us.

There have arisen two camps as to whether Jesus was able to sin or not. Some argue that Christ was 'able not to sin' (*potuit non*

---

34 Monophysitism is the heresy that asserts that Jesus only had one nature – the divine – and he just took on human form.

35 Appollinarianism is the heresy that asserts that Christ had a human body and a divine soul.

36 Wright, N. T. (2012), *How God Became King: The Forgotten Story of the Gospels*, SPCK, p. 12: 'the one thing that the creeds do not do . . . is to mention anything that Jesus did or said between his birth and his death'.

peccare, otherwise known as 'peccability'), while others argue that Christ was 'not able to sin' (*non potuit peccare*, or 'impeccability'). Some of the debates that surround whether Jesus could or could not have sinned appear to be an attempt to impose systematic and philosophical categories on what Scripture holds in paradox. We have to let Scripture guide us, and in this case it teaches both that God cannot sin (James 1:13) *and* that Christ suffered when he was tempted (Hebrews 2:18). The tension between these two truths is what makes faith live: it is in the wrestling, not the easy answers, that we will find God. The Bible does affirm the full divinity of Jesus, but it also affirms his humanity and it does not attribute his ability to fight sin to his divinity. Rather, as D. G. Bloesch argues, 'the sinlessness of Jesus is pictured as a result of conscious decision and intense struggle rather than being a formal consequence of his divine nature'.[37]

This brings us back to our original paradox. Jesus is presented both as fully human and fully divine. Therefore Jesus is both unable to sin, and at the same time capable of sin. This is not a paradox that can be resolved. Rather it is a tension that we have to learn to accept. This may seem like a cop-out but there are parallels in the world of science, where seemingly contradictory pieces of empirical evidence force scientists to create new conceptual frameworks to understand them. Strangely enough, the best example of this is the exact image John chose to introduce the paradox in the first place – that of light.

When I was studying A Level physics, I was pretty sure I knew what light was and what it looked like. But that was before I was

---

37 Hebrews 4:15; 5:7–9; 12:2–4. See Bloesch, D. G. (1997), *Jesus Christ: Saviour and Lord*, IVP, p. 55.

exposed to the paradox of wave particle duality. During our very first lecture at university, seventy students, newly kitted out with lab coats, goggles and glassware, waited expectantly to be inspired for our initiation into the exciting world of chemistry. We had had our tour of the laboratories. We had all oohed and aahed when we were shown the analytical machines – the mass spectrometer with the magnet so strong it would stop the pacemaker in your chest at ten metres. We were ready to mix potions, create pyrotechnics and discover the cure for cancer. Then Professor Kemp, with his mad-scientist haircut and beer-bottle-bottom glasses, walked into the room and, to the palpable disappointment of everyone present, wrote this equation on the board:

Schrödinger's Equation

$$i\hbar \frac{\partial}{\partial t} \psi (r,t) = - \frac{\hbar^2}{2m} \nabla^2 \psi (r,t) + V (r,t) \psi (r,t)$$

i is the imaginary number, $\sqrt{-1}$.

$\hbar$ is Plank's constant divided by 2π: 1.05459×10^{-34} joule-second.

$\psi (r,t)$ is the wave function, defined over space and time.

m is the mass of the particle

∇^2 is the Laplacian operator, $\frac{\partial^2}{\partial x^2} + \frac{\partial^2}{\partial y^2} + \frac{\partial^2}{\partial z^2}$.

$V (r,t)$ is the potential energy influencing the particle.

It scared the living daylights out of us.

Professor Kemp then tried to explain how this equation, coupled with something called Heisenberg's uncertainty principle, meant that you couldn't know the position and speed of an electron at the same time; that observing an electron would change its position and measuring its speed would also change its speed. Are you lost yet? We were. In short, science suddenly became speculation – certainty became uncertainty – and we had to learn to live within a paradigm of paradox.[38] Basically we were told to mentally throw away everything we had been taught about how light worked, and adopt a new model. We were shown two different sets of experiments: one set showed conclusively that light is particular, solid and can hit things. The other set of experiments showed conclusively that light is a wave: it can be in two places at the same time. Human beings have no mental categories within which to explain this paradox. Rather than take the easy route and ignore or discount one or the other set of data, scientists decided to take the humble route and acknowledge that their brains were not wired up to be able to picture what this looked like. As there were no analogies, they just called it 'wave particle duality'.

Some argue that this is just nonsense, not too dissimilar from the old joke: 'When is a door not a door? When it is a jar.' But this is just a play on words; it only works if you know that a door, while still being a door, can also be left slightly open or 'ajar'. The theory of wave particle duality is not nonsensical technospeak; the light actually does act simultaneously as waves and particles. Similarly,

---

38 Later my philosophy lecturer explained it in terms of an animal cruelty experiment involving Schrödinger's infamous cat. For a discussion between Stephen Hawking and Roger Penrose on this subject, see Penrose, R. & Hawking, S. (2010), *The Nature of Space and Time*, Princeton University Press, p. 121.

when we say that Jesus is both fully human and fully God, it is not just nonsense, or a puzzle to be worked out, or a play on words – Jesus is actually and simultaneously both God and man, and neither his divinity nor his humanity are compromised. Early church leaders came up with a way of expressing this in the Chalcedonian Creed – 'the two natures of Christ'.[39]

The Bible teaches quite a number of things that our brains struggle to comprehend. For example: Jesus is both God and with God; the Holy Spirit is also God; so God is three persons in community and yet there is only one God, not three. The simple route would be to ignore one or more of these direct teachings of Scripture because they are too hard for us to integrate. Instead theologians, like the scientists in describing the behaviour of light, have taken the humbler and more honest route. They created a new concept and gave it a name that doesn't occur in the Bible – the Trinity. It is a neologism – a new word (at least, it was new when Theophilus of Antioch first used its Greek equivalent in the second century).[40] It was not, however, a new idea – it is simply trying to accurately describe the paradoxical tensions of what the Bible teaches. Because Jesus is fully human he can fully sympathize with us in our temptations and struggles; he knows what it is like to be

---

39 See the Chalcedonian Creed from AD 451 which states, 'one and the same Christ, Son, Lord, only begotten, to be acknowledged in two natures, inconfusedly, unchangeably, indivisibly, inseparably; the distinction of natures being by no means taken away by the union, but rather the property of each nature being preserved, and concurring in one Person and one Subsistence, not parted or divided into two persons, but one and the same Son, and only begotten God, the Word, the Lord Jesus Christ; as the prophets from the beginning concerning Him, and the Lord Jesus Christ Himself has taught us, and the Creed of the holy Fathers has handed down to us.'

40 Cross, F. L. & Livingstone, E. A. (2005), *The Oxford Dictionary of the Christian Church*, Oxford University Press, p. 1652.

single and childless and poverty-stricken and hurt and hungry. He made sacrifices in order to fulfil his mission. We should treasure Jesus' humanity, because it means we have someone who pleads for us in God the Father's presence, someone who can empathize with our weaknesses: 'one who has been tempted in every way, just as we are – yet did not sin'.[41] We should treasure Jesus' divinity because it is only through his divinity that Christ is able to live for us and die on behalf of all of us.

Jesus himself, therefore, is a paradox – he cannot be reduced to fit our thinking. Knowing him means having our assumptions and misconceptions reinstalled, revised and redeemed. Christ the God-Man is simultaneously the most attractive and most repugnant person in history. The split reaction to him explains why the crowds either flocked to him or rallied against him, why some disciples abandoned or betrayed him and others were willing to leave everything to follow him, and face death because of their allegiance to him. He is repugnant to many people because his divinity makes an absolute claim on us – that is why his enemies, such as the Jewish religious elite and the Roman imperial powers, joined forces to crucify him. For the humble his attraction was overwhelming, but for the powerful his claims were too demanding.

Worshipping God in Hoxha's modern-day pyramid in downtown Tirana, Albania with a host of brand-new believers helped me grasp a little more of the strength and depth of who Jesus is and what he's come to do. Converted from nominal Islamic backgrounds, these new followers illustrated the challenge and the value of living like him, and commending him to others. Similarly, I remember sheltering from the scorching sun in the porch of the village church

---

41 Hebrews 4:18.

in Burkina Faso, and feeling the challenge of watching local Christians serving the poor of their community day in, day out in 50°C heat. They did it because of Jesus – the one who was Lord of heaven and earth and yet chose to become human and live on our dusty, dysfunctional planet. For them, working off the beaten track in a small West African country, Christ's two natures as fully God and fully human were not just a theological paradox. They gave a pattern for a life calling, the spiritual and the earthbound intertwined to show and share God's love. It taught me a great deal about worship. As one East African creed eloquently puts it:

We believe that God made good His promise by sending His Son, Jesus Christ, a man in the flesh, a Jew by tribe, born poor in a little village, who left His home and was always on safari doing good, curing people by the power of God, teaching about God and man, showing the meaning of religion is love. He was rejected by his people, tortured and nailed, hands and feet, to a cross, and died. He lay buried in the grave, but the hyenas did not touch him, and on the third day he rose from the grave. He ascended to the skies. He is the Lord . . . This we believe.[42]

---

42 Cited in Sanneh, L. (2003), *Whose Religion is Christianity? The Gospel Beyond the West*, Eerdmans, pp. 59ff. See also Jacobsen, D. (2011) *The world's Christians and how they got there*, Wiley & Sons pp.168–9.

Chapter 10

The Judas Paradox
The God who determines our free will

There are days when I wake up and I am halfway to work already. How did that happen? The alarm must have gone off, presumably. I obviously woke up and jumped out of bed. I must have stared at my face in the mirror when I brushed my teeth. I must have been alert enough when I cycled to the station, navigating that tricky roundabout and bustling A-road. I must have been conscious when I bought my ticket, too. By the time I wake up I am just sitting down on the 7.32 a.m. train to Marylebone, and realize I have been on autopilot for the last forty minutes. When I get off the train I quickly find myself falling into step with those around me and as I join the queue to stick the ticket into the exit barrier, I watch as we all plug our headphones into our smart phones. We all have the same expression. We all wear the same clothes. As I join the ranks of commuters I feel like a tiny little cog in the big machine of money-making and production that takes place in London. Life around me is not that dissimilar from the quasi-robotic life lived by the people of the future world Fritz Lang predicted in his classic 1927 silent movie *Metropolis*. Am I really making my own decisions or making them through habit and a constant barrage of media input? Am I being programmed on a daily basis by my family history, my genetics, my media diet or my peers to conform to a set of standard goals, hopes and aspirations? Am I human, or am I robot?

Modern cinema has reversed the theme of *Metropolis*. More recent science fiction is not about humans becoming more robotic, but about robots or strange otherworldly creatures becoming more human. I have watched virtually every episode of every series of *Star Trek* and its spin-offs, and I have lost count of how many times this idea has cropped up. Remember Spock the Vulcan struggling with the idea of experiencing emotions, or Data the android who wants to develop a sense of humour, or Odo the shape-shifter who usually lives in a bucket as a glutinous blob, trying to see the attractions of walking upright? These questions intrigue us. Can a machine ever develop personality? Can a computer ever become self-aware? If you gave an android memories, could it come to believe it was a person? From *Frankenstein* to *Wall-E*, it is a near-ubiquitous science-fiction trope to have someone wrestling with these basic existential questions of what it means to be human.[1] Most of the movies home in on the ability to make free choices and being self-determining as the basic quality that makes beings authentically human. Strangely, the idea of robots becoming self-aware becomes the ultimate doomsday scenario in films like *Terminator*, *The Matrix* and *Blade Runner*. By contrast, it is the robot in *Metropolis* that shows the workers that they can choose not to comply but escape the monotony and destroy the machine that is taking away their humanity.

Whichever way you come at this issue, whether you feel like a cog in a machine or enjoy reflecting on whether our new technologies are changing our perception of what life is about, we are

---

1 Don't forget *2001: A Space Odyssey*, *Blade Runner*, *Total Recall*, *Robocop*, *Alien*, *The Matrix*, *I, Robot*, *Prometheus*, *Oblivion* – and many more.

continually confronted with the question of what it means to be free and choose freely. The question comes in other guises too: Are we free to take our children on holiday in term-time? Are we free to wear what we like in a court of law? Is a woman free to choose to abort the foetus in her womb? (Is a foetus allowed the freedom to live?) There are constant debates on talk radio and television panel shows, and answers are hard to find because, while talk-show hosts might have a glib response, philosophers and theologians alike struggle with the basic dilemma of what human freedom really is.

We saw in the Job Paradox that God created human beings and gave us the ability to make free decisions because he wants a genuine relationship with us. Human freedom is at the heart of a classical Christian response to the problem of suffering. But now we come to the Judas Paradox, where we are forced to question whether we are genuinely given freedom of choice or not.

I have been wrestling with the question of Judas since the very first time I read the story for myself. His name has become a byword for betrayal. Was he intrinsically evil, or did the devil make him do it? Even more controversially, did God *plan* for Judas to betray Jesus? Was Judas born for damnation? Was his future already mapped out when he was an embryo? While he was a toddler learning to walk and talk, was his fate already decided – was it predetermined that he would betray the Son of God? Is Judas a tragic hero of the providence of God, a man to be pitied more than any other, or is he the master villain of the gospel story? Had God pre-programmed him as the robot assassin of the Son of God? If he had no choices, was Judas truly human?

In short: was Judas pushed – or did he jump?

If you have read the story in the Gospels you will know that Judas' betrayal of Jesus in the Garden of Gethsemane with a kiss is one of the most poignant moments in all of history. Judas ran out of patience with Jesus and his mission and so betrayed him to the temple authorities, Jesus' worst enemies. The man who goes around healing and helping people, welcoming the outcasts, offering hope and eternal life, is traded in by one of his closest friends for the measly amount of thirty pieces of silver. That was the same amount of money you would remunerate someone if you accidentally killed their slave.[2] This apparent coincidence is pregnant with meaning. Jesus failed to bow as a slave to Judas' desires and agenda, and so Judas conspires to get him killed. It's a cruel and bitter twist in the gospel story – a great wrong, done to a man who did not deserve it in any way. But it is not the whole story. This betrayal of Jesus *has* to happen. His death on the cross is described in the Bible as an event that was planned before the creation of the world.[3]

Seen in this light, Judas' betrayal seems like a necessary act. Perhaps he is just another cog in the divine plan to deliver up a crucified Saviour at just the right time and in just the right way to fulfil the Old Testament prophecies. But if Judas was always part of the plan – if he was a mere pawn – how can anyone blame him for what he did? Surely, in that case, God himself is to blame for the death of his Son, not Judas? Is the remorse and regret that Judas feels indeed only a further display of the cruelty of God, since it wasn't Judas' fault? Peter became an apostle despite his betrayal of Jesus, while Judas threw the silver back into the temple and went to a field and hanged himself.[4] Should we sympathize with Judas, simply another innocent victim caught up in the complex

---

2 Exodus 21:32.

3 1 Peter 1:18–21.

4 Matthew 27:1–5.

clockwork of God's master plan? Or should we take heed of this cautionary tale as to the corrupting power of greed to destroy even our most valued relationships?

The Judas Paradox is more than just a philosophical conundrum like the one ostensibly debated by schoolboy philosophers about the number of angels that can fit on a pinhead. It is more than just a good dilemma-based plotline for the *Star Trek* writing team. The question of whether Judas had a real choice about what he did is highly significant for how we understand the character of God. Is God some kind of moral monster who guides innocent people into situations where they are led astray? Is he uncaring that they become collateral damage in the cause of his bigger purposes, casualties for his grand scheme?

Judas' plight has implications for all of us. If Judas' betrayal was pre-ordained, if he did not have free will – we have to ask, do any of us really get to make decisions in our lives? Or are we all caught up in a clockwork universe where it is the watchmaker's purposes that are accomplished, and it only feels like we are making choices? Are we all predestined to act in the way we do? What does it mean for us to be subjects in God's kingdom?

Let's take a closer look at the Judas story, to make sure that it is the Bible that is setting the boundaries for the debate, rather than just our conjecture. Once again, Jesus' close friend and disciple John will be our guide. Here are Jesus' own words about how Judas' betrayal happened, in a passage which records a very intimate moment as we eavesdrop on a conversation between God the Son and God the Father:

I will remain in the world no longer, but they are still in the world, and I am coming to you. Holy Father, protect them by the power of your name, the name you gave me, so that they may be one as we are one. While I was with them, I protected them and kept them safe by that name you gave me. None has been lost except the one doomed to destruction so that Scripture would be fulfilled.[5]

This prayer is a rare opportunity to catch a glimpse of the relationship between Jesus and his heavenly Father. We see the Jesus Paradox up close and personal, as two members of the Godhead speak to each other. Jesus is not just another 'phase' of God, or a different mode of being. Jesus speaks to his Father, because he is a different person from him; yet he affirms that 'we are one', even in this context. Jesus asks God to protect his disciples when he is not physically with them during his death, resurrection and ascension, just as he himself has been protecting them while he has been with them. There is a clear unity in their aims, but their roles are shown to be different.

As Jesus reports back to his Father on his faithful protection of his disciples, he explains how he has discharged his duties as a good shepherd of his flock.[6] But he also mentions what is going on with Judas – who at this point in the narrative has already disappeared into the darkness of the night to go and betray Jesus.

Jesus explains that no one has been lost except 'the one doomed to destruction', or as some translations, such as the RSV, put it, 'the son of perdition'. Translators are split on this phrase, as to whether Jesus' description of Judas refers to his character or to his destination. Does he carry the family trait of someone caught up in sin, or is Jesus simply referring to Judas' eventual fate? Was his

---

5 John 17:11–12.

6 John 10.

betrayal due to some sin in the past – or some verdict of guilt in the future? Either way, we cannot assume from this that Judas was pre-programmed to betray Jesus – this reference does not prevent us understanding his act of betrayal as stemming from something he freely chose to do.

The bigger difficulty comes as Jesus asserts that Judas' status as a lost cause is 'so that Scripture would be fulfilled'. Jesus is clear that everyone in his care has been kept safe, except the one who was predicted in the Scriptures to be 'the one that got away'.[7] Now there seems to be no way of escaping it. God knew in advance what Judas would do, and he wrote it into the biblical texts circulated hundreds of years before Jesus' birth. Judas had no chance. He just did what he had to do.

To be able to predict the future, God must know the future. Theologians call this 'foreknowledge'. The question that remains is whether foreknowledge is the limit of God's relationship with the future. Is God like a time traveller who journeys through history, remembering every detail – and who is therefore able to predict events in what appears to be the future? Or is God like the ultimate chess grandmaster,[8] who can effectively and accurately predict all the moves an opponent will make, and in that way see all the future outcomes beforehand? Or perhaps God is like a director of a movie, who knows where he wants the film to end, and directs all his characters and plotlines to fit into that grand finale? The key question is whether God not only knows the future but makes it happen – what is known

---

7 The Scripture in question seems to be Psalm 49:8: 'Even my close friend, someone I trusted, one who shared my bread, has lifted up his heel against me.'

8 This is the view of the eighteenth-century French philosopher Pierre Simon Laplace.

as determinism or predestination. These debates have been raging between different Christian thinkers for hundreds of years.[9]

Before we can wrestle further with the Judas Paradox, we need to pause and take note that Christians are far from alone in navigating the relationship between freedom and determinism.

Materialistic atheism, for example, which may seem like it ought to be the polar opposite of Christianity on this, also has a problem with the nature of freedom. If everything in the universe is governed by natural laws, then those laws must also govern our brains. So the question arises: are we free to make decisions or are our choices determined by the oscillation of electrons or the interactions of chemicals in our brains? Are we like the replicants in Ridley Scott's *Blade Runner*, who think they are human but are really just androids with self-awareness, possessed of an illusion of freedom? Scientists articulate this dilemma by asking if there really is a difference between the physical reality of our brains and the ephemeral reality of our personalities, characters and decision-making processes. This is known as the brain/mind debate. If there isn't a difference between brain chemistry or neural physics and our minds, then human beings are basically biologically determined automatons responding by reflex rather than through conscious choice. Militant atheist Sam Harris argues exactly this:

Free will is an illusion. Our wills are simply not of our own making. Thoughts and intentions emerge from background causes of which we are unaware and over which we exert no conscious control.[10]

---

9 In recent days the debate has raged under the title of 'open theism'.
10 Harris, S. (2012), *Freewill*, Free Press, p. 5.

This makes our belief and experience of making decisions simply a figment of our pre-programmed imaginations. 'Qualities of character like courage, villainy, leadership'[11] disappear in a puff of deterministic smoke. Another of my chemistry lecturers held this view. He was researching the olfactory process; that is, how our brain responds to different scents and aromas. He believed that love was purely a chemical reaction – triggered not by *seeing* someone across a crowded room, but by *smelling* someone across a room. For him, love at first smell was not only possible but likely, because on first contact with someone from the opposite sex, our brains are designed to compute our biological compatibility, and calculate our ability to reproduce physically healthy offspring.[12] Because my lecturer for Inorganic Chemistry believed that romantic love was reduced to a chemically induced state of euphoria that is motivated by the process of finding a genetically appropriate mate, he was convinced he could design a perfume that would make anyone he wanted to fall in love with him.[13] It did not appear to have worked thus far.

A more common belief, which also has its origins in materialistic atheism, is that even if our lives are not primarily determined by our nature – biological factors or our genetic makeup – then they are driven by our nurture – sociological factors. In other words, our choices are limited because of family traits, or because of influences in society around us.

In other religions there are views that are not dissimilar to this

11 Menaker, D. (2012), 'Have it Your Way', in Sunday Book Review, 15 July 2012, *New York Times*.

12 See the work of Dr Martha McClintock, described in Clark, W. & Grunstein, M. (2004), *Are We Hardwired? The Role of Genes in Human Behavior*, Oxford University Press, pp. 41ff.

13 Lynx turned this idea into a successful but overtly sexist advertising campaign.

kind of fatalism. Islamic scholars posit that our choices are limited because of what they call Kismet[14] or fate; that whatever happens must be the will of Allah. This can lead to a fatalistic acceptance of whatever life brings. Hinduism has the notion of karma – an impersonal and unstoppable cycle of cause and effect. Knowing that other thought systems also wrestle with how to relate free will and determinism helps us to have more patience, recognizing that the philosophical grass is not in fact greener on the other side. But how does the Christian faith attempt to reconcile this paradox?

The Judas Paradox exemplifies two classic philosophical and theological challenges. The first is more general: what is the relationship between human free will and God's control over the universe? The second applies this question to whether God predetermines who will be given eternal life and who is doomed to damnation. We will look at each of these in turn and see how Judas' story sheds light on them.

First of all, then, we need to ask if we really do have free will, or whether God is in control of everything. Are humans genuinely responsible for their actions? Throughout the Scriptures there is a clear understanding that crimes have their appropriate punishments. This only makes sense if human beings have the ability to decide what they are doing. For example, the account of the origin of evil in the Bible describes a perfect environment and two human beings given the opportunity and freedom to explore the world, and a mandate to make something of it through scientific exploration and cultural innovation. The only prohibition was that the first humans were not to eat from the tree of the knowledge of good and evil. This was an opportunity for humanity to express their allegiance to

---

14 Kismet comes from the Arabic *Qisma*, which means 'lot' or 'portion'.

God by choosing to obey him – sadly, however, we did the opposite. Instead we used our freedom to disobey God, and we have been living with the negative consequences of this event ever since. The Genesis narrative describes God holding Adam and Eve accountable for their actions – which only makes sense if they genuinely did have the opportunity to choose this course for themselves.

Another argument for human free will is that the Bible is very clear that God is not the author of evil. This seems difficult because the Bible is equally clear that everything was created by God. Classically the way that this has been reconciled is by arguing that evil is not a thing in itself but a potentiality made possible by free will. This is known as the doctrine of privation and was championed by the fourth-century bishop Augustine.

In Judas' story, we are left in no doubt that Judas both felt responsible and was made to feel responsible by others:

> When Judas, who had betrayed him, saw that Jesus was condemned, he was seized with remorse and returned the thirty pieces of silver to the chief priests and the elders. 'I have sinned,' he said, 'for I have betrayed innocent blood.'
>
> 'What is that to us?' they replied. 'That's your responsibility.'
>
> So Judas threw the money into the temple and left. Then he went away and hanged himself.[15]

The Bible is clear that the responsibility for the execution of Jesus is due to human betrayal. However, the fault does not lie solely with Judas. In the book of Acts, Peter addresses a large crowd in Jerusalem and accuses them all collectively of Jesus' betrayal:

---

15 Matthew 27:3–5.

You handed him over to be killed, and you disowned him before Pilate, though he had decided to let him go. You disowned the Holy and Righteous One and asked that a murderer be released to you. You killed the author of life, but God raised him from the dead. We are witnesses of this.[16]

This is a stinging indictment. In poetic language but with real emphasis Peter hammers home the fact that the death of Jesus is the responsibility of the crowd that bayed for Christ's blood. Some of the people present for Peter's sermon may indeed have been part of the mob that called on Pilate to release the zealot brigand Barabbas and crucify Jesus – Jerusalem was not a large community by the standards of today. But equally, many of those listening could not have been present when those events took place, as Jerusalem was full of people from all around the world gathered for the feast of Pentecost. Peter seems to be implying a communal responsibility and blame for the death of Christ. He then outlines the proper response to this collective guilt in his subsequent call for repentance.[17] Judas is not even mentioned, so cannot be pinpointed as having sole responsibility for the death of Christ. This does not mean, though, that 'the Jews' as a people are guilty of Jesus' death, as has been claimed too often through Christian history, leading to unconscionable anti-Semitic acts. Indeed, Peter himself later argues that it was Jews and Gentiles conspiring together that brought about the death of Jesus.

Implicit in this escalation of blame is the conclusion that the whole of humanity together shares full responsibility and will be

16 Acts 3:15.
17 Acts 3:19.

held accountable, since all have sinned. The sixteenth-century artist Caravaggio captures something important in his masterpiece *The Taking of Christ*. There are seven people in the picture: the apostle John, who is running for his life; three soldiers; Judas, caught in the act of betraying Jesus with a kiss; and then a final man. This unnamed figure is in fact a self-portrait of Caravaggio himself. In this way the great artist acknowledged his, and our, complicity in the events that led to the death of Christ. Peter brings this same insight into his Pentecost address. He is not singling out the Jews as having special responsibility for the death of Jesus, but rather emphasizing humanity's corporate responsibility.

Peter then adds another perspective on the same events that helps us as we consider the second element of the question of free will: to what extent is God sovereign? Peter continues:

> this is how God fulfilled what he had foretold through all the prophets, saying that his Messiah would suffer.[18]

The handing over of the Son of God to the authorities, his trial, his torture and his crucifixion, were all part of God's way of fulfilling what he had promised through the Old Testament prophets. This is underlined by the astounding level of detail describing the death of Jesus in ancient prophecies. For example, Psalm 22 seems to predict not only the method of execution but also apparently incidental details such as the mocking crowds,[19] the abandonment by his disciples,[20] his physical distress, including his thirst and the

---

18 Acts 3:13–18.

19 Psalm 22:7.

20 Psalm 22:12.

dislocation of bones that is common among crucifixion victims,[21] the public nature of the event,[22] and even the fact that the soldiers gambled for his clothes as he died.[23]

For these details to be foreseen and then fulfilled indicates a substantial divine involvement in fine-tuning the events of history. God is clearly in control – in fact, he had a plan. This verse from Peter's Pentecost sermon brings these two elements, of God's sovereignty and human responsibility, together:

> This man was handed over to you by God's deliberate plan and foreknowledge; and you, with the help of wicked men, put him to death by nailing him to the cross.[24]

It would be nice to think that Judas' cowardly kiss and the crowds' complicity were 'helping' God, that somehow, via a film-like twist in the plot, the bad guys turn out to be the good guys working undercover. But what God took as 'help' in the Judas story was not meant as such; there was no deliberate intent to support God's plans. Neither Judas, nor Pontius Pilate, nor the clamouring crowds knowingly co-operated with God's grand rescue scheme for the world. Peter states clearly that they acted 'in ignorance'.[25]

This paradox seems to go back and forth like a see-saw. Humans are responsible, but God had a plan. Humans helped, but they did it in ignorance. And still we are not off the hook. We may have been ignorant of God's grand scheme, but we cannot claim ignorance

---

21 Psalm 22:14.
22 Psalm 22:18.
23 Psalm 22:20.
24 Acts 2:23.
25 Acts 3:17.

of our crime. It seems perfectly clear from the Gospel accounts that everyone concerned knew very well they were conspiring together to falsely accuse and execute a man who had claimed to be God in the flesh – and had provided more than enough accrediting miracles to give substance to his claims. As far as these individuals were aware, each one was responsible for their own choice when it came to the death of Jesus.

Judas freely chose to betray Jesus with a kiss; in return he received his thirty pieces of silver. The crowds chose to betray Jesus by calling for a murderer to be released. Pontius Pilate chose to betray Jesus by acquiescing to the Jewish religious leaders' demands, despite having found Jesus innocent of all charges. The Jewish leaders chose to betray Jesus by deliberately conspiring to have him executed, even though they had seen ample evidence that God's power was at work through him, through the miracles he performed. We ourselves have all sinned, necessitating Christ's death for the sins of the world.[26] Thus each guilty party brought their own self-serving motive; and yet each one, in ignorance, was fulfilling God's plan. Scripture is clear that not just in Judas' case but in every aspect of life God has ultimate control. The degree of control of human events demonstrated in the fulfilled prophecies of Jesus' death reflects what the book of Proverbs claims about God's super-intendence of history: 'The lot is cast into the lap, but its every decision is from the LORD.'[27] So there can be no doubting that God is in control – as we have seen in our discussion of suffering in Chapter 4 (the Job Paradox). Although God is in control, he chooses not to exert his control in a way that robs us of freedom. In one

---

26 Romans 5:6–8, for example.
27 Proverbs 16:33.

sense or another, all of us must bear some responsibility for the death of Christ.

Paradoxes allow seemingly contradictory statements to be held in tension. In the Jesus Paradox we saw how we can accept the dual natures of Christ because of the overwhelming evidence, even though we can't necessarily picture or describe how the divinity and humanity of Christ work out together. We do not have the mental categories to handle it, but Scripture gives us clear guidance – and just enough support – to enable us to hold on to both realities.[28] Again here, in the Judas Paradox, we have to hold together two apparently irreconcilable concepts – that human beings have genuine and accountable freedom, and that God is working out his perfect purposes.

This brings us to the second level of the Judas Paradox: does a good God choose to doom people to eternal punishment? I have shared already the way in which, when I look back over my life, I can see that I became a Christian because God intervened in my life. I know from my experience that I didn't seek God out, but that he came to find me. Every time I think about this, I want to thank God, because I know that, left to my own devices, I wouldn't be a Christian. I am continually grateful for what God did to help me come to faith. And yet I can see, too, that there came a point where I had my own decision to make. Faced with the evidence for the Christian faith, with the challenge to pledge my allegiance to Jesus, with the example of a friend who was radically transformed by becoming a Christian, and with the profoundly moving Gospel accounts, I made a conscious decision to become a follower of Jesus.

---

28 J. I. Packer argues that this is an antinomy, but Wayne Grudem argues that the word 'paradox' is a better term for this state of affairs. See Grudem, W. (1994), *Systematic Theology*, p. 35.

This two-pronged process is exactly how the Bible describes conversion, too. Both in the Gospels and in the Acts accounts, people come to faith as they are persuaded by the evidence. In the Pentecost sermon we have been exploring in this chapter, Peter explains the events that have taken place in Jerusalem regarding the death of Jesus, and he uses the fulfilment of Old Testament prophecies as part of his argument. Peter also draws attention to the miracle of people hearing their own mother-tongue languages spoken by unschooled men. Yet whenever Luke records the number of people that became Christians that day, and then on subsequent occasions, he always says, 'the Lord added to their number'.[29] So the Scriptures seem to support the idea that both God's direction and the individual's choice are involved in the journey to faith. There is both divine sovereignty at work and human responsibility.

If that isn't hard enough for us to grasp, there is a further complication. If God chooses some to become Christians – if he predestines and 'elects' those who will be saved – there is an unspoken implication that God must choose for others *not* to be saved. Peter was chosen to be an apostle. Isn't it therefore logical that Judas was chosen for damnation? But looking around at our friends and family, it seems unfair that God would choose some of them for eternal life, and others for destruction. This fear of rejection by God has led some people to reject God's goodness altogether – after all, who would want to worship a God like that?[30]

The Bible, though, seems to teach an asymmetry in the sovereignty of God. Whenever it talks about people coming to believe,

---

29 Acts 2:47; 5:14.

30 An 'unbeliever was really offered life in the gospel, and could have had it if he would . . .' Packer, J. I. (1961), *Evangelism and the Sovereignty of God*, IVP, p. 105.

receiving forgiveness from God, being adopted into God's family – this is attributed to the grace of God at work. But when it speaks about someone refusing God's grace, being condemned or receiving judgement, there is no avoidance of human responsibility. God does not make plans for someone to face judgement in the same way that he plans for someone to inherit eternal life.

J. I. Packer argues that the offer of salvation is genuinely offered to everyone. When someone chooses not to accept his offer of grace in Jesus, God leaves them to their own devices and desires.[31] There are, it is true, occasions in both the Old Testament and New Testament where the text speaks of God actively 'hardening' people's hearts – Pharaoh perhaps most famously. But even then this seems to be God confirming an individual's desire to resist him.[32] At no point does the Bible say that sinners will miss eternal life because they are not chosen, but always because of their actions, and because they 'neglect the great salvation'.[33]

As we wrestle with this extremely difficult and delicate area of theology, it is worth us heeding the warning the apostle Paul raises when he reflects on this subject. Paul goes out of his way to warn us about arrogance:

> One of you will say to me: 'Then why does God still blame us? For who is able to resist his will?' But who are you, a human being, to talk back to God? 'Shall what is formed say to the one who formed it, "Why did you make me like this?"' Does not the potter have the right to make out of the same

---

31 Matthew 22:37–38.
32 Exodus 9 and Romans 9.
33 Hebrews 2:3.

lump of clay some pottery for special purposes and some for common use?[34]

God can, of course, choose to do whatever he pleases. Just as Job was challenged by God to recalibrate his mind, so we need to find our place in front of the Lord of all the earth. We are the creatures and he is the Creator. God is God and we are not. He does not have to answer to us; he does not have to fit into our understanding. But nevertheless, we are not being instructed to stop thinking, or to let sleeping (theological) dogs lie. We are called to love God with our minds,[35] so it is fitting to seek to understand these things as best we can – whether we come at it humbly and reverently, or kicking against the pricks. What we see in the Scriptures is a God who genuinely offers salvation and grace to everyone, and yet is sovereignly in control of who ultimately will be saved and who won't.

We see this principle at work in John's account of the Judas story:

His disciples stared at one another, at a loss to know which of them he meant. One of them, the disciple whom Jesus loved, was reclining next to him. Simon Peter motioned to this disciple and said, 'Ask him which one he means.'

Leaning back against Jesus, he asked him, 'Lord, who is it?'

Jesus answered, 'It is the one to whom I will give this piece of bread when I have dipped it in the dish.' Then, dipping the piece of bread, he gave it to Judas, the son of Simon Iscariot. As soon as Judas took the bread, Satan entered into him.

---

34 Romans 9:19–21.
35 Matthew 22:37.

So Jesus told him, 'What you are about to do, do quickly.' But no one at the meal understood why Jesus said this to him. Since Judas had charge of the money, some thought Jesus was telling him to buy what was needed for the Festival, or to give something to the poor. As soon as Judas had taken the bread, he went out. And it was night.[36]

This is a dark moment in the Gospel of John and yet we see spotlighted in it a beautiful moment of grace. This is the Last Supper,[37] an intimate meal where Jesus explains to his disciples the significance of his death on behalf of the sins of the world. The meal they share together prefigures the communion meal which Christians around the world celebrate to remember the death of Christ. So when Jesus offers Judas a piece of bread, this is an act of generous hospitality. It was a moment of genuine free will. Judas could have chosen not to take the bread, or having taken it, not to walk out into the night.

Some have flippantly dismissed this offer of bread as a 'magical morsel' or a 'satanic sacrament',[38] especially as we are told that Satan entered Judas the moment he opened his mouth. So how do we assess whether this was some kind of trick, or the act of generous hospitality and choice on Jesus' part that it appears to be on the surface?

First, consider the guest list. Bearing in mind Jesus' apparent

---

36 John 13:21–30.

37 'The precise nature of this meal and its relationship both to the Passover family meal, and to the Last Supper described in the synoptic gospels, has long been debated. The many points of parallel to the synoptic descriptions make it highly likely that this was the same occasion.' Milne, B. (1993), *The Message of John: Here is your King!*, The Bible Speaks Today, IVP, p. 196.

38 See Carson, D. A. (1991), *The Gospel According to John*, The Pillar New Testament Commentary, IVP, p. 474.

knowledge of what he was going to do, the fact that Judas is not precluded from this intimate setting to celebrate the Passover meal with Jesus is a big deal. Just as being invited to Christmas dinner with a friend makes you part of their inner circle, so Jesus' invitation to share this meal with Judas is an act of love. Second, feeding somebody directly, as Jesus does Judas, was also considered an honour such as a host might pay a valued friend. Third, Jesus does not reveal to the other disciples what Judas is going to do or why – this is a private, whispered conversation which apparently includes Simon Peter and John, but no others. Judas leaves the room without being questioned, blocked or otherwise accosted by the other disciples. William Temple comments that Judas left 'under the Lord's protecting silence'.[39]

Jesus thus demonstrates his love for Judas in this final encounter. He has included Judas in his final meal, he has washed his feet, he has sat with him, fed him and he has kept quiet about his plan. Although we are told that Jesus' enemy Satan has taken hold of Judas, Jesus retains his authority and control and dismisses Judas to go and do what he has planned. The great missionary thinker Lesslie Newbigin describes this moment:

> that final act of love becomes, with a terrible immediacy, the decisive movement of judgement . . . So the final gesture of affection precipitates the final surrender of Judas to the power of darkness. The light shines in the darkness, and the darkness has neither understood it nor mastered it.[40]

---

39 Newbigin, L. (1982), *The Light has Come: An Exposition of the Fourth Gospel*, Eerdmans, p. 174.
40 Ibid., p. 173.

Jesus offers Judas genuine love, starkly contrasting the fake affection of Judas' later kiss. Jesus seems to be genuinely offering Judas every opportunity to receive his love and affection, but Judas decides not to receive it. Even in the tragic events of Judas' betrayal we see the balance and beauty of both God's sovereignty and human free will.

Before we leave our consideration of this paradox it is important for us to review what we can definitely affirm about human freedom and divine sovereignty so we can be guided as to how to worship the God who seems to determine our freedom to choose. Let me offer three instincts that might help to demonstrate to us that, at a basic level, we do believe in human freedom.

First, when we break God's laws, when we fail to live out his grace and compassion, we have an inbuilt sense of guilt and a desire to say sorry. In fact we are told that confession of our sin is the right response to God for our moral failings. This instinct betrays the fact that we believe we have responsibility for our actions.

Second, when presented with decisions about our futures, our natural reaction is deliberation. The instinct to not rush headlong into situations but to reflect and work out what we ought to do is endorsed by Scripture.[41] When it comes to decision-making, the wisdom literature in general and the book of Proverbs in particular instruct us not to blindly abandon ourselves to the will of God but to make wise decisions and choose the right path. Wanting wisdom and deliberating carefully before we make decisions is not by any means contrary to faith in God. In the same chapter that we are instructed to 'Trust in the LORD, and lean not on our own understanding', we are also told to 'not let wisdom and understanding out

41 See Proverbs 3:5–6, for example.

of your sight, preserve sound judgement and discretion.'[42] The instinct to make informed and wise decisions is approved of by Scripture and is another sign that we do know that we have genuine human freedom.

Third, we instinctively make plans for the future. This desire to look ahead demonstrates that we believe our choices have consequences and that they make a genuine difference to how things work out.

There are, however, also three instincts that demonstrate a natural belief in the sovereignty of God.

First, we are drawn to say thank you to God – for what we know he has done for us and for all the good things we have in life. We know that it was God who opened our blind eyes to see 'the light of the knowledge of God's glory displayed in the face of Christ'.[43] We naturally respond in grateful praise to the God who sought us and found us.

Second, we pray. We believe in a God who can intervene in our world. A God who is powerful enough to change things, no matter how bad the situation or dire the circumstances. Specifically, we pray for other people to know this God of ours, to come to faith; because we believe that what God has done for us, he wants to do for others, too.[44]

Third, we look to the future with a sense of trust. We are inclined to believe that in the end God's will will indeed be done on earth as it is in heaven, and in that we are demonstrating that we believe in a God who is truly the Lord of time and history.

---

42 Proverbs 3:5–6, 21.

43 2 Corinthians 4.

44 For an articulation of this argument see Packer, J. I. (1961), *Evangelism and the Sovereignty of God*, IVP.

We praise a God who rules by his word, who speaks to make things happen, just as he did at the beginning according to the creation accounts.

How do we come to terms with these contradictory and yet powerful inclinations?

I believe that God really wants to be in relationship with us, and I also believe that genuine relationships are only possible with genuine freedom. Human freedom, though, is a sacred gift from God, not to be taken for granted. If we have come to a living relationship with God, this is something to be treasured – but it should drive us on as well, fighting for God's purposes to be more fully realized in this world, pleading with God in prayer that he intervene to bring his good into the world, just as Jesus taught in the Lord's Prayer: 'Your kingdom come, your will be done on earth as it is in heaven.'

But while we should lift up our prayers to God, pleading for his intervention, at one and the same time, wherever we have opportunity we should champion these same good purposes with the strength God has given us.

Worshipping the sovereign God means resisting the future that Fritz Lang depicted in *Metropolis*, where the machinery of modern life turns us into another cog in the wheel of consumer capitalism. Honouring God means we resist mere conformity. We should speak out against – for example – advertisers who turn women into either super-neat and obedient 'Stepford Wives', or sexualized objects of lust. We should fight against the global slave trade which robs men and women, boy and girls of their God-given freedom of choice. Worshipping God means standing up to dictators, fighting for freedom and for the religious liberty of everyone on the planet. Worshipping God means waking up to a world in need and refusing to trade Jesus' concerns for a hurting world for thirty pieces of silver. This is the Judas Paradox – that it's never over till it's over, but if we know the truth, we must be willing to fight for it.

Chapter 11

The Cross Paradox
The God who wins as he loses

It was the best of times, It was the worst of times . . . It was the season of Light. It was the season of Darkness. It was the spring of hope. It was the winter of despair. We had everything before us. We had nothing before us. We were all going direct to Heaven. We were all going direct the other way.[1]

With these immortally paradoxical lines Charles Dickens introduces his epic novel *A Tale of Two Cities*. The contradictory sentiments they invoke point at the coexistent extremes of life in so-called 'enlightened' eighteenth-century London and Paris, at a time just before the French Revolution. These lines hint at the contrasts and tensions that will unravel in the book, and the conflicting values that will be portrayed. Love and hate. Wealth and poverty. Good and evil.

They make for an apt description of another time in history, too; one where Light and Darkness, hope and despair smashed into each other, and the world was changed forever.

If ever there was a paradoxical moment in time, it was three

---

1 Dickens, C. (1859), *A Tale of Two Cities*, Collins, p. 1.

o'clock on that Friday afternoon outside the city of Jerusalem, atop a hill that had been given the nickname 'the Place of the Skull'. It was the middle of the day, and yet it became the middle of the night. It was humanity's darkest hour, and yet divine love never shone brighter. An innocent man had been found guilty and was being given his – or, rather, everyone else's – punishment. A man screamed out to God, asking why he had been abandoned, and at the same time the curtain in the temple was ripped open, welcoming the world into the very presence of God. The death and distress of the one offered life and hope to the many. To the world, it looked like utter defeat, but in fact it was God's greatest victory. In this picture of abject weakness, the power of God is revealed.

The cross of Christ has to be the biggest paradox in Scripture. It is so difficult to grasp that it is described as a stumbling block to faith to some, foolishness[2] to others, and yet for some of us it is the turning point of history and the foundation of our faith.

The paradoxes of the cross are manifold. In this chapter we will explore three of them. First, the paradox of particularity – how can this single event, however singular, alter the course of every other event in history? Can the cross really change everything? Second, the paradox of barbarity – how can what is supposed to be the most perfect act of love that God has ever shown appear so barbaric, cruel and unnecessary? How can such a cruel cross rescue anything – let alone everything? And third, the paradox of exclusivity – how on earth can the cross be the only way for people to find forgiveness, rescue and hope? How can the cross be claimed to fix everything?

First, why do Christians make such a big deal about the cross?

---

2 1 Corinthians 1:18–25.

How can an event in a forgotten backwater of the Roman Empire two thousand years ago have any significance for my situation and yours? How can an eternal God be so concerned about the temporal affairs of humans as to make history turn around one particular man, one death, in this way?

There have been various turning points in history where specific events in very particular situations have had a global impact. Whether it is patient zero in a global epidemic, or the murder of a man looking for a hospital, which would spark World War I, our history books are littered with examples of seemingly minor events that have huge repercussions. In the field of physics, chaos theory proposes that small changes in complex systems can have huge and unforeseen consequences. The classic example is of a butterfly flapping its wings in one hemisphere, resulting in a hurricane being generated on the other side of the world. Some argue that if the tuning between weak and strong nuclear forces in atoms were off by the tiniest amount – 1 in 10,000,000 – then no elements heavier than hydrogen would be able to exist. So science is certainly willing to consider that a lot could hinge on something that seems inconsequential; that something very particular can have a significant universal effect.

But what is it about the cross of Christ that makes it so significant?

Part of the answer to this is to do with who it was that was on the cross. If we take the Jesus Paradox and the Cross Paradox and think of them in a unified way, we will be far more likely to be able to understand just what the big deal is. It was not just anyone who took a wrong turn down the wrong street looking for Sarajevo Hospital and thus came within range of Gavrilo Princip's gun, but Archduke Franz Ferdinand himself. It was the assassination of the heir to the Austrian Empire which ignited the atrocities of World War I. Similarly, this was not just anyone dying on a cross. The Romans used crucifixion widely as a means of public execution, so it was not crucifixion that was unique. Rather, the identity of the crucified person holds the key. Remembering that Jesus was the unique God-Man sheds light on why his death matters. As hymn-writer Charles Wesley put it, "'Tis Mystery all, the Immortal dies'. What a paradox: the eternal God, the author of life, experienced the worst of deaths.

Unlike the death of Franz Ferdinand, however, the cross was no accident of history. God had been building towards this moment from eternity past and had written markers into human history to guide us to the right understanding of this event – this was no ordinary death.

Imagine watching the ultimate heist movie with, of course, a priceless diamond arriving at a museum. The alarms are set to cover every inch of the display hall, and weight sensors are sensitive to the nearest gram. Extremely careful planning is necessary by the prospective thieves so that at the decisive moment an unnoticed switch or substitution can occur. The diamond has to be replaced by something that is exactly its weight, or all the alarms will sound and the caper is over.

This image gives us an inkling of what was going on when Jesus died on the cross. This particular substitution had been planned in minute detail since before the beginning of time itself, and sign-posted throughout the Jewish Scriptures. You can see those signposts from the moment that sin entered the world. God had promised that if humanity sinned, death would result, but in the Garden of Eden the first thing to die after the fall were not sinful human beings but animals, sacrificed to provide fallen people with the clothes they needed to cover over a nakedness that was no longer appropriate in a world contaminated by sin. We saw in the Abraham Paradox that the ram caught in a thicket which took the place of Isaac was a signpost to Jesus, who would be described as 'the Lamb of God that takes away the sin of the world'.[3] We saw in the Moses Paradox that the Holy of Holies in both the Tabernacle and then in the temple was barred to all but the High Priest, and then only on the right day and with the shedding of sacrificial blood. We saw in the Job Paradox that whether for a cosmic purpose or not, there are times when an innocent person will suffer. We saw in the Jonah Paradox that when the sailors threw God's prophet ostensibly to his death, that was when they were saved.

All of these paradoxes along the way are signposts to the Cross Paradox, the place where we see resolution through the picture of a God who wins when he loses.

God was building up to the exact moment that his Son Jesus was born in Israel, at a time when the country was under Roman occupation. The death of Jesus involved the ultimate substitution. Jesus' death did not just satisfy but fulfilled the sacrifice system set up in the Old Testament. It satisfied God's righteous anger not just once but for all. It paid for the sins of the entire world. The death of Jesus was not an isolated and random event in a forgotten corner of the Roman world. The cross of Jesus is the place where all of God's plans come together. X marks the spot: this place, this time is where God is resolving the great paradox of history. God uses the tiny details of history to solve the riddle of the universe, demonstrate his perfect love and redeem his broken world.

---

3 John 1:29.

The death of Jesus for the sins of the world has brought comfort and hope to millions of people through history and around the world. But for some, the idea of Jesus as a substitute only leads to another paradox, one they find even harder to grapple with – the paradox of barbarity.

The cross of Jesus, the Son of God giving his life to save ours, is supposed to demonstrate the greatest love of all. But it's God's own Son hanging there. How can a loving God meticulously set out a plan that will lead to the death of his own Son? What we found inconceivable for Abraham to consider doing to his only son, God had planned to do to Jesus since before the beginning of the universe. How can the love of God and the barbarity of the cross be reconciled?

The details of how crucifixion worked bring home its cruelty. The Romans had engineered a lingering form of torture that displayed its victims as macabre visual aids showing the futility of opposing the might of the empire. It was designed to make a lasting impression on the occupied population; to show that Roman law would destroy all those who opposed its hegemony. Even before he got to the cross Jesus had experienced excruciating pain from a Roman scourging. Each lash of the whip was extremely severe; the long leather strips had weights on their ends, and sharp protrusions sewn into their lengths, to rip through the flesh of the victims.[4] There are records of people dying from this alone. But Jesus survived this, and then after being beaten, scourged and forced to carry his cross until he collapsed, he was nailed to it and left to die, painfully and slowly. Worn out from all they'd suffered even before being nailed up there, victims would be unable to hold themselves up and

---

4 McDowell, J. (1993), *The Resurrection Factor*, Alpha, p. 60.

– perhaps with a little helping hand from a soldier breaking their legs to make it even harder to extend themselves enough to breathe – death normally occurred through suffocation.

Jesus' death was painfully slow, excruciatingly agonizing, and publicly humiliating. It is hard to imagine how it could have been worse. This cruel death was a gross injustice against an innocent victim. How can this possibly be the means through which the ultimate justice in the universe is satisfied?

Why did God 'need' appeasing anyway? The idea that God the Father pours out his anger on his Son has led some critics to ask if the crucifixion is some form of divine abuse:

> Christianity is an abusive theology that glorifies suffering. Is it any wonder that there is so much abuse in modern western society when the predominant image of the main religion of the culture is of 'divine child abuse' – God the Father demanding and carrying out the suffering and death of his own son on a cross? If Christianity is to be liberating for the oppressed, it must itself be liberated from this theology.[5]

These statements come in a paper arguing that the violence at the heart of the atonement story informs the use of violence as a means to an end, and that has then been used to legitimize domestic abuse in Christian families. As someone who works with neglected and abused children, I have a great deal of sympathy with the motivations of the author, and I agree that Christianity must be bunk if it does not prove to be liberating for the oppressed. Having said

---

5 Brown, J. C. and Bohn, C. R. (1989), *Christianity, Patriarchy, and Abuse*, Pilgrim, p. 30.

that, I have come to very different conclusions on the import of this paradox of the barbarity of the cross.

I want to set out three perspectives that may help resolve the paradox of the love of God and the cruelty of the crucifixion, and they are to do with our view of Jesus, our view of sin, and our view of justice. The charge of 'divine child abuse' undervalues the dual natures of Christ. As we have already discussed, the Bible is clear that Jesus is fully human but also fully God. As the second person of the Trinity, Jesus, with God the Father, co-planned the rescue mission to deal with the sin of the world. Jesus was fully signed up to every aspect of the mission of the cross. He was not a helpless casualty, an innocent victim or simply collateral damage, but a willing sacrifice. There is a beautiful painting by the Pre-Raphaelite painter Holman Hunt called *The Shadow of Death*. The painting depicts Jesus working in Joseph's carpentry shop. As he stretches out his arms at the end of the day, the shadow of the sun setting forms a crucifix on the wall behind him. What this painting captures beautifully is the sense that through his whole life Jesus lived with the knowledge that the cross was his destiny: he knew what was coming and, despite the anguish of the Garden of Gethsemane, walked willingly towards it. Jesus frequently predicts his death on the cross. Indeed, in the famous 'Good Shepherd' section of John's Gospel Jesus states:

I lay down my life – only to take it up again. No one takes it from me, but I lay it down of my own accord. I have authority to lay it down and authority to take it up again.[6]

---

6 John 10:17–18.

Looking at the biblical account, there is no way we can miss that Jesus knowingly chose to face crucifixion on our behalf. He did not consider himself a victim at God's hands, or a martyr for a cause – he knew he was the means by which salvation could be offered to all.

The charge of divine child abuse not only underrates Jesus' nature as God, but also underestimates the problem of sin and the need for justice. The idea that God needs human sacrifice in order to fully satisfy his anger at sin is difficult to accept. It appears to be a concept borrowed from the movie *King Kong*, where the angry giant gorilla's terrible temper can only be mollified by an innocent and beautiful young maiden who is tied up and offered to the beast while the rest of the people hide in fear behind the city walls.[7] Nothing could be further from the truth. God requires sacrifice not because of his nature, but because of the nature, extent and consequences of the problem of human sin.

When we watch suffering at close hand or see it unfold on our television screens, there is something there that tears at our hearts. Children who are starving, women who are kidnapped and kept hidden for decades, the brutalities of war, the conscription of child soldiers, bullying that brings teenagers to the point of wanting to end their lives. Whatever it is, something inside us shouts out that this is wrong; that there *is* a moral fabric to the universe and this is a violation of it. We instinctively want justice, crying out for the perpetrators of these atrocities to be made to answer for the suffering they have caused. This moral sense is God-given. When we are incensed by these things we are exhibiting a part of God's

---

7 See Stott, J. (1990), *The Cross of Christ*, IVP, p. 173 for a discussion on the difference between the moral anger of God and an animistic view of sacrifice and appeasement.

character, because he is a moral and perfect God, who is moved with compassion for the suffering of the world. God does not turn a blind eye. He reassures us that there will be a final accounting for people's selfish acts and cruel words – for everything that displays insolence to and ignorance of their Creator, and violence towards his people.

Sometimes our moral sense is not as finely tuned as it ought to be, and its scope is too limited. Our moral outrage functions extremely well when it is directed at other people, but seems to malfunction somehow when we consider our own actions. We are far more likely to spot moral deficiencies in other people, as Jesus ably pointed out.[8] When we look at ourselves, we can evince a moral myopia. If we were to apply the same criteria to ourselves when it comes to selfish motives, ignorance of God or hurtful words, we would have to demand the same judgement we demand of others. Russian dissident Alexander Solzhenitsyn realized this:

if only there were evil people somewhere insidiously committing evil deeds, and it were necessary only to separate them from the rest of us and destroy them. But the line dividing good and evil cuts through the heart of every human being. And who is willing to destroy a piece of his own heart?[9]

God's moral sense, by contrast, is perfectly attuned. He sees both the beauty and the brokenness in everything. God sees the contamination that sin causes, and understands that every human heart is shot through with both good and evil. God loves with an infinite

---

8 Matthew 7:1–3.
9 Solzhenitsyn, A. (1974), *The Gulag Archipelago*, Collins, p. 17.

love, yet at the same time will not turn a blind eye to even a speck of evil, a single act of injustice or bad motive. God's judgement is perfect in its clarity. And yet God is at one and the same time a loving judge, a merciful creator, a gracious king. These ought to be, but are not, mutually exclusive categories. There is no tension, no inner conflict in the heart of God. The cross of Jesus is the place where love and justice meet, where wrath and compassion combine; as the Psalmist puts it, 'Love and faithfulness meet together; right-eousness and peace kiss each other.'[10]

This is indeed a paradox; another instance where God is too big and too absolute for us to wrap our minds around his intentions, and how he can possibly hold these two things together. God will both punish sin and forgive sinners. He will give the just and appropriate punishment to every act of human sin. Yet he will also offer amnesty to all those who will receive it. God the Father does this by allowing his Son to face the depths of humanity's depravity. God the Son does this by volunteering to receive the worst that humanity can throw at him. God the Spirit does this by sustaining Jesus through the ordeal, but also by sharpening our moral sensi-tivity so we might realize our need for Jesus' death to count for us. We may only see the tip of the iceberg in terms of our understanding of it, but the barbarity of the cross is intended to match the barbarity of sin.

The cross brings into the light the darkest parts of human nature. The more we reflect on it, the more we realize our guilt. It was human beings who dreamed up the torture of crucifixion. It was human beings who decided to drive nails through an innocent man's hands, to prolong his life so he could be left in a pitiful state for

---

10 Psalm 85:10.

as long as possible, to drive a spear through his side to make sure he was dead. It is we human beings who continue to disregard the life and words of Jesus, and who make our own paths. The unfathomable extent of human sin is revealed in the extreme cruelty of the cross. God let this moment of violent depravity happen, to be the arena where he would display the full extent of his love. As one theologian puts it: 'The crucifixion was both a heinous act of human sin perpetrated at Jerusalem and a most loving, gracious, holy and wise act of God conceived in eternity.'[11]

We have seen that the charge of divine child abuse not only underrates Jesus' nature as God, but also underestimates the problem of sin and the need for justice. As we begin to grasp these two things more fully, our minds can start to recalibrate and understand that the cross is not a place of tragedy, but of victory.

Every summer, Hollywood saves up its best and biggest action blockbuster movies of the year for the holidays. Our teenage children find them irresistible; mostly we go to enjoy the developments in computer graphics and special effects, as the acting is pretty poor and the plotlines are predictable. It doesn't matter whether it is a superhero movie, a western, a science-fiction drama, or a zombie/vampire film – we know how it is going to unfold. In the first few scenes the baddies establish themselves, enacting some terrible violence that cries out for justice. Enter the heroes. Often from downtrodden backgrounds themselves, ideally they have actually suffered at the hands of the baddies. Once this initial conflict is set up, the rest of the film moves inexorably towards its happy – if violent – resolution. We are cheering for our hero to unleash

---

11 Grogan, G. (2008), 'Atonement in the New Testament', in Tidball, Hilbourne & Thacker (eds.), *The Atonement Debate*, Zondervan, p. 95.

his[12] just revenge. The worse the violence at the beginning of the movie, the longer the villains seem to get away with it, the stronger our urge to see the final moment when vengeance is exacted. The more pain the villains have inflicted, the more pain we want inflicted on them. As long as resolution comes, the hero survives and the baddies get what they deserve, we'll be happy.

Some people think the Christian story runs to a similar plotline – sometimes described as the 'myth of redemptive violence'.[13] It is perhaps possible to recast the gospel as the victory of God's violence over evil, where our hero, Jesus, suffers at the hands of the bad guys, and, despite his initially peaceful resurrection and institution of a church that eschewed rather than pursued violence, will one day turn from victim to victor, as he comes into town with all guns blazing to claim his rightful place. You have to come at it somewhat unconventionally to make it come out right, but you can have a good go if you want to.

But when Jesus submitted himself to the barbarity of the cross, he did not outdo evil, he undid evil. He triumphed over the powers of evil at the cross by disarming them, not outgunning them. He was cancelling the debt, not collecting it.[14] Unlike in the action movies, we are not looking at Jesus, the victim on the cross, and left waiting for it all to be put right at the end. No, Jesus put everything right on the cross – that was the moment of ultimate victory. When he seemed to lose, that was when he actually won. Rather than glorifying

---

12 Sadly, too often it is a 'he'. As Tad Friend observed in the *New Yorker* magazine: 'Female-driven movies aren't usually blockbusters.' *New Yorker* magazine, April 2011, p. 52.

13 See Wink, W. (1992), *Engaging the Powers: Discernment and Resistance in a World of Domination*, Fortress Press.

14 Colossians 2:13–15.

the violence, Jesus undermines it, disables it; turns it against itself. Theologian Steve Holmes writes: 'God has so ordered the world that the inevitable consequences of sin is violence, suffering and death; and rather than let us suffer these things, God takes them on himself.'[15]

Sometimes a heist movie does end with a variation on this. After an hour or so of action and suspense, the meticulously prepared diamond thieves get caught by a gang of rival crooks and punished for their cheek in daring to think they'd succeed; they go away with their tails between their legs and nothing to show for all their hard work, leaving the bad guys ogling the diamond and, quite likely, a case full of dollars. End of film. Except an extra scene shows the protagonists pulling out the real diamond from a secret hidey-hole, the bad guys discovering the case is actually full of note-shaped pieces of newspaper, and everyone is left wondering how they managed to pull it off. They seemed to lose, but at some point right in the middle, they had done exactly what was going to turn out to be necessary – and won.

Finally we come to the paradox of exclusivity. The Bible claims that it is only through the cross of Jesus that anyone can be saved. There is no other way, no other means by which human beings can be put into right relationship with God.[16] But what about other faiths? Aren't their teachings valuable too? Why would God exclude people from other religions from knowing him? Is God just a narrow-minded bigot, intolerant of other faiths? Why shouldn't a star, a moon, a flame, or the yin and yang symbols be just as worthwhile to follow as the cross?

---

15 Holmes, S. R. (2007), *The Wondrous Cross: Atonement and Penal Substitution in Biblical History*, Paternoster, p. 107.
16 John 14:1–6; Acts 4:8–12; 1 Timothy 2:3–7.

Let's come back to the Bible and reflect on the moments before Jesus was crucified. As he sweats blood in the Garden of Gethsemane he prays to God and asks his Father if there is any way his coming death can be avoided. All four of the biographies of Jesus record this desperate, fateful prayer vigil – it is that significant. Jesus cries out: 'Father, if you are willing, take this cup from me.'[17] Many martyrs through history have faced death with much more bravery and resolve. Was Jesus weaker than them? Or was there more to the cross than just social exclusion and physical torture? Jesus' distress in anticipation of the cross was because he knew he would experience carrying the weight of the world's sins. As the second person in the Triune Godhead, who had lived in eternal unbroken fellowship as Father, Son and Holy Spirit, he knew he was going to experience exclusion from this relationship because of the shattering effect of the evils of sin. It was this, more than the external physical suffering, that made the cross the most significant event in all of human history and the most difficult challenge anyone has ever faced.

Jesus asks for his Father to take his cup of suffering away. Any true father hates to see their child suffering, and would do everything in his power to take that suffering away. If I were held captive in my home by criminals who were threatening to hurt my children, I wouldn't be able to give them my bank details, laptop, or jewellery fast enough. I would trade anything so that my children could avoid suffering. On the occasions when my children have been in hospital, I would have swapped places with them in an instant if it were possible. I would have done any deal with God to relieve their pain. Here at the turning point of the gospel story we have the

17 Luke 22:42.

opportunity for just such a deal. God the Father is being asked by his Son that the ordeal ahead of him may be removed.

Two important things happen here.

First, God the Father does not remove the cup of suffering. Would God really have made his Son go through the agonies of the cross if all he was doing was giving people an extra option in terms of what to believe – an alternative route to restoration in relationship with himself for people who didn't like Judaism or Hinduism? Would God have been so callous as to let his own Son die if we could put ourselves right with God through religious observance, social justice work, personal piety, or being born into the right religious community? If God knew there were other ways humanity could have been saved and yet did not rescue his Son, the cross would indeed be a travesty and demand that we seriously question the integrity of God the Father. God the Father's decision not to answer his Son's prayer, not to remove his suffering, is one indicator that the absolute exclusivity of the cross was intended.

Second, Jesus' prayer ends, 'yet not my will, but yours be done'.[18] This is our evidence that what is being done here is not divine child abuse, but the voluntary submission of the Son to his Father's will. This is not abuse but a partnership, one that both parties have signed up for. Jesus' personal yet public prayer in the Garden of Gethsemane reveals something of the depth of suffering the cross will involve. But it also reveals the love that Jesus has both for his Father, and for us. Jesus is willing to submit his desires to his Father's plans, for the sake of the salvation of humanity. Jesus' willingness to put aside his own desires in order to suffer the pain

---

18 Luke 24:42.

and shame of the cross only really makes sense if there was no other way that sin could be forgiven.

The paradox of exclusivity claims that there is no other way to God than through trusting the death of Jesus.[19] For many this seems unacceptable, intolerant – a viewpoint that we have no right to impose on the rest of the world. However, if it is in fact true and there *is* no other way to be made right with God, then it is no more intolerant than claiming that Paris is the capital of France. It is not controversial to insist that something can be true even if not everyone agrees. If somebody insists that Paris is the capital of Austria, it is unacceptable and unhelpful to try and arm-twist them into accepting that Paris is really the capital of France. But it doesn't make them any the less wrong. It is not intolerant to hold the view that salvation comes exclusively through Christ; intolerance is more than possible, though, if we do not respect the fact that others have the right to disagree.

Believing in the exclusivity of the cross, coming to terms with the barbarity of the cross and recognizing the particularity of the cross all bring us back to the absolute centrality of this cruel Roman torture instrument as the place where, despite indications to the contrary, God won the decisive battle against darkness, evil and injustice.

The final words at the end of Charles Dickens' novel *A Tale of Two Cities* echo the opening lines cited at the beginning of this chapter:

It is a far, far better thing that I do now, than I have ever done; it is a far, far better rest that I go to than I have ever known.[20]

---

19 John 14:1–6; John 10:1–9.
20 Dickens, C. (1859), *A Tale of Two Cities*, Collins, p. 456.

Here are the words of a man who took the place of a friend in prison awaiting execution. His willingness to die for another is an incredibly powerful story of love and selflessness. How much greater, though, is the story of the cross – an act of terrible betrayal and yet at the same time God's great and willing sacrifice for the world, an act of divine love and mercy. It was, paradoxically, the very best of times and the very worst of times, met together in one man's death – a death that would save the world.

Chapter 12

The Roman Paradox
The God who is effectively ineffective

I have a confession to make. My own life is a paradox. I am not half as Christian as I want to be, despite having attempted to follow Jesus for over half of my life. I would love to tell you that my life is a worked example of the character of Jesus, but the fact of the matter is that I am a walking contradiction. A two-faced hypocrite – and I know it. Yet I cannot seem to change.

Some people talk about how they found peace when they came to know God. Other people talk about the battles they have faced as a result of following him. Some people talk about internal comfort, others about internal conflict. Some talk about the gift of grace; others about the struggle with sin. Some walk confidently in peace and victory. Others drown in defeat, doubt or despair.

Most of us perhaps know both sides of the story – our Christian life is itself a paradox. We know both joy and pain, faith and doubt, peace and frustration. We are declared holy, but we struggle to *be* holy. Our sin and guilt are washed away, but we fall for temptation time and time again. Whether we are new to the faith, or have been Christians for decades, we know the struggle of longing to be like Jesus, and we know all about feeling like we fall short. Like a corrupt army officer on dress parade, externally we might put up a good show, but inside it's a different story.

These are the sort of issues that are raised by the Roman Paradox. Paul's letter to the Roman church contains many verses people love to quote at one another – here are some examples:

There is therefore now no condemnation for those who are in Christ Jesus . . .[1]

Since we have been justified through faith, we have peace . . .[2]

We are more than conquerors . . .[3]

God works for the good of those who love him . . .[4]

You have been set free from sin . . .[5]

If God is for us, who can be against us?[6]

But Paul's letter to the church in the capital of the Roman Empire also contains verses that make for significantly less easy reading, passages that seem to indicate an exactly opposite view:

---

1 Romans 8:1.
2 Romans 5:1.
3 Romans 8:37.
4 Romans 8:28.
5 Romans 6:18.
6 Romans 8:31.

I do not understand what I do. For what I want to do I do not do, but what I hate I do.[7]

What a wretched man I am! Who will rescue me from this body that is subject to death?[8]

Those who are in the realm of the flesh cannot please God.[9]

Each of us will give an account of himself to God.[10]

The letter to the Romans allows us to explore this more personal faith paradox, as Paul shares his own personal battle with holiness – in what some argue is his finest theological work. Paul wrestles with very real questions:

Why can't God just deal with our sin the instant we come to faith?
(Surely we would be better advocates for him if he did?)
Why can an absolutely holy God only manage to make us relatively holy?
If we can never please God through good deeds, and we know he loves us unconditionally, why even bother trying to be holy?
Does God get some sort of pleasure out of watching me fail over and over? Is it a ploy to keep me reliant on him?

---

7 Romans 7:15.
8 Romans 7:24.
9 Romans 8:8.
10 Romans 14:12.

When it comes to making us more like himself, is God, in effect, ineffective?

Let's try and wrestle with these questions alongside Paul.

I once met an elderly lady at a bus stop. Tears were trickling down her cheeks, so I asked if I could be of any assistance. She explained to me that she had just been to visit her husband in the nursing home, as she had done every day for the past ten years. They had chatted for a while and then as she left he said: 'Could you send my wife in now, please?' She knew her husband's condition meant he was often confused and disoriented and even physically violent to her, but that day he didn't even recognize her. I learned from that stranger at a bus stop a wonderful lesson of genuine love. The kind of sustained and sacrificial love that doesn't give up, whatever happens. The longer I sat talking to her, the more this lovely old lady grew in my estimation and admiration. The more unlovable her husband seemed to me, the brighter his wife's love shone.

Going back to the dandruff illustration we used in considering the Hosea Paradox, God does seem to have a habit of choosing the most unlikely, unfaithful people – which does mean that his faithfulness to us is all the more obvious. Paul tells us to look back and see that this is true in our past:

Brothers and sisters, think of what you were when you were called. Not many of you were wise by human standards; not many were influential; not many were of noble birth. But God chose the foolish things of the world to shame the wise; God chose the weak things of the world to shame the strong. God chose the lowly things of this world and the despised things – and the things that are not – to nullify the things that are, so that no one may boast before him.[11]

This new faith, Christianity, deliberately set out to turn the world's values on their heads; God does indeed take delight in making something out of nothing, making saints out of nobodies. God chose Israel, the least of all nations; now, from across society, Jew or Gentile, he chooses the weakest individuals to be his flag-bearers. By rescuing the most broken, rejected and despised of society, God provides a living example of what his character is like and turns upside down the hierarchies and strata of society. Jesus did not choose the most powerful or intelligent disciples. Instead, he chose a ragtag group of dysfunctional followers who often seemed to get more wrong than they did right.[12] Paul argues that when we look around the church, it is obvious that God did not choose people because of their social significance or influence; his business is to take broken things and make them beautiful, to take the weak and make them strong, to choose the despised, the marginalized and the outcast and to include and welcome them in his family.[13] These gracious, loving, compassionate characteristics of God are treasured in all of Scripture.[14] We too are called to be like God in this: when we demonstrate his love to the most vulnerable and needy in society, as we are called to do,[15] we make the character of the invisible God visible.

---

11 1 Corinthians 2:26–29.

12 See Kandiah, K. (2007), *Dysciples: Why I Fall Asleep When I Pray and Twelve other Discipleship Dysfunctions*, Authentic.

13 See Kandiah, K. with Kandiah, M. (2012), *Home for Good*, Hodder.

14 Exodus 34:6; Psalm 103:8; 111:4.

15 James 1:27; Matthew 25:31–46; Luke 10:30–37.

Maybe, though, we feel that the rules must change after we have become Christians: now we're in, we need to show this by being perfect. This is not the case. Post-conversion, we are still just as fallible as human beings, yet this is not a barrier for God to demonstrate his compassion through and to us. Let me tell you about a father I know. He reads his children stories at bedtime, drives them to school on rainy days, and gives them treats occasionally for no reason. You might think he sounds like a good dad. But imagine he adopted another child who, because of his past abuse, was often vindictive, unpredictable, rude or worse. Would this man's reputation as a good father suddenly be destroyed? No, surely it would be affirmed as he continued to love this new troubled son, read to him, drive him around and give him treats, despite his bad behaviour.

God's compassion was clearly shown in the fact that he adopted us into his family. But it shines even brighter as he continues to love us and forgive us despite our continued rebellion and sinfulness – which, at risk of repetition, do not disappear post-conversion. But this raises new questions for Paul as he continues working through this logic of the gospel of grace: 'Shall we go on sinning so that grace may increase?'[16] This is such an attractive argument. Resisting temptation feels like a fight against our most basic desires.

Paul gives us three reasons why we should not give up our struggle:

1. We are dead to our past wrongdoing and its effects.
2. We are alive to Christ.
3. We live in the power of Christ.

---

16 Romans 6:1.

None of these are simple concepts; let us consider each of them in turn.

Immediately following his rhetorical question, Paul states that we have 'died to sin'.[17] In other words, becoming a Christian means there has been a decisive change in our lives, not so that we are immune to the influence of sin, but so that we no longer live 'under the domination of sin'.[18] This sounds good in theory – but in practice, resisting temptation seems to be as hard as ever. So what does Paul mean when he says that we have died to sin? The story of John Darwin might have something to say to us on this.

John Darwin was seen paddling his red canoe into the sea on 21 March 2002.[19] When he failed to report for work later that day a huge air and sea rescue was launched. Sixty-two miles of North Sea coastline was combed for clues as to the fifty-two-year-old's disappearance. The next day, the broken hull of Darwin's canoe was discovered, but no sign of its owner. It was considered very strange that an experienced canoeist would have run into trouble on such a calm day. A month later, when there was still no sign of his body, a death certificate was issued.

Years later, however, it was discovered that Darwin was alive and well. He had been living initially in a bedsit next door to his family home, and then, just a year later, he had moved back in with his wife, after which they moved to Panama to invest in the property market. Darwin had faked his death to escape the consequences of the financial difficulties he had found himself in and so that his wife could claim over £150,000 in life insurance. Darwin's deceit

---

17 Romans 6:2–3.

18 Moo, D. (2000), *Romans*, NIV Application Commentary, Zondervan, p. 196.

19 http://www.telegraph.co.uk/news/uknews/crime/9188424/Canoe-man-how-John-Darwins-obsession-with-becoming-rich-led-to-audacious-plan.html

was only discovered after he went home to visit his sons, who all believed he was dead.[20] He explained his disappearance and absence as being due to acute amnesia. The story did not convince either the police or the courts and in 2009 he was sentenced to six and a half years in prison for fraud.

Darwin showed a clear understanding of a principle that drives Paul's argument here in Romans: death sets us free. You can't ask a corpse to pay what it owes, so the debt collectors had written off the bad debt. Sadly, Darwin's freedom was illusory, because his death was a fake. Christians, however, have had their spiritual debts written off once and for all through their connection with the actual physical death of Christ.[21] To deliberately get back into debt again after all the lengths that Jesus went to in order to redeem us is as ridiculous as a drowning man jumping straight back into turbulent water the moment after he has been rescued. Choosing to continue to sin devalues the grace that has been shown.

So why do we believers continue to sin after we have been rescued? Surely no one would choose to make things worse in their lives? Isn't the reality of the situation that it is just too hard to change, to break the old habits?

Imagine you are a prisoner of war in an internment camp deep in enemy territory. After years of imprisonment, you hear rumours that your entire camp is going to be executed. But in a daring rescue your camp is liberated, although the captain of the rescue effort who led the charge is tragically killed in the process. Your liberty has been bought at great expense and you are now free to leave.

---

20 http://www.theguardian.com/uk/2012/feb/14/canoe-man-prosecutors-recover-assets

21 Galatians 2:19–20.

But your fellow captives have become your family, and you don't know what you will do for food if you strike out across country. You have a familiarity with the land and the routines. The captain died for your freedom, but in practice you are tempted to stay living under the fear of the old regime.

The grace of God was demonstrated when Jesus, the commanding officer in our rescue, died to liberate us from imprisonment and slavery to sin. Jesus' death for us has brought about a decisive change already.[22] But only if we make the journey out of the camp will we begin to more fully enjoy the benefits that Christ has won for us. Continuing under the old regime does not bring greater honour to Jesus. Continuing to sin does not make grace increase. In fact, continuing to live in sin devalues the grace we have been given, and dishonours Jesus. But deciding to leave our sin behind is as difficult as deciding to leave behind a place of captivity that has become all we can remember. Prisoners who write of surviving experiences such as these describe how hard it is to get rid of a concentration-camp mind-set. Habits, fears, values and priorities ingrained under those extreme conditions are not easily dismissed.

Once you become a Christian, your status has changed. You were once a prisoner, enslaved by wrongdoing, unable to escape its consequences. But now you are dead to sin, freed from prison – yet you struggle to live out this new status. This is why Paul also talks about another status, one which is positive: we are alive in Christ. This

---

22 As Australian scholar William Dumbrell puts it: 'Christ's death announces the annihilation of the power of sin to dominate and enslave the human race through the fear of death.' Dumbrell, W. J. (2005), *Romans: A New Covenant Commentary*, Wipf and Stock, p. 68.

little term 'in Christ' is used by Paul on numerous occasions here,[23] as he wants to hammer home that this is the place where we now belong. Thinking back to that prisoner freed from an internment camp, imagine they make it back to their family. But, suffering from post-traumatic stress disorder, they wake up screaming in the middle of the night. We can imagine their family reassuring them that they are now 'at home', deliberately dropping that fact into their conversation whenever possible to reinforce the understanding that they are now somewhere safe. Similarly, Paul wants us to know that we are 'in Christ', and so vitally connected to Jesus that all his accomplishments and characteristics become ours.

How does this help us in our struggle with temptation and wrong actions? Parenting experts teach us that telling a child to 'stroke the cat' is more effective than saying, 'Don't pull the cat's tail' when it comes to ensuring good behaviour around pets. Shifting our focus so that we live up to our positive identity in Christ, accessing his resources and accomplishments, is much more effective in forging our new life than constantly worrying over past temptations and trying not to get sucked in again. Looking at the one who died to rescue us motivates us to live in the light of his grace, rather than in the shadow of our sin.

Paul tells us to practise living out our resurrection life:

> In the same way, count yourselves dead to sin but alive to God in Christ Jesus. Therefore do not let sin reign in your mortal body so that you obey its evil desires. Do not offer any part of yourself to sin as an instrument of wickedness, but rather offer yourselves to God as those who have been brought from

---

23 See Romans 6:11; 8:1; 8:39.

death to life; and offer every part of yourself to him as an instrument of righteousness.[24]

A preacher friend of mine used to tell the story of a man named George who woke up one morning in a strange bed in a hotel room, with a woman by his side. He had been single his whole life and had tried hard to live by Christ's standards of purity – but now he was in love with a woman he did not want to let down. So, shocked at this apparent indiscretion, he immediately jumped up, grabbed his clothes and headed for the door. As he was turning the door-handle he heard a voice from behind him say, 'George, it's OK! It's me, your wife. We are on our honeymoon!' George's new circumstances had not yet embedded themselves in his consciousness. He was still thinking of himself as a single man despite being a newlywed. Similarly, many newly married women continue to sign using their maiden name, as it is second nature to them. But as they very deliberately sign using their new name, however counter-intuitive that may feel, they are reminded of their new identity.

In the same way, Paul calls on Christians to increase their consciousness of their new status by practising it. Craig Keener in his commentary on the letter to the Romans summarizes this point well:

Paul summons them to be what he declares they are . . . Through faith one receives a new identity, and through faith one must also continue to embrace and live in that new identity, so that obedient works become expressions of living faith.[25]

---

24 Romans 6:11–13.
25 Keener, C. (2009), *Romans*, New Covenant Commentary, Cascade, p. 82.

The internal battle that we experience is part and parcel of our transformation from one identity to another. We have seen that it in no way undermines God's love for us; rather, his grace is seen more clearly as a result. But we choose not to continue to sin, because we are dead to sin and alive in Christ, a status which was won for us at great cost. If we become comfortable in our discipleship, we should expect God to come in and disturb us, to try and make us more like him. We are supposed to struggle with sin in this life, in order that we worship God more effectively through our efforts to be holy. We worship the God who freed us, united us with Christ and helps us in our struggles.

Paul describes the Christian faith using forceful metaphors such as running the race or fighting the good fight, which implies the continual need for discipline, exertion and stamina to live lives of worship to God.

God has shown that he could not love us any more than he has already. He has proven beyond all doubt that despite the sin we have committed and are committing, he remains committed to us.[26] But it still feels like he is leaving us to it, rather than really helping us to deal with sin and temptation. To help us understand why sin remains such a problem for us, Paul goes on in this same chapter to offer three arguments. He explains the addictive nature of sin, the destructive nature of sin and the relational nature of sin.

He uses a number of metaphors to help us understand what Jesus accomplished on the cross; one powerful metaphor is that of redemption. He begins by introducing the idea of sin as slavery: we have been freed from slavery and liberated from captivity. Slaves on sale in a marketplace go to the highest bidder – only by paying the highest

---

26 Romans 5:8.

price can one buy the right to own the slave, or to set him or her free. Jesus paid the ultimate price for us when he offered up the most precious thing in the universe – himself – to redeem us. He offered himself, outbidding any other claim. We were given a preliminary glimpse of this idea in the Abraham story as we considered how precious the life of Isaac was to Abraham. Now the intensity of the image is increased as we consider the value of Christ, the true Son of God, to God the Father. Our redemption price was nothing less than Christ himself. But now that we have been freed, what will we do with our freedom? If we choose to carry on as we were and not give our future actions to God, then we effectively sell ourselves back into slavery. Paul explains: if you 'offer yourselves to someone as obedient slaves, you are slaves of the one you obey'.[27] Douglas Moo summarizes this passage simply: 'Sin, then, is a serious matter. Though set free from it, we can in effect become its slaves again if we give ourselves to it.'[28]

C. S. Lewis creates a wonderful incident to illustrate this in *The Lion, the Witch and the Wardrobe*. Edmund had become enslaved to the despotic White Witch whose sorcery meant that in Narnia it was 'always winter and never Christmas'. Edmund should have been part of the rescue team to restore Narnia to its true glory, freeing the land and its citizens from the clutches of the Witch. But instead, he took the Turkish Delight she offered him and he was instantly addicted, so the White Witch controlled Edmund for her own ends. Edmund was now trapped and there was only one way that he could be freed – if Aslan, the true king of Narnia, offered himself as a substitute. Aslan's

---

27 Romans 6:16.

28 Moo, D. (1996), *Romans*, New International Commentary on the New Testament, Eerdmans, p. 210.

life was the ransom price for Edmund, and he willingly paid it. Once Aslan had died a grizzly death at the hands of the White Witch, her power over Edmund was broken. Never again would he choose to eat her Turkish Delight. What an insult to Aslan's kindness it would be, what a desperate plight to be once more under the Witch's control. Once ransomed, Edmund joined Aslan's revolution to bring liberation to all of Narnia so that winter might end and Christmas could come (though how you could have Christmas without Christ being born in the first place is not explored – it is only a children's book, after all!). Although sin is addictive, Jesus has effectively dealt with its power. With his help we can break free of those things that enslave us.

This leads to the second argument that Paul uses to further challenge the view that because we are recipients of grace, sin does not matter. He asks his readers to remember the results of sin in their lives. 'What benefit did you reap at that time from the things you are now ashamed of? Those things result in death!'[29] What good did it do you when you were living under the power of sin? Sin promises so much but delivers so little. Like a moth drawn inexorably to a flame, so we are drawn to sin. If only a moth were able to think through what is happening to it – that its urges are leading it to death. But, sadly, there is no reasoning with moths. Paul honours his readers by assuming they are not just unthinking insects incapable of reflection, restraint or redirection. He asks his readers to consider the trajectory that sin takes them on. When we offer ourselves up to sin, we are being controlled and manipulated not by a gracious king who loves us and wants the best for us, but by an enemy who wants to destroy life and inflict as much pain and chaos on us as possible.

---

29 Romans 6:21.

Paul's arguments relate directly to the character of God. As we have been exploring throughout this book, the character of God is perhaps the most fundamental paradox of the Christian faith. In the end, all these questions come back to one, central question: is God trustworthy, or not? Sin is not just a legal status, or a physical addiction, but is a relational state of being. Sin is a decision to turn away from a God who has not turned away from us.

A student in a hostile debate setting asked me why we should bother trying to change our behaviour, if the God I had been describing was so loving and compassionate. I was encouraged – I felt that I must have communicated something if antagonistic atheists were asking these questions.[30] I explained using an illustration about my grandmother. She was a lovely and gracious old lady and I am sure loved me unconditionally. I am pretty sure that she would have found it in her heart to forgive me, whatever I did. But, knowing her character and her depth of graciousness, what should my response be? Should I deliberately punch her in the face, just to make the most of her forgiveness? Should I carry on playing my music loudly, even though I knew it upset her? Of course not. The only fitting response to this kind of love is to give love in return. The appropriate response to God's forgiveness is love towards him and forgiveness towards everyone else. The grace of God is not an

30 Martyn Lloyd-Jones once claimed, 'The true preaching of the gospel of salvation by grace alone always leads to the possibility of this charge being brought against it. There is no better test as to whether a man is really preaching the New Testament gospel of salvation than this, that some people might misunderstand it and misinterpret it to mean that it really amounts to this, that because you are saved by grace alone it does not matter at all what you do; you can go on sinning as much as you like because it will redound all the more to the glory of grace.' Lloyd-Jones, D. M. (1973), *Romans: An Exposition of Chapter 6*, Banner of Truth, pp. 8–9.

excuse to take advantage of him, but a motivation to live a life of worship worthy of the calling we have received.

Our experience of the Christian life is always going to feel paradoxical, because we are people in transition. We are like slaves, learning to be free. We are addicts coming off our dependencies. We are newlyweds getting used to our new identity. We are prisoners of war venturing out of the camp. We are bankrupts, rebuilding our lives now that our debts have finally been paid. We are people sentenced to death who have been given new life.

We are living between two realities – who we used to be, and what God is making us into. God has done the work that was needed: he has rescued, justified, redeemed, liberated and accepted us. Now he calls us to work out the implications of what he has done in the day-to-day reality of our lives, and empowers us to do so by his Spirit. God inspires us to do so by helping us to remember our identity in Christ.

In the end, it comes down to fundamentals: Who are you, really? When times are hard, where will you turn? To God, or against him? That is what is really at stake here.

A young woman from a wealthy background became a Christian and started attending an introductory course about living a Christian life, as a preparation for baptism. But fierce persecution broke out against Christians and her whole baptism class were arrested and put on trial. The young woman had just given birth to a son and she was not allowed to nurse her baby in prison. On the day of her hearing her father came into the courtroom carrying the baby and begged his daughter to deny her faith so she could raise her son herself. What would you and I have done?

This young woman held fast to her faith, and she, along with her friends, was sentenced to death. First they were publicly whipped, then they were gouged by wild animals, and finally they were stabbed to death by soldiers. That was in AD 203. The young woman's name was Perpetua, and she was twenty-two years old when she was killed.[31]

Sadly, this kind of persecution didn't end during Roman times. Even today, all around the world in places like North Korea, Pakistan and South Sudan, Christians are facing imprisonment, beatings and execution. Day by day Christians make courageous choices to live for God despite great temptation to compromise to avoid suffering and death. In the light of this kind of courage our attempts at faithfulness seem pretty feeble. Yet the reality of temptation and struggle is not restricted to believers facing martyrdom. All of us need a rationale for fighting sin, resisting temptation and persevering in the Christian faith.

Not long before Perpetua was martyred, her father visited her in prison and begged her to denounce her claim to be a Christian. She answered him:

'Father, do you see this vase here?' she replied. 'Could it be called by any other name than what it is?'

'No,' he replied.

'Well, neither can I be called anything other than what I am, a Christian.'[32]

For anyone who believes, their new identity of being 'in Christ' shapes and directs their life. The problem we face is that we live

---

31 Galli, M. (2000), *131 Believers Everyone Should Know*, B & H Publishing, p. 361.
32 Ibid., p. 362.

in the paradoxical moment (in God's long timescale) of disparity between our identity in Christ and the reality of our daily experience. This paradox can be difficult to live with – but nevertheless, God wants us to learn to live in the reality of who he has made us and what he has done for us, even in this temporal life, surrounded as we are by trials and temptations. Learning to live in the tension of the now and the not yet is the challenge we must face.

Chapter 13

The Corinthian Paradox
The God who fails to disappoint

The stand-up comedian Jack Handey is well known for his quasi-philosophical one-liners, which seem to make people laugh, although nobody really knows why. Here is his take on disappointment:

> I was going to take my little nephew to Disneyland, but instead I drove him to an old burned-out warehouse. 'Oh no', I said, 'Disneyland burned down.' He cried and cried, but I think that deep down he thought it was a pretty good joke. I started to drive over to the real Disneyland, but it was getting pretty late.[1]

The easy reference to what his nephew thought 'deep down' made me laugh precisely because we feel this let-down so often in our everyday lives. There often seems to be a huge disconnect between our hopes and aspirations for tomorrow, and the grim reality of today. Advertisers promise their products will transform our lives, but they rarely do. Trusted public institutions proffer total security – until the latest scandal shakes that trust to the core. We feel let

---

1 Handey, J. (1994), *Deep Thoughts*, Berkley Publishing, p. 2.

down by revelations of corruption in the banking services, allegations of abuse by respected broadcasters, the blatant greed of some politicians who were caught with their hands in the till, and reports of cruelty and neglect in hospitals and care homes. We seek comfort in social media, but there we discover that our friends all have better lives than we do, as they post about another fantastic party, another perfect holiday, another delicious meal, or boast about their wonderful spouse and their cute or talented children. We know these are only the edited highlights of their lives, but we can't help negatively comparing our own experiences with the 'best of' experiences of our friends and feeling that our own lives fall hopelessly short.[2]

Our experience with the church follows a similar path. Bill Hybels, leader of the large and successful Willow Creek Church in Chicago, eloquently describes the church at its best:

There is nothing like the local church when it's working right. Its beauty is indescribable. Its power is breathtaking. Its potential is unlimited. It comforts the grieving and heals the broken in the context of community. It builds bridges to seekers and offers truth to the confused. It provides resources for those in need and opens its arms to the forgotten, the downtrodden, the disillusioned. It breaks the chains of addictions, frees the oppressed, and offers belonging to the marginalized of this world. Whatever the capacity for human suffering, the church has a greater capacity for healing and wholeness.[3]

---

2 See Niequist, S. (2013) 'Instagram's Envy Effect', *Relevant Magazine* http://www.relevantmagazine.com/culture/tech/stop-instagramming-your-perfect-life; also Bottone, A. (2005), *Status Anxiety*, Penguin.

3 Hybels, B. (2002), *Courageous Leadership*, Zondervan, Chapter 1.

It's a compelling vision, but sadly, there are churches that are ugly, that hamper healing and cause discomfort, that smash down any bridges to seekers, that close their arms to the forgotten, that walk all over the downtrodden and disillusioned. There are churches that have put up chains to keep out the addicts. Some churches have been the cause of oppression and marginalization.

For many of us, our disappointment with life is never more acute than in thinking about the church. Surely God's own people ought to do better than the rest of the world? Yet the press reports details of scandal and abuse in the church itself with depressing regularity. I have met far more people who have been put off the Christian faith by Christians than by atheist propaganda. I have known church leaders who behave like tyrants or bullies, and congregations that seem to breathe gossip and judgementalism. Even if we are lucky enough to go to vibrant, welcoming, growing churches full of good men and women all earnestly seeking to serve their communities, we know how much hard work it takes to maintain that, and to manage both our expectations and those of others. Our radical gospel makes such little headway into our common life together; things seem to change so slowly; our relationships cause such heartache; our corporate worship is often so half-hearted. To be honest, church often feels like a huge let-down.

How are we to understand the paradox that the church, God's chosen instrument of blessing to the world, is crushing Christians and chasing many out of or away from the body of Christ?[4] How are we supposed to live with the gap between our hopes of church as the family of God, and the reality of what sometimes amounts

---

4 For a systematic study of why many people leave church and what happens to them afterwards, see Jamieson, A. (2002), *A Churchless Faith*, SPCK.

to little more than a room full (or not so full) of people who barely seem able to find a word to say to one another over coffee. Is God so hopelessly devoted to the church that he fails to see its flaws? Or can he really help the church become the hope of the world?

Once again, the character of God is at stake. The discrepancy between promise and reality is felt most acutely by those of us who believe in a faithful God and yet are painfully aware of the brokenness of our world, our church and our lives. Even when our present culture's addiction to instant gratification and immediate consumption is factored in, the slow progress towards fulfilment of the promises of God is a constant challenge to believers. We worship either like those who are hopelessly romantic – with our eyes closed to the reality around us – or like those who are simply hopeless – with our eyes turned away from the promises of God. If we can't resolve this problem, we must ask if there is any future for belief, and what belief we can possibly hold on to for the future?

Before we look at a Christian response to the paradox of the contradiction between the promise and reality of the church, let us consider two alternative ways in which humanity typically tries to cope with disappointment.

The first way of eliminating the gap between hope for a better world and disappointment at its non-arrival is to settle for the world as we find it. If we don't cling on to a belief that things could get better, we can simply get on and enjoy life, or, as the hedonists say: 'let us eat and drink, for tomorrow we die'.[5] This quote comes from Isaiah and was then used by Paul to point to the folly of consumption. Nowadays the same quotation is used to point to the folly of religion! Hedonism as a philosophy argues that the highest good we

---

5 Both Isaiah 22:13 and Greco-Roman thought.

can achieve on earth is our personal pleasure; life is temporary and transient, so we should stop living for a higher purpose and instead simply live for the satisfaction of our own basic appetites.

Hedonism has been around for centuries, if not millennia, but the consumerism[6] of many societies today is in a different league. We are defined by what we buy, what we eat, what we wear, what we drive. In the words of the Dean of King's College London: 'Tesco ergo sum' – I shop, therefore I am.[7] This compulsion to consumption is driven by a fixation on the present. The future is assumed to be full of disaster, whether personal or global, so it is viewed with fear, rather than with hope. Zygmunt Bauman, the world-renowned sociologist, argues that our spending habits are a marker of these larger cultural shifts:

> We live on credit . . . no past generation was as heavily in debt as we are . . . the future is beyond control. But the credit card magically brings that vexingly elusive future straight into your lap. You may consume the future, so to speak, in advance – while there is still something left to be consumed . . . if the future is designed to be as nasty as you suspect it may be, you can consume it now, still fresh and unspoiled, before the disaster strikes . . .[8]

But what if we do 'spend our future' through consumption and on credit, and we still can't make the present satisfying enough? It

---

6 Sociologist David Lyon describes consumerism as 'the lifestyles and cultures structured around consumption'. Lyon, D. (2010), *Jesus in Disneyland: Religion in Postmodern Times*, Oxford: Blackwell, p. 77.

7 http://www.timeshighereducation.co.uk/95931.article

8 Bauman, Z. (2006), *Liquid Fear*, Polity, p. 6.

would seem we are doubly doomed: we have traded our future hope for our present pleasure, only to find that it still comes up short.

Richard Dawkins and the British Humanist Society famously launched a publicity campaign buying up space on the sides of buses and running the slogan: 'There's probably no God. Now stop worrying and enjoy your life.' Their insinuation was that religion in general and the Christian church in particular exert some kind of joy-inhibiting influence on society – effectively arguing that if hedonism isn't getting results, it's religion's fault. John Lennon obviously had a similar idea; in his song 'Imagine', he preaches that a world without religion equals a world of peace.[9]

It has to be said that this way of experiencing life in general does affect our attitude to church. Consumerism has become an unconscious mode of operation when it comes to our thinking about church and faith just as much as our clothes and our houses. When we move to a new area we 'shop around' for a church, until we find a 'brand' we like. We evaluate services by whether we 'got anything out of them', as if we were calculating the cost-benefit ratio in a business transaction. And we accessorize our faith with the latest podcasts, worship songs, blessings, teaching, ministry, small-group material, T-shirts and Bible apps. Yet despite the availability of an unprecedented amount of resources, we still live with an underlying dissatisfaction, even disappointment, with life, with church, perhaps with God himself. We expect our faith to

---

9 See Spufford, F. (2012), *Unapologetic*, Faber and Faber, pp. 12–13, for a critique of John Lennon's anthem 'Imagine': 'Imagine there's no heaven. Imagine there's no hell. Imagine all the people, living life in – hello? Excuse me? Take religion out of the picture and everybody starts living life in peace? I don't know about you, but in my experience peace is not the default state of human beings . . .'

serve our 'felt needs' and if it doesn't deliver, we want our money back . . .

A second way of dealing with the discrepancy between promise and reality is to try and ignore the reality. We saw in the Job Paradox that Buddhist thought sees the world around us with its pain and suffering as an illusion or *maya* – if reality does not exist, how can we be disappointed by it? But, unable to resist taking it a step further, Buddhism then attempts to explain how to switch off our desires as well. Perhaps this double-barrelled attempt at disappointment-busting is because on the one hand, the resilience of our hope for a better future is so strong, and on the other, the power and reality of suffering kicks so hard against any attempt to ignore it.[10]

The plain fact of the matter is that however much we try and suppress the mirror-twin experiences of hope and disappointment, they just won't go away. They are like that big beach-ball the children play with in the swimming pool – no matter how hard they try to push it down under the water, sooner or later the ball will bob up to the surface.[11] Perhaps we need to recognize that the resilience of both hope and disappointment points to something true. This is a line of argument that C. S. Lewis pursues:

Creatures are not born with desires unless satisfaction for those desires exists. A baby feels hunger: well, there is such a thing

---

10 Remember, in Chapter 8 we saw how C. S. Lewis famously wrote: 'We can ignore even pleasure. But pain insists upon being attended to. God whispers to us in our pleasures, speaks in our conscience, but shouts in our pains: it is his megaphone to rouse a deaf world.'
11 Illustration from Dan Strange, Oakhill College.

as food . . . If I find in myself a desire, which no experience in this world can satisfy, the most probable explanation is that I was made for another world.[12]

Our appetites point us to God, as we saw back in the Abraham Paradox at the beginning of our journey. Christianity promises us an outrageous hope for the future – true peace, genuine happiness, restored relationships. But the danger is that we focus solely on these promises in an attempt to avoid facing our disappointment with the present reality. We are tempted to maintain a certain detachment in church relationships, so we don't get deep enough to allow anyone to hurt us; this may apply especially if we have been hurt in the past. When we go to church we just go through the motions, present in body but absent in spirit. Or we try and open up spiritually only to God, closing our eyes as we sing and pray in an attempt to shut out the disappointment we feel if we look around with our eyes open and have to confront the other people we're supposed to be on the journey with. Perhaps we tell ourselves that we are connected to what Augustine of Hippo in the fourth century called the invisible church – the true church of all believers throughout history, that only God can see. But that doesn't justify our abdication of responsibility to be part of the church as God set it up – visible local communities that exist to encourage one another and share his message in word and deed.

We cannot deny the reality of the church as we know it, just as

---

12 'This is the greatest conclusion of any argument I know, since it argues not only for the existence of God, but for the existence of Heaven as well, including thereby the possibility of personal immortality.' Williams, P., (2001), 'Aesthetic Arguments for the Existence of God' in *Quodlibet Journal*, Vol. 3, No. 3.

we cannot deny the future of the church that God promises. We have to live with the tension of feeling both disappointed and hopeful. Paul's first letter to the church in Corinth gives us an important opportunity to wrestle with this paradox. It is a relatively long letter covering many issues, and preachers have tended to focus a lot on some paragraphs, leaving most of the rest almost entirely ignored. Frankly, the letter as a whole is difficult to explain, precisely because of the paradox we are determined to face.

This particular letter is best known for articulating a beautiful description of the nature of genuine love – there is hardly a wedding where these words are not read aloud:

> Love is patient, love is kind. It does not envy, it does not boast, it is not proud. It does not dishonour others, it is not self-seeking, it is not easily angered, it keeps no record of wrongs. Love does not delight in evil but rejoices with the truth. It always protects, always trusts, always hopes, always perseveres.[13]

This is such a lofty picture of love. Proof of its significance is that it finds such a resonance with most marrying couples, whether they are Christians or not. They choose to have this passage read publicly on their wedding day, one of the most important days in their lives. But these inspiring words are set in a letter addressed to a church that is far from able to demonstrate this love. I wonder if these lines would be so popular if the context was understood. These words were written to a church that was racked with dispute, disunity and disintegration. That's why Paul had to write so boldly about the

---

13 1 Corinthians 13:4–7.

characteristics of love – precisely because the people he was writing to didn't seem to get it one bit.

The Corinthian church was neither loving nor kind. The letter begins by addressing the divisions in the church, with different factions arguing over which leader to follow. This church certainly did 'dishonour others': it was wracked with sexual immorality, including one man sleeping with his father's wife,[14] and others visiting prostitutes.[15] So far were they from not keeping a record of wrongs that some of the church members even took each other to court. They were certainly not patient with one another – instead they were jumping the queue in communion, and those who got there first scoffed all the food before others even had a sight of it.[16] Then they went about criticizing each other for what they were eating outside of the church.[17]

There is a reality gap between the life of the Corinthian church and God's intention for his people. Nonetheless, Paul calls these Christians to live out exactly this kind of radical love *now*, even in the middle of the messiness of our present world. I have visited a lot of churches all around the globe, and this tension is to be found everywhere I've been. Within the same congregation there will be people who bear testimony to an extremely patient and self-sacrificial love towards others, and others whose actions blatantly contradict it. I have seen just as much bullying, manipulation, and false accusations in the church as anywhere – or what can be worse, a detached coldness, a lack of welcome, whispering behind people's hands, a nagging feeling of discontent.

---

14 1 Corinthians 5:1–13.
15 1 Corinthians 6:12–20.
16 1 Corinthians 11.
17 1 Corinthians 8 –11.

It is not unusual to find people who have lost faith in church because it has become a toxic place for them, preventing their faith from developing. Now, there are indeed toxic churches, with abusive leaders, bullying elders or corrupt practices – such can be found both in the church's history and the church's present. Jesus himself, in the book of Revelation, issues ultimatums to churches that are living in persistent contradiction to God's good news – he says he will snuff them out.[18] But that's not what we're talking about here – this problem is to do with the ongoing problems that beset all churches everywhere, all groups of people coming together to worship God, however committed they may be to peace, love and unity.

What the Corinthian Paradox shows us is that even in the best churches there will be a disconnect between what the church is called to be and what the church actually is; between the lives that God deserves from us and what we actually give him; between the character of God and the character of his people. Even in the earliest churches, those that were closest in time to the time of Christ, and which were overseen by an apostle, there was already this falling short. The fact that so close to the time of Jesus himself, so soon after the miraculous explosion of the church across the Near East, this church in Corinth has so much wrong with it, demonstrates such a degree of dysfunction in its communal life that it must surely quash the myth that dysfunction won't be seen in our churches today.

So how are we to navigate the discrepancy between hope and disappointment, between the promise and the reality of the church?

Before Paul closes this first letter to the Corinthian church, he

---

18 Revelation 2:5–6: 'Repent and do the things you did at first. If you do not repent, I will come to you and remove your lampstand from its place.'

has one last major lesson to set out and apply to its messy life. It is this final theme that can help us to find at least some resolution for the paradox of how the promise of God rubs up against the reality of the world, the church and our lives. Paul began his letter by exploring the significance of the crucifixion of Jesus,[19] and he ends with a reflection on the significance of Jesus' resurrection. Paul and the Corinthian church can be under no illusion about their problems, and in this context he shows us that the resurrection of Jesus is the key to living in the place of the hopelessly hopeful.

First of all, Paul argues that the resurrection is the foundation of the good news of Jesus and the reason for our hope. But many of us struggle to understand the resurrection – what was the need for a resurrection, if the victory was won on the cross? There is plenty of evidence pointing to the historical fact of Jesus' life and death, but isn't the resurrection just a matter of conjecture? Does it really matter whether Jesus physically rose from the dead, or just came back as an angel in disguise? Paul forces us to face the logic of this. Without the resurrection, he argues, the Christian faith has no claim to be good news.[20] This is the point where Paul argues that we might as well give up hope and simply follow the hedonist mantra: 'eat and drink, for tomorrow we die'.[21]

If the resurrection did not take place, there is no reason to believe that Jesus accomplished anything on the cross, and thus no future to look forward to. If Jesus did not conquer death, then the church's preaching is useless and faith in Christ is futile. If Jesus simply died on a cross, then remained in the tomb, we cannot make any

---

19 1 Corinthians 1:13–22.
20 1 Corinthians 15:14.
21 1 Corinthians 15:32.

claim to forgiveness of sins.[22] In fact, Paul goes so far as to say that if we are following an unrisen God, then everything we claim is a sham, and (in the words of one commentator) 'those who struggle for the gospel are the most-to-be-pitied members of the human race, since they are undergoing the present hardships for the sake of a future which is not going to happen'.[23] After showing what is at stake, though, Paul goes on to assert that the resurrection of Jesus is not a myth, a legend or a fable, but a much-witnessed-to historical event. It is therefore not a false hope but the very key to the validity of the claims of the Christian faith. This line of reasoning is an important riposte to the likes of Richard Dawkins, who argue that faith is a blind leap of ignorance rather than the informed step of trust we explored in the Abraham Paradox.

We have already seen that on its own, Jesus's death on a Roman cross was nothing unusual. Thousands were killed in this cruel manner, a gory visual aid to show the power of the empire and the futility of resistance. But only Jesus was raised from the dead. The resurrection shows that Jesus' willing self-sacrifice was effective, and that our sins really have been forgiven. The New York pastor and theologian Tim Keller summarized this idea wonderfully in a single tweet: 'The Resurrection is a giant receipt stamped across history saying your debt has been paid for and you don't have to pay it ever again.'[24] Resurrection was not wish fulfilment – absolutely no one was expecting someone to rise from the dead, at least not before the end of history, when God would resurrect all of his

---

22 1 Corinthians 15:17.

23 Wright, N.T. (2003), *The Resurrection of the Son of God*, Fortress Press, p. 332.

24 @timkellernyc tweet on 28 June 2013.

people.[25] The resurrection was not a hallucination: eye-witnesses reported Jesus cooking and eating at a lakeside cook-out. Hallucinations happen individually, so the chance that over 500 people would all hallucinate their own individual and collective encounters with the same person over a forty-day period is almost non-existent.[26] The resurrection was not a fabricated story – the disciples had everything to lose; propagating a claim they knew to be a lie with their country under Roman rule was surely dicing with death.

But how does any of this help us cope with the paradox of disappointment? The resurrection of Jesus happened two thousand years ago, and we are still waiting for God to finally come good on his promises. The hope he offered the disciples back then – those rooms in his Father's house, that kingdom which was so near, the end to their suffering – feels like a rather hopeless cause after all this time. The resurrection seems to disprove, not prove, the promises God makes.

Paul uses a powerful metaphor to help us understand why the resurrection resolves the paradox of disappointment. He argues that Christ is the 'firstfruits'[27] of those who have fallen asleep. The 'firstfruits' was the first and best of the crop, which under Jewish law must be offered to God as a recognition that the best belonged to God; but it also proved their expectation of receiving the remainder of the harvest. It was a way of showing their trust in God for what was yet to come, as well as thanking God for the fullness of the harvest. The definition 'firstfruits' implies 'later

25 Wright, N. T. (2003), *The Resurrection of the Son of God*, Fortress Press, p. 205.

26 Craig, W. L. (1984), *Apologetics: An Introduction*, Moody, p. 200.

27 See Wright, N. T. (2003), *The Resurrection of the Son of God*, Fortress Press, p. 339.

fruits',[28] as New Testament scholar Leon Morris puts it. Jesus' resurrection gives us a glimpse into the future – a taste of things to come. The resurrection of Jesus not only acts as a receipt, pointing backwards to the effectiveness of the crucifixion, but operates as a guarantee, pointing forwards to the general resurrection from the dead and the restoration of all things.

As a father of a growing family, I seem to spend a lot of time in supermarkets. And I often have a trail of children behind me as we snake up and down the aisles – something which amuses, perplexes or annoys fellow shoppers. We all get quite excited when the supermarket have those little tasting booths out. In the middle of a shop filled with all kinds of tasty treats they are not allowed to help themselves to, they get a miniature polystyrene cup of whatever new ice cream or cheese or sausage is on trial. The samples don't last long with my swarm of locusts in tow – especially when they go back for seconds! If we time it correctly, we can get pretty close to a free meal between the different tasting booths positioned in the various aisles. The point is, though, that these samples have to be the genuine article – they are actual pieces of the product they sell in the shop. But they are only a taste – not enough to fully satisfy our hunger, just enough to give us an authentic experience of the food, in the hope that we will want more. Similarly, the resurrection of Jesus is a foretaste of the resurrection of the whole of creation – it is God's promise of restoration of the whole universe, and yet it deliberately leaves us hungry for more.

The nuances here are important to note. Paul is not promising that every aspect of the life to come is or should be fully realized

---

28 Morris, L. (1985), *1 Corinthians: An Introduction and Commentary*, Tyndale New Testament Commentaries, IVP, p. 250.

now. But neither is he willing to admit that the Christian hope for the future is futile or unrealistic. He is utterly realistic about the state of the world today, yet very optimistic about the future. It can be tempting to take this the wrong way – and on this there are (at least) two directions in which we can head off down a blind alley.

First, we may assume that, because Christ has promised that everything will one day be sorted out, we ought to be able to claim that in advance now. This approach to faith can lead to the 'prosperity gospel'. There are various forms of this prosperity teaching, but at the heart of all of them is the claim that the fullness of life can be experienced today. These churches and their leaders teach that we should expect to see heaven invade our lives in constant healings and consistent success in life, through material blessings and miraculous provision. If we do not see these results, then our faith is lacking. But this theology is effectively claiming not just the firstfruits but all the harvest. It is tantamount to accepting a financial gift from your parents on your birthday and then demanding your entire inheritance right there and then. Paul knows that we have to wait for some things – including physical healing,[29] life free from sin, and the face-to-face company of Jesus.[30]

The opposing viewpoint states that in our time we will see nothing of the coming grace of God, only disaster and doom for our planet. Thus the church should expect to have very little impact and success in the world. This approach, though, denies the importance of the resurrection, and the idea of the firstfruits as a taste of the coming kingdom of God here in our times. There are two other New

29 2 Corinthians 12:7.
30 1 Corinthians 13:12.

Testament references, one in Romans and one in James's letter, which help to bring home the idea of the firstfruits:

> We know that the whole creation has been groaning as in the pains of childbirth right up to the present time. Not only so, but we ourselves, who have the firstfruits of the Spirit, groan inwardly as we wait eagerly for our adoption, the redemption of our bodies.[31]

> He chose to give us birth through the word of truth, that we might be a kind of firstfruits of all he created.[32]

In both these passages, we feel a sense of the Corinthian Paradox – we may experience a taste of what is to come, but not its fulfilment. Through the presence of the Holy Spirit in us, we too are a kind of firstfruits. But in the Romans passage Paul also argues that we groan as we long for what is yet to come. The pain of labour is a somewhat disturbing metaphor – the pain is intense, even unbearable; and yet it is made more bearable because something good is happening: new life is being brought into the world.

We live in this time of transition: too late for this world to satisfy our longings fully and yet too early for the new age. We are an anomaly. We are time travellers, who have to live with the contradiction of our destiny and our present reality. It is critical to our understanding of both these passages that they reference the firstfruits as a taste of the future not just for our own personal benefit, or even for the benefit of humanity, but for all of creation. Despite our frustrations, we

---

31 Romans 8:23.
32 James 1:18.

should therefore expect to see and be part of bringing tasters of God's coming kingdom in this world: fragments of justice, beauty, healing and restoration throughout the created order.

The Corinthian Paradox reminds us to hold on to the reality of Jesus' resurrection as the promise of the coming future. This is vitally important as we look around at the mess that our lives, our relationships, our churches, our world are in, and have to try and reconcile that with these passages that talk about God's family from all the nations of the earth worshipping God one in spirit, mind and purpose, loving each other in a way that is patient, kind and selfless.

Come with me as I take you to a very special place, a property in which I have invested all my life savings, the place that I one day plan to retire to. As we drive down a long country track, I spend the time explaining all about my new home – its size, features, the fantastic views, its radical layout. And then I pull over into a muddy field, a huge space ripped up by bulldozers, with piles of girders and patches of concrete and haphazard collections of bricks and scaffolding. This scene of chaos looks nothing like the dream home I had been describing in the car. Yet you understand that the development, and the little bit of it that will be mine, is a work in progress. Then, as I drive further into the site, you can see that in the middle of the rubble and mess there is one beautiful home, fully equipped and wonderfully decorated. It seems strange that they bothered with curtains and vases here when the foundations are not even laid for the building next door. But this set-piece perfection in the middle of the mess is a time machine. As you enter its four walls you are transported into my future, given a glimpse of what is yet to be, a visual aid of how my home will also look one day.

Standing inside the show-home looking out, you see nothing but chaos all around, you see the past of the field that once was there, dug up, overturned and dumped in piles. But from the outside, this house captures your attention, your imagination. You can see something of the future. In the same way, the church is a work in progress – it is filled with broken and damaged people who break and damage other people.

Sometimes, though, in our worship – not necessarily the loud singing kind, but the real and practical ways in which we honour God and show our determination to follow him – the kindness that is shown to the needy, the acceptance that is shown to the outcast, when we share communion, when we baptize a new believer – we give those present a taste of the future. We experience a glimpse of what is to come on the day when all are raised to life, and Jesus brings together all those who belong to him and restores every square inch of his universe. Entering our church communities should be like entering a time machine or a show-home, as those who see our hopeful worship see what is yet to come.

Christians believe in resurrection as a way of life. We may not be very good at it, but with God's help, we try. Most of all, we believe that God will not abandon or discard his creation, but restore all things. We believe that God will one day answer the prayer that Jesus taught all of his followers to pray. One day God's kingdom will come, God's will will be done on earth as it is in heaven. We believe that the resurrected Jesus will return.

Epilogue: Living with Paradox

I was sitting at our kitchen table, laptop open, working on this book. The phone rang – it was my neighbour, calling from her work. I could hear the panic in her voice as she explained that her husband was working at home, had fallen down the stairs and was lying on the floor unable to move. I rushed round as fast as I could and managed to make my way into the hallway of the house next door. There was my good friend, lying on the floor, in pain and barely conscious. I dialled 999 and the telephonist talked me through how to make sure my neighbour was in a safe position. Then we waited together. Time seemed to drag. We were in the limbo between the reality of tragedy and the hope of rescue. I tried to remain calm. Trying to help my friend stay conscious, I talked to him, cracked some silly jokes, offered prayer, phoned 999 again to check on progress and reassured him with the promise that the ambulance was only a few minutes away. Still we waited – and waited. Time seemed to stretch out, minutes felt like hours.

That in-between time was difficult to live through. I thought about people in other parts of the world where there is no ambulance service. There would be no impatience there – just resignation. But as my neighbour and I waited in his hallway in a small Oxfordshire town, our faith that an ambulance would eventually arrive was not a blind leap but rather an informed belief based on evidence. My struggle to be patient was precisely because I believed an ambulance would eventually come. Paradoxically, my complete confidence that help *was* really coming created the tension we were living through.

We live with a similar paradox. It is precisely because we are convinced that God is good, compassionate and gracious that we face such challenges and tensions when our hopes and the reality of life do not match up.

In so many of the paradoxes we have explored, it is the waiting that is the most difficult part. Whether it is a romantic teenager waiting to see if the phone will be answered in Germany, a helpless pastor waiting in the hospital to see if a little boy would regain his sight and hearing, or an inconsolable son waiting with his family to see whether the cancer would take his mother, it is an age-old tension. We can think back to Queen Esther waiting to see if she would be able to plead her people's cause before the king, or Habakkuk waiting to see if God would rescue his people from invasion. And it is a worldwide tension: we read about Gyeoung waiting to see if her father will ever return from prison in North Korea. In the paradox of hope and history, promise and reality, the challenge is really in the waiting.

As we have seen, the Christian faith throws up all sorts of experiential and intellectual challenges as we live in the tension between what is and what should be, between promise and fulfilment, between partial and complete knowledge of God, between limited access to him and the promise of complete intimacy, between the judgement to come and grace to live fully in the now.

It is precisely *because* we believe in God and in his plan of redemption that working through, walking through and waiting through the challenges of living in the paradox can be so difficult.

But, as we have seen time and time again, it is by experiencing the tension of these paradoxes that our understanding and our intimacy with God grows. Abraham, Moses, Job, Esther, Hosea, Habakkuk – even, arguably, Jesus – all seem to experience a greater depth, a fuller authenticity and a stronger relationship with God because of and not, as we tend to expect, in spite of their struggles.

When the ambulance finally arrived I nearly hugged the paramedics: we had been longing for them to come and put things right and bring their wisdom and expertise to help my friend. We will experience relief like this when Jesus returns. In the meantime, we long for the fulfilment of his promises, for the restoration of all things, and for the new heavens and the new earth that the returning Jesus will restore out of their present broken condition into his perfection. We long for the resolution of these paradoxes that only face-to-face knowledge of God will give us. That is the promise of the Scriptures:

> For now we see through a glass, darkly; but then face to face: now I know in part; but then shall I know even as also I am known.[1]

The paradoxes of our faith will not be resolved by this book, or any other book. They can only be explained – indeed, they will be fulfilled – when Christ himself comes again and all things are resolved in him.

But in the meantime, it is good and proper for us, far from papering over the cracks, as we have done too often in so many different ways, to keep straining to see through that dark glass, in

---

1 1 Corinthians 13:12, King James Version.

the hope that we may discern clues and comfort from a loving God whose ways are so often inscrutable to us.

Christianity was never meant to be simple – after all, it is about relationship, and what true relationship is ever simple?

My prayer is that we continue to discover that our faith is worth fighting for and that it can stand up to the most difficult questions and challenges. I pray that we continue to discover a willingness to obey God, even when it is uncomfortable and costly. I pray that as we engage heart, soul and mind in tough worship, we will find ourselves drawing closer to our Maker and our Saviour.

Through the power of paradox, may we come closer to his kingdom.